The Struggle for Health

This book is dedicated to the children of the poor in Zimbabwe and their mothers who made me learn something about the struggle for health.

THE STRUGGLE FOR HEALTH

Medicine and the Politics of Underdevelopment

DAVID SANDERS

with

RICHARD CARVER

MACMILLAN
EDUCATION

First published 1985
Reprinted 1986, 1988

Published by
MACMILLAN EDUCATION LTD
Houndmills, Basingstoke, Hampshire RG21 2XS
and London
Companies and representatives
throughout the world

Printed in Hong Kong

British Library Cataloguing in Publication Data
Sanders, David, 1945
The struggle for health.
1. Medical care—Developing countries
I. Title   II. Carver, Richard
362.1′09172′4   RA395.D44
ISBN 0—333—37529—7
ISBN 0—333—37530—0 Pbk

Contents

Foreword

Why do people, especially children, still die in large numbers throughout the world, from wholly preventable diseases? Why is it that appropriate provision for health care is not available to every individual in the world? What changes can be made to improve this situation? These are the major themes of this book. David Sanders analyses the social context of ill health, the pattern of health-care systems in different countries of both the 'developed' north and the 'under-developed' south, and shows clearly that existing medical systems are consistently ineffectual in providing for all people in most countries of the world.

There has been a succession of eminent scientists, including MacDermott and McKeown, who, over the past twenty years, have questioned the relative importance of 'curative' health care in the overall improvement in health of people in the countries of the northern hemisphere. Far more significant are the improvements in nutrition, water supplies, sanitation, housing and education. Similar evidence is now available from the less-well-developed countries of the south, where often a heavily doctor- and cure-oriented system of health care has been adopted, which reaches only a small and usually privileged minority of the population. But comparable improvements in nutrition, living conditions and education have not been achieved in the south. This failure, combined with and partly resulting from the unequal distribution of resources and political power within nations, leaves many millions of people suffering and dying from easily preventable conditions.

Writers such as David Werner in the USA, Malcolm Segall in the UK and Susan Rifkin in Asia, have emphasized to us the strong influence of politics on health care; not only the politics which decides the distribution of resources, but also the political strength of the medical profession which is responsible for moulding health care in such a way as to benefit the profession. David Sanders argues that improvements in health can only be made by popular progressive political struggle, which must involve health workers, against the international forces which cause underdevelopment.

The idea for this book began with the need for appropriate information on the health and development debate for health workers travelling to work abroad under the British Volunteer Programme. However, the potential readership is now much wider, and the book will be of value to health workers training and practising throughout the world, and to people involved with the administration of health-care systems. In the past, and still today, the medical schools and their students have been a conservative group who are usually more than satisfied with the status quo. However, as doctors these medical students will have to deal with the results of maldistribution of resources and with political decisions throughout their lives. Perhaps books such as this will awaken those, particularly in the less-developed countries of the world, to realize that improvement in the health of the vast majority of their patients in the shanty towns and rural areas will come largely through political change rather than through pills and injections.

David Morley
Professor of Tropical Child Health
University of London

Preface

Some time ago a British volunteer agency published a recruiting poster which carried a picture of Albert Schweitzer and the legend: 'You won't be the first long-haired idealist to go into the jungle and teach his skills.' Unwittingly perhaps, this expressed a sentiment that has always underlain the relationship between developed and underdeveloped countries — the notion of the West's civilizing mission. The atrocities and excesses of colonialism are now routinely condemned. No longer could that poster bear the face of Cecil Rhodes or Clive of India. Instead, the 'white man's burden' has been taken up by a new and subtler civilizer: the individual volunteer, often with a vast agency apparatus behind him or her. Different heroes, Schweitzers and Livingstones, are revived to give the volunteer a sense of historical tradition.

This book began life as a manual for the volunteer health worker going to the underdeveloped world. Over the years it has grown into something rather broader, which I hope will be of use to others as well — indeed, to anyone concerned with 'development'.

In recent years there has been increasing debate about the sociology of health — this book is, in part, a contribution to that debate. It may also be of value to health workers in underdeveloped countries who are starting to explore the roots of ill health in their societies and to question their roles.

Many aspects of the work of aid agencies have been given an unsparing critique in recent years. Not only has this confirmed the suspicion that such agencies were not tackling the root causes of poverty; on occasions they can also do clear harm. Consequently, many aid agencies have received an overhaul. More of them now stress campaigning and education on the causes of hunger and homelessness and begin to point towards solutions.

Illness, health and medicine have almost escaped this critique. Many people in the West can see that much ill health is the result of hunger or unsanitary conditions. And of course commonsense tells us that 'prevention is better than cure' — an idea that has been enthusiastically taken up by the international health bureaucracy.

But there is still a firmly entrenched belief that the highly trained health professional is important to the well-being of those who live in tropical climates with their 'reservoir of disease'. Conventional 'health indicators', for example,

You won't be the first long haired idealist to go into the jungle and teach his skills.

Tradesmen and craftsmen, graduates and teachers, engineers and technicians, agriculturalists and foresters, medical auxiliaries, librarians and accountants, surveyors and architects, urgently needed for voluntary service overseas. If you would like more information please contact: **Voluntary Service Overseas**, 14 Bishop's Bridge Road, London W2. Tel. 01-262 2611

Hard work. Long hours. Low pay. The most memorable year of your life.

(Photograph courtesy John Topham Picture Library.)

measure not health but the number of physicians and hospital beds per head of the population.

This book offers a far more radical approach than simply the need for more preventive medicine. It argues that medicine of any sort plays a very minor role in improving the health of peoples — that their health is inextricably linked to underdevelopment and the struggle against it.

In so far as Western professional medicine has had an impact on the mass of people in underdeveloped countries, it has largely been a negative one, reinforcing a political and economic system that is the root cause of their ill health. This does not mean that the health worker has no positive role to play. A large section of the book explores ways of combining more appropriate health care with the struggle against underdevelopment.

This, then, is no conventional tropical health manual — though it has a similar starting point. Mainly through visual images, Chapter 1 gives an impression of the diseases that most commonly affect people in underdeveloped countries — 'tropical diseases'.

Chapter 2 then asks whether our conventional ideas of tropical health hazards are correct, whether the problem is simply one of hot countries where disease breeds more easily. It looks by comparison at the disease pattern of European countries, especially England and Wales, when they were less developed and finds that many diseases we now regard as 'tropical' were once prevalent in the northern hemisphere.

Chapter 3 asks why this is so. How were the industrialized countries of the West able to eradicate those illnesses which were still prevalent in the early nineteenth century? Why are underdeveloped countries not able to? Why indeed are they underdeveloped? Is there a connection between development in some countries and underdevelopment in others? In any given country are health standards roughly equal for the whole population? Finally, this chapter discusses the question of population — so often seen as the crucial factor for explaining underdevelopment. Again it compares the population structure of England and Wales in the eighteenth and nineteenth centuries with that of underdeveloped countries today. Is there a lesson to learn?

Chapter 4 looks at how the health services of developed countries evolved and asks how appropriate they are. And how appropriate are they when they are transferred wholesale to underdeveloped countries?

Chapter 5 isolates the various influences that shape this medical model. It looks at the role of doctors, of business interests and of the State — and at the areas where all three interact. Is it possible to make the necessary changes in this model, in either developed or underdeveloped countries, while these influences are still at work?

Chapter 6 is an examination of possible alternatives to this Western medical model. Particular attention is paid to China and Cuba as examples of countries where massive social transformations have succeeded in destroying the old pattern of underdevelopment. How has this affected the health of the people? And what changes have there been in the 'medical contribution' as a consequence? It suggests some new approaches to health promotion and care which might themselves stimulate and be part of necessary social transformations.

Chapter 7 outlines the difficulties faced by the health worker who wishes to adopt a different approach to that of the 'foreign expert'. It cites several projects where such approaches have been successfully used and reaffirms that the struggle for progressive social change both in developed and underdeveloped countries is also a struggle for health.

Some readers might object to the use of the word 'underdeveloped' to describe the countries of the 'Third World'. This book takes the same approach as John Berger:

> 'The term "underdeveloped" has caused diplomatic embarrassment. The word "developing" has been substituted. "Developing" as distinct from "developed". The only serious contribution to this semantic discussion has been made by the Cubans, who have pointed out that there should be a transitive verb: to underdevelop. An economy is underdeveloped because of what is being done around it, within it and to it'.

John Berger and Jean Mohr (1975)[1]

This book is dedicated to the proposition that problems of health, development and underdevelopment are intimately linked. It is for that reason that it might sometimes read like a lesson in history or politics rather than a health-care manual. There is no reason to apologize for this. For too long health has been widely looked upon as an issue apart from the real problems of society. The time has come to redress the balance.

Harare, Zimbabwe, 1984   D.M.S.

Reference

1. John Berger and Jean Mohr (1975). *A Seventh Man*, Penguin, Harmondsworth, p. 21.

Acknowledgements

In the mid-1970s the development and aid agencies, particularly those sending personnel to work in underdeveloped countries, began to recognize the need to provide their representatives and recruits with a deeper understanding of the socio-economic and political context of the often frightening problems they were supposed to help solve. This book was born of such a recognition within the BVP (British Volunteer Programme), the umbrella body for four British volunteer-sending agencies: VSO (Voluntary Service Overseas), CIIR (Catholic Institute for International Relations), IVS (International Voluntary Service) and UNAIS (United Nations Association International Service). Specifically, Professor David Morley (a member of the BVP Council) believed that health workers 'going abroad', while often relatively well prepared technically for the daunting tasks ahead by an increasing wealth of information, resources and such useful books as those by himself, the Kings and David Werner (to cite only a few), were relatively ill-equipped to understand and tackle the underlying causes of the health problems. This recognition coincided with my own ongoing quest to understand what I, a doctor, should and could do about the terrible injustices I was aware of — injustices which for me were (and are) most poignantly revealed in the children's wards of hospitals in Zimbabwe, later in London's East End and still later in St Thomas's Hospital, London, where the disparities with and inappropriateness to surrounding Lambeth seemed as stark as those which had forced my departure from white Rhodesia. In late 1976, the BVP commissioned me to develop 'an information pack on health and development' for their health volunteers.

Soon after commencing my research it became clear to me that a 'pack' or collection of separate materials on the subject would not adequately cover the complex background or bring together the diverse areas relevant to the subject. Gradually and painfully the 'pack' became a booklet and eventually a book. David Morley was always a staunch supporter of my efforts despite the long periods of inertia, especially during the years following my return to Zimbabwe. The BVP — and especially within it CIIR — were very supportive, CIIR housing me for several years and, together with RVA (Returned Volunteer Action), affording me the opportunity to learn from the experiences of their organizations and from prospective and returning volunteers — an experience that I hope has helped me to ask and start to answer the questions that preoccupy the concerned health or development worker. During this period, Paddy Coulter, Jane Mackay and Fedelma Winkler, who had the unpleasant task of acting as the 'editorial group', were immensely helpful, as were Jenny Pringle who was a constant source of encouragement and an expert 'reserve' typist. Later, Gill de Wolf of the BVP and particularly Trish Silkin of CIIR were very patient and energetic in ensuring slow forward movement.

Many changes have been made to the text during its halting metamorphosis. These have often been as a result of the very helpful comments made by those either silly enough to volunteer, or too polite to resist pressure, to read the various draft manuscripts. I here mention and thank Jenny, Kasturi, Ann, Janet Aitken, Luise Parsons, Jonny Myers, Tony Klouda, Hermione Lovel, Sue Hunt, Liz Mason, Anthony Zwi, John Sanders, Bill and Angie Vennells, Gill Walt and Aubrey Sheiham. Many insights were derived from my involvement with the Politics of Health Group and later the OXFAM Medical Team in Zimbabwe.

Special thanks are due to David Werner and Lesley Doyal, both very busy people, but both of whom went to a lot of trouble to put their extremely helpful comments down on paper. Chris Welch was a very patient and painstaking illustrator whose influence will be clear to all who peruse this book, and whose mantle was comfortably and ably inherited by Colleen Crawford who prepared the later drawings. Richard Carver, whose task was initially to edit the manuscript, became an important contributor; without his expert help and humour the final manuscript would never have emerged. To him I am immensely grateful. Thanks are also due to Liz Horne, my editor, who pleasantly kept things moving.

I am also most grateful to OXFAM, War on Want, Christian Aid and SIDA (the Swedish International Development Authority) who have variously subsidized the writing of this book and assisted in its production at a cost within the means of the majority of health and development workers in underdeveloped countries. They of course bear no responsibility for its contents.

Finally, I want to acknowledge the contribution of Sue Fawcus whose comments, advice and enduring and loving support have ensured this book's eventual appearance.

1 The Child's Name is Today

Figure 1.1 To him we cannot answer, 'Tomorrow'. His name is 'Today'. (Courtesy Oxfam.)

We are guilty of many errors and faults,
but our worst crime is abandoning the children,
neglecting the fountain of life.

Many of the things we need can wait.
The child cannot.

Right now is the time his bones are being formed,
his blood is being made and his senses are being developed.
To him we cannot answer, 'Tomorrow'.
His name is 'Today'.

Gabriela Mistral[1]

The little boy in *Figure 1.2* is receiving fluid replacement for dehydration caused by severe diarrhoea. The intravenous and nasogastric routes are being used since the child is both urgently ill and too weak to drink. The first of these methods entails inserting a needle into a vein – in this case on the forearm. The second requires the insertion of a polyvinyl tube into the nostril and down into the stomach. The intravenous route requires sterile, accurately prepared solutions of glucose, salts and water, and both routes require trained personnel. The child is obviously very undernourished. He has a form of protein–energy malnutrition (PEM) called marasmus.

1.2 A boy receives fluid replacement for dehydration. (TALC, courtesy Institute of Child Health, London.)

Figure 1.3 shows another form of PEM — kwashiorkor. One of the differences between these two forms of what is essentially the same disease — PEM — is the age distribution, although this varies somewhat from country to country (*Fig. 1.4*).

Figure 1.3 Kwashiorkor. (TALC, courtesy Institute of Child Health, London.)

Figure 1.5 shows the distribution of undernutrition in the world. In the underdeveloped countries children aged under 5 years may be divided into the groups shown in *Figure 1.6*.

At least one-fifth of all the world's children are undernourished.[2] The two girls pictured in *Figure 1.7* are exactly the same age: the taller one is of normal height and weight. The small, miserable girl is much too short and light for her age.

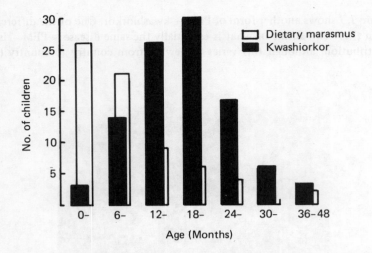

Figure 1.4 Age distribution of children admitted to Lagos Hospital with dietary marasmus and kwashiorkor. (TALC, courtesy Institute of Child Health, London.)

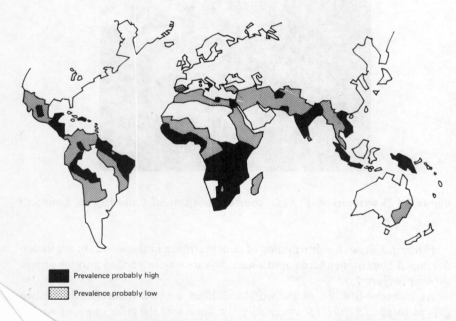

5 Geographical distribution of protein–calorie deficiencies in young children. (Courtesy World Health Organization.)

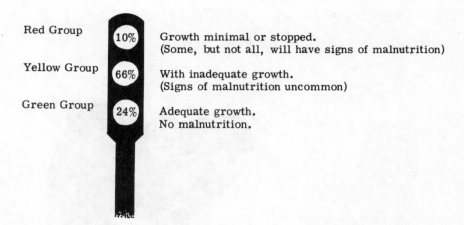

Red Group 10% Growth minimal or stopped.
(Some, but not all, will have signs of malnutrition)

Yellow Group 66% With inadequate growth.
(Signs of malnutrition uncommon)

Green Group 24% Adequate growth.
No malnutrition.

Figure 1.6 Children aged under 5 years in underdeveloped countries may be divided into these groups. (TALC, courtesy Institute of Child Health, London.)

Figure 1.7 These two girls are the same age. (TALC, courtesy Institute of Child Health, London.)

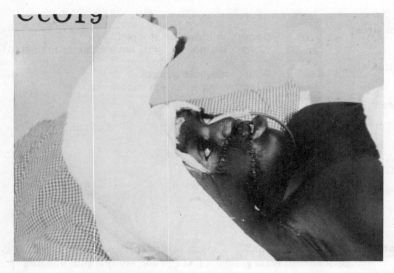

Figure 1.8 Plastic surgery for cancrum oris. (TALC, courtesy Institute of Child
Health, London.)

The little girl in *Figure 1.8* is a patient in the plastic surgery unit at a university hospital in an African city. She is undergoing repair of a facial defect caused
by cancrum oris (*Fig. 1.9*), an acute condition characterized by gangrene of the
gums, mouth, mucosa and facial tissue, also frequently destroying adjacent skin
and bone. Measles is the commonest cause.[3] Cancrum oris was once common
both in Europe and in America but has now virtually disappeared from these

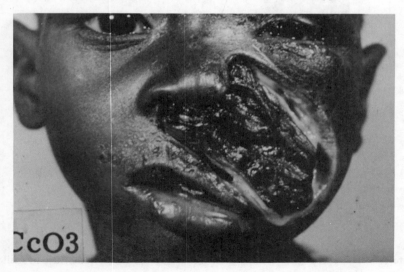

Figure 1.9 Cancrum oris. (TALC, courtesy Institute of Child Health, London.)

areas. However, it is still seen in the underdeveloped areas of Asia, Africa and South America. If it is not treated, maiming and death are all too common.[4]

The child in *Figure 1.10* closes his eyes to avoid light since he is photosensitive — bright sunlight hurts his eyes. He is carried by his mother because he cannot see well and is weak. He has xerophthalmia (*Fig. 1.11*) — a deficiency disease

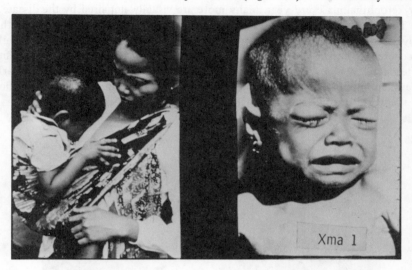

Figure 1.10   Child with xerophthalmia — bright sunlight hurts his eyes. (TALC, courtesy Institute of Child Health, London.)

Figure 1.11   Xerophthalmia — caused by lack of vitamin A. (TALC, courtesy Institute of Child Health, London.)

caused by lack of vitamin A, usually combined with too little food to supply the necessary calories, proteins or both (PEM). It occurs most often in young children because they require large quantities of vitamin A for growth and development.

It is estimated that 100 000 children, most under 6 years of age, are blinded by xerophthalmia every year. Many more are visually impaired by the disease.[5]

The X-ray in *Figure 1.12* shows tuberculosis (TB), which has hospitalized this boy and is responsible for his wasted appearance. *Figure 1.13* shows a child recovering from abdominal TB. In the underdeveloped world it is a common and often fatal disease, affecting about one per cent of people. It is particularly prevalent and also more dangerous in the under-5 age group. At least 50 million of the world's people suffer from TB.[6]

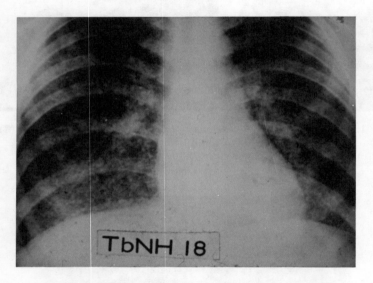

Figure 1.12   Tuberculosis. (TALC, courtesy Institute of Child Health, London.)

In underdeveloped countries skin disease is extremely common, especially in young children (*Fig. 1.14*). Infection with bacteria and fungi and parasitic infestations cause much suffering and, indirectly, death because of the effects of certain bacteria. Streptococcal infection of scratched scabies lesions has been responsible for six epidemics of severe kidney disease — acute glomerulonephritis — in Trinidad over the last 25 years, and similar epidemics are frequent in Africa and Asia.[7]

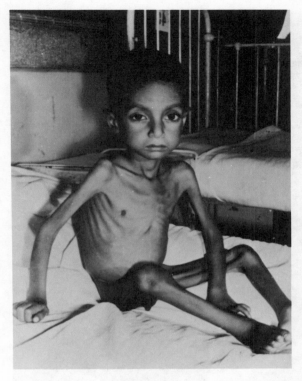

Figure 1.13 A child in India recovering from abdominal TB. (Courtesy Oxfam.)

About 200 million people are affected by malaria and approximately 70 million children under 5 are seriously at risk. Where it is endemic, malaria may cause up to 10 per cent of all deaths in children.[8]

'. . . . Children under 5 years of age in Brazil constitute less than one-fifth of the population but account for four-fifths of all deaths; in India, for 65 per cent of the deaths; in Egypt, for 68 per cent. (In the United States, the children at this age account for 8.8 per cent of the population and 4.8 per cent of deaths.) In Pakistan the percentage of 1–4 year olds who die is 40 times higher than in Japan and 80 times higher than in Sweden. In rural Punjab, one of India's strongest and healthiest areas, the death rate at that age is 72 times higher than in Sweden; in Egypt 107 times higher; and in The Gambia 111 times higher.'

Alan Berg[9]

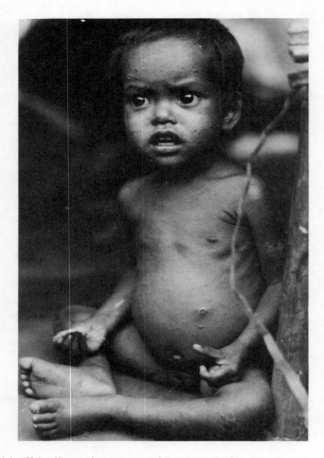

Figure 1.14 Skin disease is common. (Courtesy Oxfam.)

Of the 500 million children under the age of 5 years, 400 million live in under-developed countries, and it is there that 97 per cent of all deaths in that age group occur.[10]

There is no single indicator of health in a community. However, a number of statistics taken together give a rough idea of the level of *disease*. These include *life expectancy* and *infant mortality rate*. The latter, for reasons that will be discussed later, is a particularly sensitive index.

Population and disease statistics in underdeveloped countries are notoriously inaccurate, the degree of under-reporting of births, deaths and illness being most marked in rural areas where services are sparse. Thus while the following statistics are 'official' and of the correct magnitude, many are only approximations.

The burden of disease and death falls on small children. In the underdeveloped world a majority of all deaths often occurs in children under 5 years, who make

Table 1.1 **Deaths of children aged under 5**

Country	Deaths of children under 5 as % of all deaths	Children under 5 as % of population
Guatemala	57	17
Jamaica	38	17
Thailand	34	16
USA	7	11

Source: J. Bryant (1969). *Health and the Developing World*. Cornell University Press, Ithaca and London, p. 35 (*see* chapter 4, reference 32)

up only 17 per cent of the total population. Official data for three underdeveloped and one 'developed' country are shown in Table 1.1.

Data on infant mortality — deaths in the first year of life — are especially pertinent as they refer to the population most vulnerable to health hazards (*Fig. 1.15*). Life expectancy at various ages gives some insight into the health of populations (Table 1.2). Surviving the hazardous first year of life increases the expected life span in underdeveloped countries where the vulnerable young run the gauntlet of nutritional deficiency and infectious disease. But even if a child clears the obstacles of the first few years, she or he can expect to live only to 45 in some parts of the underdeveloped world.

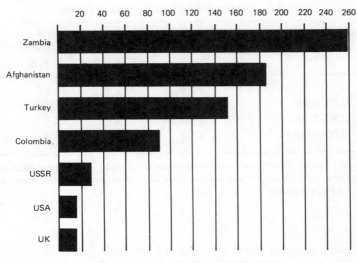

Infant mortality rates (per 1000 live births)

Figure 1.15 Infant mortality rates (per 1000 live births). (*UN Statistical Yearbook 1978*, courtesy United Nations.)

The Struggle for Health

Table 1.2 **Life expectancy in selected countries for males at specified ages (in years of life remaining)**

Country	Age					
	0	1	5	10	15	20
Togo	31.6	36.4	40.1	37.4	33.8	30.3
India	41.9	48.4	48.7	45.2	41.0	37.0
Guatemala	48.2	52.5	54.5	51.3	47.2	43.2
Sweden	72.1	71.9	68.0	63.1	58.2	53.5

Source: *UN Demographic Yearbook* (1977)

Within each country, whether rich or poor, ill health does not affect everyone equally. In Bangladesh for example, in 1975, a child whose family had no land was five times as likely to die between the ages of 1 and 4 years as a child whose family had 3 acres or more (Table 1.3). And even in Britain, between 1975 and

Table 1.3 **Death rates by landholding of family**

Land per family (acres)	Crude death rate per 1000 people	Death rate per 1000 infants aged 1–4
0	35.8	85.5
0.01–0.49	28.4	48.2
0.50–2.99	21.5	49.1
3.00 or more	12.2	17.5

Source: Colin McCord, 'What's the Use of a Demonstration Project?' quoted in *Basic Service Delivery in Developing Countries and a View from Gonoshasthaya Kendra*. United Nations Economic and Social Council

1977, the infant mortality rate was more than 12 per 1000 higher among children of unskilled manual workers than among those of 'professional' families (Table 1.4).

Table 1.4   **Stillbirths and mortality rates in the first year of life for legitimate births 1975-7 by social class**

Rate	Social class						
	All	*I*	*II*	*III NM*	*III M*	*IV*	*V*
Stillbirth*	9.5	7.0	7.7	8.6	10.0	11.1	13.4
Infant mortality†	13.6	9.8	10.9	11.5	13.3	15.9	21.9

Source: *Perinatal and Infant Mortality: Social and Biological Factors 1975-77,* HMSO (1980)

NM = Non-manual; M = Manual.
*Per 1000 live and stillbirths.
†Per 1000 live births.

References

1. Poem by Gabriela Mistral (Chilean Nobel prizewinner).
2. Susan George (1976). *How the Other Half Dies*, Pelican, London, p. 31.
3. Michael N. Tempest, 'Cancrum Oris', TALC slide series, Tropical Child Health Unit, Institute of Child Health, 30 Guilford St, London WC1.
4. *Ibid*.
5. Oomen and Beyda, 'Xerophthalmia', TALC slide series.
6. *New Internationalist*, April 1977, p. 8.
7. David Morley (1973). *Paediatric Priorities in the Developing World*, Butterworths, London, pp. 279-83.
8. *New Internationalist*, April 1977, p. 9.
9. Alan Berg (1973). *The Nutrition Factor and its Role in National Development*, the Brookings Institution, Washington.
10. Morley, *Paediatric Priorities*, p. 1.

2 Disease in Underdeveloped and Developed Countries

Diseases of the underdeveloped world are often talked of as *'tropical'*, bringing to mind such grotesque images as leprosy cripples, stuporose sleeping-sickness sufferers and victims of ever-present parasites. Exotic disease-transmitting insects swarm past our mind's eye and swampy undergrowth conceals lurking health hazards (*Fig. 2.1*). But is this commonly held caricature correct? Are diseases in tropical and subtropical countries really 'tropical'?

Figure 2.1 'Exotic, disease-transmitting insects. . .'. (Courtesy Chris Welch.)

DISEASE IN UNDERDEVELOPED COUNTRIES

The diseases that account for 50–90 per cent of illness and death among the poor in the underdeveloped world fall into two main groups — *nutritional deficiencies and communicable diseases*. These sometimes act separately but more often they act together and aggravate each other. The conventional groupings for childhood deaths are shown in Table 2.1. A study in two projects in North America and 13 in Latin America, comprising urban and rural areas, has yielded the most reliable information on the causes of childhood mortality.[1]

Table 2.1 **Groupings for childhood deaths**

Term used	Age
Infant:	Under 1 year
Neonatal	0–28 days
Postneonatal	28 days–1 year
Child	1–5 years

Causes of Disease and Death in the First Month of Life

Immature babies or those with low birth weight are most vulnerable to disease and death. In the Latin American countries studied, immaturity was 2–3 times as common as an associated cause of death as it was in North America (*Fig. 2.2*).

The nutritional state of the mother before and during pregnancy is important in determining the size of her baby at birth. Undernourished mothers have small, and therefore more vulnerable babies. The mother's size and nutritional status depend not only on genetic factors but also on her own diet in infancy, childhood and pregnancy (*Fig. 2.3*). They also depend on her age. In undernourished communities growth may not be completed until the age of 18 or 19 by which time many women are or have already been pregnant.[2]

Anaemia in the tropics is extremely common and results from general chronic undernutrition, recurrent infection and infestation by parasites such as malaria and hookworm. It causes premature labour and yet again an immature and extra-vulnerable baby.[3]

Malaria in pregnant mothers is an acknowledged cause of infection of the placenta and thus of low birth weights, especially in first and early pregnancies. The reduction in fetal growth comes towards the end of pregnancy, when brain cells are multiplying rapidly. The child's potential for intellectual development may be irreversibly impaired.[4]

In the 'developed' world smoking during pregnancy is one of the most important factors in reducing the baby's weight and potential for intellectual development.[5]

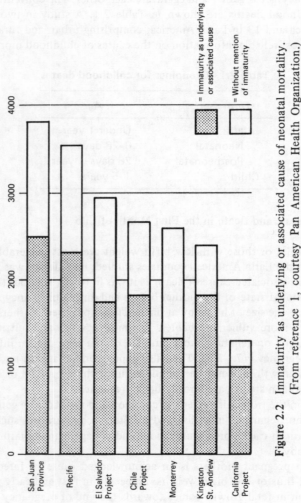

Figure 2.2 Immaturity as underlying or associated cause of neonatal mortality. (From reference 1, courtesy Pan American Health Organization.)

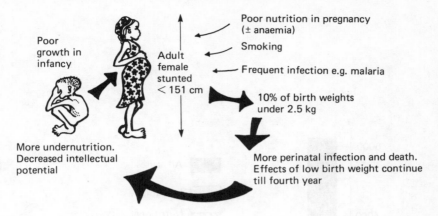

Figure 2.3   The cycle of malnutrition.

Causes of Disease and Death in Infancy and Early Childhood

Small babies surviving the first month of life often develop nutritional deficiency.[6] This was an associated cause of death of 35 per cent of the children under 5 in the Pan American study. The problem was especially severe in the postneonatal period (1 month to 1 year) and during the second year of life.

Nutritional deficiency and immaturity were the direct cause of 6 per cent of deaths occurring before the age of 5, with one or the other factor being an associated cause in 57 per cent of all deaths (*Fig. 2.4*). In the postneonatal period and early childhood (age 1 month to 4 years inclusive) infectious diseases accounted for more than half of all deaths.

Diarrhoeal disease was the major underlying cause of death in the under-5s, accounting for 29 per cent of the total. Measles was the second most common, accounting for 9.4 per cent of deaths in those aged from 1 month to 5 years. (Measles does not occur in newborn babies.) Other diseases including TB, diphtheria, whooping cough, tetanus, meningitis, infectious hepatitis and poliomyelitis were responsible for the remainder of deaths due to infectious disease in the Pan American study. This pattern is common to all areas of the underdeveloped world (Table 2.2).

Infectious and communicable disease takes its toll of adult life too. *Figure 2.5* gives a general idea of the pattern of disease in underdeveloped and developed countries.

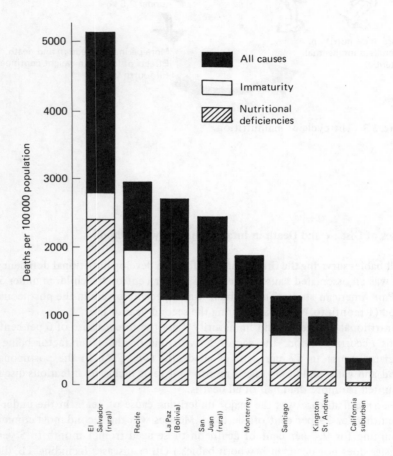

Figure 2.4 Mortality in children under 5 years of age from all causes and from nutritional deficiency and immaturity. (From reference 1, courtesy Pan American Health Organization.)

Table 2.2 **Causes of death in infants and children aged under 5 years**

Cause	London 1903	Matlab, Bangladesh 1975–7	Haiti 1979/80	Java 1978	Narangwal, India 1971–3
Diarrhoea/enteritis	13	29	15	15	39
Pneumonia/respiratory	17	6	12	21	19
Malnutrition, including low birth weight	26	—	33	22	5
Immunizable diseases:					
Tetanus	4	14	3	8	2
Pertussis	4	—	1	—	—
Measles	3	8	1	6	1
Tuberculosis	4	—	3	—	—
Other	29	57	31	28	34
Death rate per 1000	145	280	200	100	135
Age group	0–1	0–4	0–4	0–2	0–3

Source: Jon Eliot Rohde (1982). *Why the Other Half Dies: The Science and Politics of Child Mortality in the Third World*, UNESCO

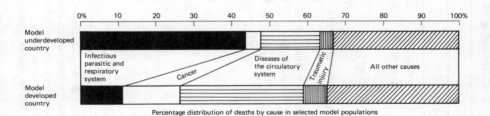

Percentage distribution of deaths by cause in selected model populations

Figure 2.5 Percentage distribution of deaths by cause in selected model populations. (From chapter 3, reference 45, courtesy World Bank.)

There is a simple way of classifying the bulk of disease in the underdeveloped world (Table 2.3).

Table 2.3 Classification of most disease in underdeveloped countries

| Nutritional | Communicable | |
	Airborne	Water-related and faecally transmitted
Undernutrition and associated vitamin deficiencies	**Viral** — Influenza, Pneumonia, Measles, Chicken-pox	**Water-borne or water-washed** — Cholera, Typhoid, Diarrhoeas, dysenteries, amoebiasis, infectious hepatitis, poliomyelitis, intestinal worms
	Bacterial — Whooping cough, Diphtheria, Meningitis, Tuberculosis	**Water-washed:** Skin and eye infection — Trachoma, Skin infection, Leprosy, Scabies; Skin infestation — Louseborne typhus
		Water-based: Penetrating skin — Schistosomiasis (bilharzia); Ingested — Guinea worm
		Water-related insect vectors: Biting near water — Sleeping sickness, Malaria, Yellow fever; Breeding in water — Onchocerciasis (river blindness)

Key: Airborne = Disease spread by breathing airborne, respiratory secretions of infected persons; Water-borne = Disease transmitted when pathogen is in water which is then drunk by person who may then become infected; Water-washed = Disease whose prevalence will fall when increased *quantities* of water are used for drinking and hygienic purposes (the water should be clean, but need not be pure); Water-based = Disease where pathogen spends a part of its life cycle in an intermediate aquatic host or hosts.

Source: Adapted from D. J. Bradley (1974). In *Human Rights in Health*, CIBA Foundation Symposium 23 (New Series), Elsevier, Amsterdam, pp. 81–98

Interaction of Nutritional Deficiency and Infection

These categories — nutritional, airborne and water related — are interrelated and interact with one another (*Fig. 2.6*). Undernutrition is a major contributing factor in communicable disease. It impairs normal body responses to disease, thus reducing any immunity created by infections. Again data from the 13 Latin American countries showed clearly how communicable diseases and nutritional deficiency work together (Table 2.4).

Severely undernourished children experience on average four times the number of attacks of diarrhoea per year as adequately nourished children.[7] Moderately malnourished children too have longer-lasting attacks of diarrhoea than their normally grown counterparts.[8] Repeated episodes of diarrhoea impair appetite and make it more difficult for the body to absorb food and also increase the body's metabolism, so causing nutritional deficiency. Thus the vicious circle is complete.

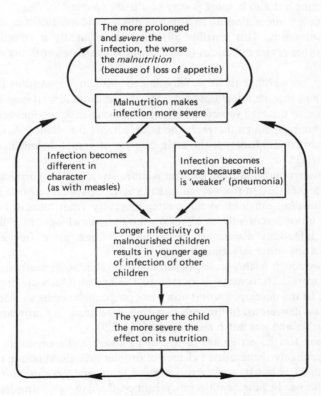

Figure 2.6 Interaction of nutritional deficiency and infection.

Table 2.4 **Nutritional deficiency as associated cause of death under 5 years of age (excluding neonatal deaths) by underlying cause group in 13 Latin American projects combined**

Underlying cause group	Nutritional deficiency as associated cause (%)
All causes	47
Infective and parasitic diseases:	61
Diarrhoeal disease	61
Measles	62
Other	59
Diseases of respiratory system	32
Other causes	33

Source: reference 1.

Studies have shown that skin infections are more common not only where water is lacking but also in more poorly nourished people.[9]

The complex interaction of an airborne disease and malnutrition is epitomized in cancrum oris. This horrible affliction is frequently a complication of measles or other severe infections (*Fig. 2.7*) and is associated with undernutrition (*Fig. 2.8*).[10]

Similarly, xerophthalmia is usually linked with undernutrition (PEM) and with acute and chronic infections of childhood that cause low vitamin A levels.[11] Regeneration of diseased superficial layers of tissue as in severe measles, chickenpox and whooping cough increases the body's needs for vitamin A which soon becomes exhausted. Measles is the main catalyst of xerophthalmia in the underdeveloped world.[12]

In the undernourished child measles is more severe and may have a mortality 400 times higher than in the well-nourished child.[13] (Recent research also shows that overcrowding can lead to far greater mortality from measles.) Measles in turn has a more severe adverse effect on the nutritional state of children than any other infectious disease. Undernutrition follows more frequently after measles than any other infection.

Whooping cough is also an important cause of childhood death in the underdeveloped world. Its severity is related to the age at which children become infected.[14] In the developed world now whooping cough occurs in older children when it is less dangerous. In the past, however, the disease in European countries occurred earlier and was much more severe (*Fig. 2.9*).

The reason for the earlier age of whooping cough and many other infectious diseases is probably the increased chance of droplet infection because children in underdeveloped countries are carried around more and because more children share one home. In nineteenth-century Europe the danger of droplet infection existed because of overcrowding. Now European children tend to receive their

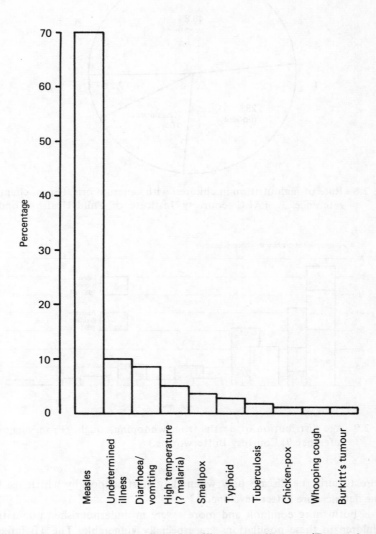

Figure 2.7 Cancrum oris: predisposing illness or disease. (From chapter 1, reference 3. TALC, courtesy Institute of Child Health, London.)

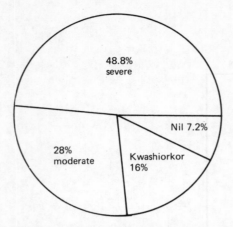

Figure 2.8 Rate of malnutrition in children with cancrum oris. (From chapter 1, reference 3. TALC, courtesy Institute of Child Health, London.)

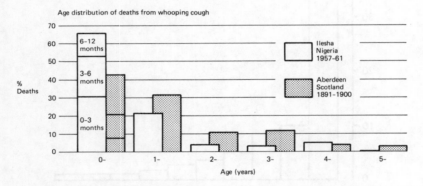

Figure 2.9 Age distribution of deaths from whooping cough. (From chapter 1, reference 7. Courtesy Butterworths.)

exposure to airborne disease only when they start school, by which age their immune defences are better developed.[15]

TB is both more common and more severe in undernourished populations, and children in these populations are especially vulnerable. The TB infection aggravates the undernourished state and this leads to a more rapid spread of the disease.[16] Yet again, the vicious cycle.

Thus communicable airborne and water-related diseases acting in the presence of and aggravating undernutrition cause most illness and death. The presence of insect vector-borne diseases such as sleeping sickness, river blindness and malaria is connected with climate, although malaria was certainly present even in England in the nineteenth and early twentieth centuries and a major cause of ill-health in southern Europe until relatively recently. However, apart from these and certain of the parasitic infestations spread by excreta contaminating water and food, for example schistosomiasis and certain intestinal worms, *the vast majority of illnesses causing debility and death in the underdeveloped world cannot be thought of as 'tropical'.*[17]

DISEASE IN NINETEENTH-CENTURY EUROPE

A look at one area of the developed world — namely England and Wales — in the eighteenth, nineteenth and twentieth centuries will put this pattern of disease in historical perspective.

In London half the infants baptized in the period 1770–89 were dead before the age of 5 years.[18] The *Health of Towns Magazine and Journal of Medical Jurisprudence* of 1847–8 gives us a glimpse of life at that time. The following extract[18] describes Snow's Rents in Westminster:

'On entering these houses you have a fine specimen of the manner in which the lower orders of Westminster live. Living by day and night in one wretched room, with scarcely any light — an intermittent supply of water, and a shocking faetid atmosphere — full of rags and filth — it is dreadful! In the corner of the room may be seen what may be termed an apology for a bed and bedding, being a mass of rags piled together, in the midst of which are the poor sickly children, whose very countenance bespeak that they will soon cease to trouble their parents; with hair uncombed, barefooted, and in rags — with their skin unwashed — the majority of them never live to manhood, while one third of them die before they attain the age of 5 years. The adult inhabitants, also, have all the appearance of being always in a typhoid state. The courts and alleys in this colony of filth and fever are chiefly unpaved and undrained, and mostly with but one privy for one court, which contains, sometimes, upwards of twenty houses. . . .

'Such is a brief sketch of a portion of what is commonly known as Lower Westminster, and which is situated midway between Buckingham palace and the House of Lords and Commons, and about 300 yards from either.

'The little girl with the saucepan in her hand [*Fig. 2.10*] is throwing on the heap a quantity of vegetable matter which is left to rot until the scavenger thinks proper to take it away. On the other side is a person following the combined callings of a chimney sweep and nightman. There is an ease in the man's appearance which shows that his calling and his residence for many years among filth have rendered him familiar with such scenes — it has almost made him love filth. His little girl has in one hand a bloater and in the other the Gin Bottle — the God chiefly worshipped among such people.'

Figure 2.10   Snow's Rents, Westminster. (By courtesy of the Wellcome Trustees.)

It was not just in Westminster that such stark differences existed. Similar conditions prevailed in all the new towns of the industrial revolution. Things were far from comfortable in the rural areas but at a number of points in the first half of the nineteenth century the infant mortality rate was twice as high in the new towns. According to Dr Turner Thackrah of Leeds, 'Not 10 per cent of the inhabitants of large towns enjoy full health.' Dr G. C. Holland of Sheffield explained that *social class* had a lot to do with it:

'We have no hesitation in asserting, that the sufferings of the working classes, and consequently the rate of mortality, are greater now than in former times. Indeed, in most manufacturing districts the rate of mortality in these classes is appalling to contemplate, when it can be studied in reference to them alone, *and not in connexion with the entire population.* The supposed gain on the side of longevity, arising chiefly from. . .a relatively much more numerous middle class than formerly existed.'

The Making of the English Working Class[19] (*see also Fig. 2.11*)

The trend of the death rate for males and females from 1841 to 1971 is shown in *Figure 2.12*. Death rates did not significantly change until after 1871, and then mainly in the 2–34 age group. There was no improvement in infant mortality or in mortality at ages over 45.[20]

Preston.

Rev. J. Clay.

TABLE showing the comparative Age at Death, &c., and the proportion of Births to Population in Preston and the neighbouring Districts of Walton-le-dale, Ashton, and Broughton.

CLASSES.	Average Age of: Total Deaths. Preston.	Walton.	Alston.	Broughton.	Deaths after 21. Preston.	Walton.	Alston.	Broughton.
Gentry, &c.	47·4	47·6	36·8	37·9	61·2	63·1	54·5	65.7
Tradesmen and Farmers.	31·6	38·8	42·7	43·	54·7	58·5	54·8	62·5
General Labourers	..	26·8	32·5	29·4	..	58·	63·5	52·6
	18·3	..	..	..	50·3	..	..	..
Weavers and Factory Hands	..	21·4	..	..	..	49·5	..	..
Σ	19·6	25·7	34·8	34·4	51·3	54·5	60·	57·1

CLASSES.	Per Centage of each Class Dying: Above 21. Preston.	Walton.	Alston.	Broughton.	Above 5. Preston.	Walton.	Alston.	Broughton.	Under 5. Preston.	Walton.	Alston.	Broughton.
Gentry, &c.	76·3	73·3	66·7	52·1	92·4	86·7	66·7	82·6	17·6	13·3	33·3	17·4
Tradesmen and Farmers.	51·8	63·5	74·5	66·5	61·8	77·8	86·3	77·2	38·2	22·2	13·7	22·8
General Labourers	..	42·7	48·9	50·5	..	57·3	60·1	67·6	..	42·7	39·9	32·4
	31·6	..	..	..	44·6	..	..	..	55·4	..	..	..
Weavers and Factory Hands	..	36·7	..	..	..	54·8	..	..	..	45·2	..	..
Σ	34·1	42·5	54·7	55·9	46·7	67·2	65·9	71·5	53·3	41·2	34·	28·5

CLASSES.	Total Number of Deaths on which the Calculations are made: Preston.	Walton.	Alston.	Broughton.	Population, 1841: Preston.	Walton.	Alston.	Broughton.	Deaths: Preston.	Walton.	Alston.	Broughton.	Births: Preston.	Walton.	Alston.	Broughton.
Gentry, &c.	148	15	6	23	50,131	8,493	4,676	6,658	2·98 per cent., or 1 in 33 annually.	2·1 ,, or 1 in 47 ,,	1·98 ,, or 1 in 50 ,,	1·8 ,, or 1 in 56 ,,	3·3 ,, or 1 in 26 ,,	3·5 ,, or 1 in 29 ,,	3·2 ,, or 1 in 31 ,,	2·9 ,, or 1 in 34 ,,
Tradesmen and Farmers.	764	126	102	158												
General Labourers	..	407	256	293												
	8017	..	..	..												
Weavers and Factory Hands	..	526	..	..												
Σ	8929	1074	464	474												

NOTE.—The above Calculations are made, as regards
Preston and Walton, on an average of 6 years.
Alston ,, ,, 5 years.
Broughton ,, ,, 4 years.

Figure 2.11 An 1844 Royal Commission showed much higher child mortality among labourers and factory workers than among the gentry. (By courtesy of the Wellcome Trustees.)

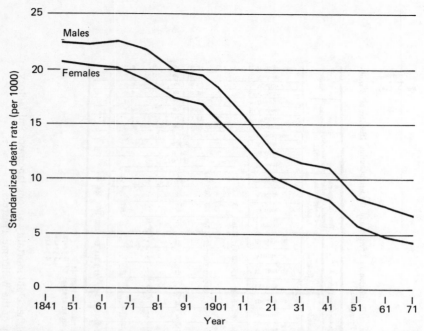

Figure 2.12   Death rates (standardized to 1901 population) England and Wales.
(From reference 17, courtesy Nuffield Provincial Hospitals Trust.)

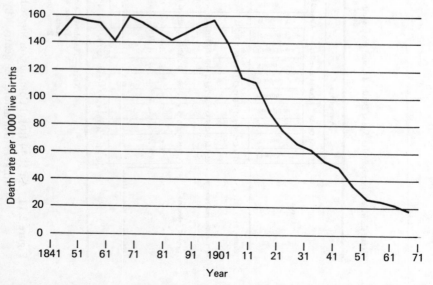

Figure 2.13   Infant mortality rate: England and Wales. (From chapter 3, reference 5. Courtesy Blackwell Scientific Publications.)

In 1846–50 the male infant mortality rate was 172 per 1000 live births and up to the end of the century did not improve. By 1947 it was a quarter of what it had been both in 1896–1900 and in 1846–50 (*Figure 2.13*). For every nine boys who died each year in 1846–50 only one died in 1947. In girls the improvement was even greater; in the group aged 5–9 it fell to 9 per cent of the original rate.[21]

Disease Pattern

Despite some difficulties in interpreting data on causes of death it has been possible to distinguish between those conditions that were attributable to micro-organisms and those that were not. In other words we can classify disease in England and Wales in much the same way as we did for the underdeveloped world (Table 2.5).

The airborne diseases most commonly responsible for death were TB, the bronchitis–pneumonia–influenza group and the diphtheria–scarlet fever group. In children measles and whooping cough were particularly common causes of death.[22]

Most important in the water- and food-borne category was the diarrhoeal group of diarrhoea–dysentery–enteritis and some cholera deaths. Also important as a cause of death was non-respiratory tuberculosis; often this was contracted from drinking infected milk and so acquiring bovine TB. Typhoid and typhus (which is louse borne) were often confused and so grouped together; they were significant causes of death in the nineteenth century (*Fig. 2.14*).[23]

Most deaths from other diseases caused by micro-organisms were in fact due to conditions such as convulsions, now known to be mostly due to airborne infections.[24]

The major conditions not attributable to micro-organisms were 'old age' and 'prematurity, immaturity and other diseases of infancy'. There is in this classification of causes of death no mention of *nutritional state*.

We know that severe forms of undernutrition occurred, and therefore moderate nutritional deficiency was undoubtedly very common especially among poorer people in nineteenth-century Britain. Descriptions of 'frightful swelling' of the bodies of children in Ireland in the potato famine of 1847 are likely to have been *kwashiorkor*.[25] Records of heights in the nineteenth century suggest that mothers and children — and therefore fathers too — were not nearly as well nourished as in Britain today.[26]

In the 1870s, 11–12-year-old boys from the upper-class public schools were on average 5 inches (12.7 cm) taller than boys from industrial schools. Public schoolboys of 11 and older all averaged 3 inches (7.62 cm) more than the sons of artisans. Similarly, although children in underdeveloped countries are *generally*

Table 2.5 Death rates (per million) in 1848/54 and 1971 in England and Wales

	1848/54	1971	Percentage of reduction attributable to each category
I. Conditions attributable to micro-organisms (communicable):			
Airborne diseases	7259	619	40
Water- and food-borne diseases	3562	35	21
Other conditions	2144	60	13
Total	12965	714	74
II. Conditions not attributable to micro-organisms	8891	4070	26
All diseases	21856	5384	100

Source: Thomas McKeown. The Role of Medicine: Dream, Mirage or Nemesis?[1,7]

Figure 2.14 Monster soup, commonly called Thames Water — an engraving of 1828. (By courtesy of the Wellcome Trustees.)

smaller than children in the 'developed' world, those from the higher socio-economic groups have grown to 'British standards' (*Fig. 2.16*).[27] Indeed the Japanese are no longer 'a small people' (*Fig. 2.16*).[28]

Clearly, *nutritional deficiency* played an important part in disease in nine-teenth-century England and prepared the way for the disastrous effects of *infections*. Disease and death in Europe in the not-too-distant past was strikingly similar to that in most of today's underdeveloped world.

Death rates in England and Wales have shown a massive decline since 1841. Death rates per 1000 in 1700 were approximately 30, and in 1971 just over 5.[29] Infectious disease acting in the presence of undernutrition caused most ill health and death, especially among infants and children.

86 per cent of the total reduction in death rate from the beginning of the eighteenth century to the present day was caused by a decline in deaths from infectious disease.

Figures 2.17–2.19 show the trend in mortality in England and Wales from some of the most important airborne and water-related infections.

Tuberculosis was the largest single cause of death in the mid-nineteenth century. The bacterium causing TB was identified in 1882 but all medical treat-ment practised before 1947 is now known to have been ineffective. Effective treatment began with the use of streptomycin in 1947 and immunization with BCG vaccine started in 1954. *By these dates mortality from TB had fallen to a small fraction of its level in 1848–54.* Drug treatment is responsible for the *more*

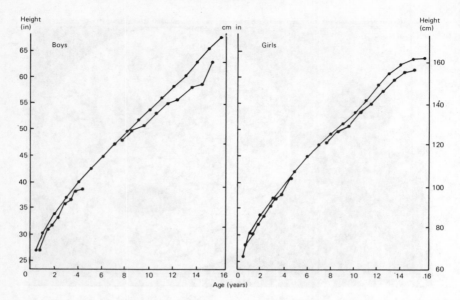

Figure 2.15 Comparison of heights of children in UK (●—●) and Lawrence Tavern, Jamaica (∗——∗). (From reference 26. TALC, courtesy Institute of Child Health, London.)

Figure 2.16 The Japanese are no longer a 'small people'. (Courtesy Colleen Cousins.)

rapid fall of mortality since 1950, but the substantial reduction occurred before the era of antibiotics (*Fig. 2.17*).

Similarly, deaths from the major childhood killers — scarlet fever, diphtheria, measles and whooping cough — had fallen to almost their present level before any effective medical treatment had been developed (*Fig. 2.18*).[30]

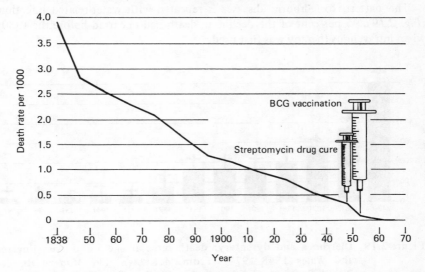

Figure 2.17 Decline in TB before drugs. (From reference 17. Courtesy Nuffield Provincial Hospitals Trust.)

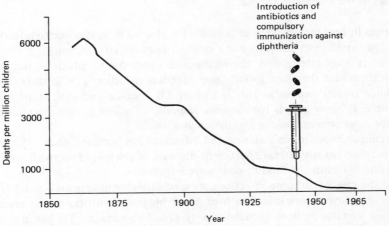

Figure 2.18 Deaths of children under 15 years attributed to scarlet fever, diphtheria, whooping cough and measles in England and Wales. (Courtesy Office of Health Economics.)

Smallpox was responsible for only a small proportion of deaths due to air-borne infections but it is the one disease in which a specific medical measure — vaccination — appears to have contributed to its decline. This will be of interest later when we consider the success of the world-wide smallpox eradication campaign and whether it can be repeated for other diseases.

The pattern for airborne diseases is repeated with water-related infections (*Fig. 2.19*). 95 per cent of the decline in death had occurred before the 1930s, when intravenous therapy was first used.

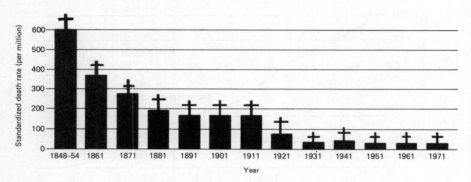

Figure 2.19 Diarrhoea and dysentery: death rates at age 5 and over, England and Wales 1848–1971. (From McKeown, *The Modern Rise of World Population*, Edward Arnold, London, courtesy of author and publishers.)

Causes of the Decline in Disease

Changes in two factors were responsible for the fall in deaths due to infections: reduced exposure to infection and a stronger response to infection.

The two are interrelated: the weaker one's response to infection, the longer one carries and therefore spreads the infection to others — who therefore experience greater exposure. This is true of TB, measles and gastroenteritis, for example. If many people have a weak response to infection then that infection will be more common in the population as a whole.

Reduced exposure to water-related infections has occurred since 1850, when (1) purification of water, (2) efficient disposal of sewage, (3) provision of safe milk and (4) improved food hygiene were introduced.

In the case of airborne infections reduced exposure has resulted mainly from fewer people carrying infection because of improved nutrition. Less cramped housing conditions have reduced the spread. Exposure to TB has also been reduced by improved living and less polluted working conditions (*Fig. 2.20*). At the same time people became better able to resist infection. There was a large increase in food supplies in Europe between the end of the seventeenth and the

(a)

THE LABOUR-YARD OF THE BETHNAL-GREEN EMPLOYMENT ASSOCIATION.

(b)

Figure 2.20 **(a)** London 1860s; **(b)** India 1970s. **((a)** By courtesy of the Wellcome Trustees; **(b)** courtesy Oxfam.)

middle of the nineteenth centuries. This coincided with a large fall in mortality from infectious diseases, especially in childhood, including airborne and water-related disease. This was because of *improved nutrition*.

Already by the beginning of the eighteenth century a revolution in agriculture had transformed food production. England in the two centuries up to the industrial revolution did not experience the famine that continued to plague continental Europe with its largely feudal agriculture.[31]

So since the early 1800s, the huge fall in illness and death resulted from the following, in order of importance:

(1) Improved living standards.
(2) Improved hygiene.
(3) Specific preventive measures (e.g. smallpox vaccination).
(4) Much later, curative measures (e.g. antibacterial drugs).

But in most of the underdeveloped world urban living conditions are not very different from those in nineteenth-century England. This account by a Canadian ex-resident of Shanghai in the 1930s is as graphic as that in the *Health of Towns Magazine* of 1847-8[18]:

'I searched for scurvy-headed children. Lice-ridden children. Children with inflamed red eyes. Children with bleeding gums. Children with distended stomachs and spindly arms and legs. I searched the sidewalks day and night for children who had been purposely deformed by beggars. Beggars who would leech on to any well-dressed passer-by to blackmail sympathy and offering, by pretending the hideous-looking child was their own.
'I looked for children covered with horrible sores upon which flies feasted. I looked for children having a bowel movement, which, after much strain would only eject tapeworms. I looked for child slaves in alleyway factories. Children who worked 12 hours a day, literally chained to small press punches. Children, who if they lost a finger, or worse, often were cast into the streets to beg and forage in garbage bins for future subsistence.'

Eastern Horizon[32]

Could this not just as well be a description of Calcutta or Nairobi, Bombay or Dacca, Lima or Lagos *today*?
The World Health Organization says of conditions in the African shanty towns:

'From the sanitary aspect Engels's description of the Manchester slums in 1844 is applicable to these shanty towns. Sanitation is non-existent, and open drains run down what passes for streets. The shanties are built of mud and wattle, old packing-cases, or kerosene tins, with tattered blankets as doors. Children crawl among the uncollected rubbish or in the drains. Water has to be fetched from a pump, well, or tap, and may be contaminated.'

The Social Organization of Health[33] (*see* also *Fig. 2.21*)

Figure 2.21 Hundreds of millions live in overcrowded conditions or slums.

Indeed, of the world's population of 4500 million[34] :

(1)   2000 million people are *undernourished*.
(2)   1100 million people or 86 per cent of the world's *rural* population and at least 25 per cent of the world's urban population do not live near a *safe water* supply.
(3)   At least 1000 million people do not have *safe sewage* and waste disposal facilities.
(4)   More than 250 million people are *homeless* and hundreds of millions live in overcrowded conditions or slums.

HEALTH DISPARITIES WITHIN COUNTRIES

Underdeveloped World

Of course not *all* parts of underdeveloped countries are underdeveloped. In fact the general pattern the world over is one of very uneven development, with grotesque inequalities, especially in the underdeveloped world. These inequalities are obvious to health workers who see and treat the *effects* of the inequalities.

In South Africa, for example, infant mortailty rates are roughly six times as high for blacks and 'coloureds' as they are for whites (Table 2.6). In other under-developed countries the poor and the rich are not distinguished by the colour of their skins and so there are not recorded infant mortality rates (or any other rates) for poor and rich, but rather rates for the population as a *whole*. This masks the vast differences in disease and death between the rich and poor. In the Pan American study, mortality was analysed according to socioeconomic status. Educational level of the mother was used as the most sensitive indicator of this (*Fig. 2.22*).

Table 2.6 **Age-specific mortality rates of different population groups in South Africa (1970) (deaths per 1000 population)**

Group	Age (years)								
	Infant	*< 1*	*1–4*	*5–14*	*15–24*	*25–34*	*35–44*	*45–54*	*55–64*
Whites	21.6	22.7	1.1	0.5	1.5	1.7	3.8	9.0	20.1
Asians	36.4	41.4	3.6	0.8	1.4	2.3	5.6	14.5	33.9
Coloureds	132.6	139.4	14.7	1.2	2.7	5.1	8.8	17.0	31.2
Blacks	(?)123.9	135.8	15.6	1.4	3.0	4.9	8.3	15.3	27.7

Source: C. H. Wyndham and L. M. Irwig (1979). A comparison of the mortality rates of various population groups in the Republic of South Africa. *South African Medical Journal*, 12 May

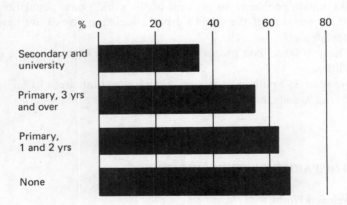

Figure 2.22 Deaths from nutritional deficiency as underlying or associated cause in children 1–4 years, by educational level of mother, in 13 Latin American projects combined. (From reference 1. Courtesy Pan American Health Organization.)

In Africa and Asia there are even more striking differences in health between poor and rich. Infant mortality rates among élite groups in many parts of the underdeveloped world are similar to European rates — approximately 20 per 1000 live births — while the poorest people's infants die at a rate of up to 300 or even 400 for every 1000 born alive.

Developed World

Nowadays most of the problems of undernutrition and infection have been overcome in the developed world by all the agricultural and environmental improvements mentioned. This means that childhood deaths are now very infrequent and our 'medical problems' are quite different (*Fig. 2.23*). Yet disparities between rich and poor still exist (*Fig. 2.24*), and this is seen too in those illnesses that do not usually cause death (*Fig. 2.25*).

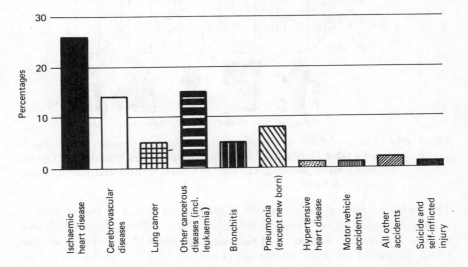

Figure 2.23 Percentage of total deaths in 1973, Great Britain. (Courtesy Office of Population, Censuses and Surveys.)

In Britain, the *General Household Survey* of 1973[35] found that:

'Unskilled men of working age were about three times as likely to say that they suffered from chronic sickness as professional men of the same age group, and younger unskilled men had higher rates than professional men of middle age.'

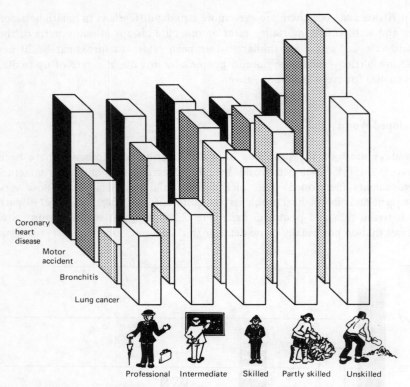

Figure 2.24 Cause of death and occupational social class (males 15–64). (Based
on a table on p. 116 of *Statistics of Inequality* (Preston, B. (1974)).
Sociological Review, **22**, No. 1. Courtesy Editorial Board, *Sociological Review*.)

This survey found that the prevalence of many illnesses rose in inverse relation
to socioeconomic status. These included bronchitis, injuries, mental disorders,
diseases of the ear, and diseases of the digestive system.[35] A study of the supposed 'diseases of affluence' such as cancer and heart disease shows some reasons
for the differences in health between social classes. Lung cancer, of course, is
primarily caused by cigarette smoking, which varies widely between different
social classes (Table 2.7).

Cancer of the colon shows a 20 per cent difference between the social classes.
Here diet seems to be the main factor — for example, the low fibre content of
the food eaten in Western industrialized societies. This is common to all classes,
but even so the reliance of the working class on 'convenience foods' makes them
even more vulnerable.

Unhealthy diets are one factor contributing to coronary heart disease. Cigarette
smoking is another. Occupational stress is another major contributor, and
contrary to mythology the main sufferers are not overworked businessmen but

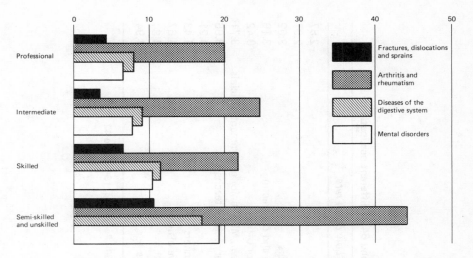

Figure 2.25   Rate per 1000 reporting selected condition groups causing limiting long-standing illness, England and Wales. (From *General Household Survey 1973*. Courtesy HMSO.)

Table 2.7   **Cigarette smoking by socioeconomic group, Great Britain 1982**

Socioeconomic group	Percentage smoking cigarettes	
	Men	Women
Professional	20	21
Employers and managers	29	29
Intermediate and junior non-manual	30	30
Skilled manual and own account non-professional	42	39
Semi-skilled manual and personal service	47	36
Unskilled manual	49	41

Source: OPCS Monitor

those involved in the repetitive, unsatisfying and highly disciplined process of production. High blood pressure is another major factor. A recent study from America shows that this is prevalent among the poor and the working class.[36]

And in Britain a recent report, commissioned by one government and hushed up by its successor, shows that those who suffer most from 'diseases of affluence' are in fact the *least* affluent members of Western society (Table 2.8).

Table 2.8 Death rate per 1000 of men in Britain aged between 15 and 64 in different occupations

High death rate		Low death rate	
Coal miners (underground)	8.22	University teachers	2.87
Shoemakers, and shoe repairers	8.98	Physiotherapists	2.97
Leather products makers	8.95	Paper products makers	3.02
Machine tool operators	9.34	Managers in building and contracting	3.19
Watch repairers	9.46	Local authority senior officers	3.42
Coal miners (above ground)	9.72	Ministers of the Crown, MPs, senior government officials	3.71
Steel erectors, riggers	9.92	Primary and secondary school teachers	3.96
Fishermen	10.28	Sales managers	4.21
Labourers and unskilled workers, all industries	12.47	Architects, town planners	4.43
Policemen	12.70	Civil service executive officers	4.67
Bricklayers' labourers	16.44	Postmen	4.84
Electrical engineers	19.04	Medical practitioners	4.94

Source: Townsend, P. and Davidson, N. (1982). Inequalities in Health – The Black Report (1980), Penguin, p. 194, Table 42

References

1. R. R. Puffer and C. V. Serrano (1973). *Patterns of Mortality in Childhood*, Pan American Health Organization Scientific Publication, PAHO No 262, Washington.
2. Morley (1973). *Paediatric Priorities in the Developing World*. Butterworths, London, p. 78; Richard L. Naeye (1983). Effects of Maternal Nutrition on Fetal and Neonatal Survival, *Birth*, vol **10**, Summer.
3. Morley, *Paediatric Priorities in the Developing World*, p. 80.
4. *Ibid*., p. 79.
5. R. Davie, N. Butler and H. Goldstein (1972). *From Birth to Seven*, Longman, London, Chap. 16.
6. Morley, *Paediatric Priorities in the Developing World*, p. 163.
7. D. C. Morley, and M. Woodland (1979). *See How They Grow*, Macmillan, London, p. 97.
8. Morley, *Paediatric Priorities in the Developing World*, p. 181; Andrew Tomkins (1981). Nutritional status and severity of diarrhoea among pre-school children in rural Nigeria, *Lancet*, 18 April, pp. 860–2.
9. A. E. J. Masawe (1975). *Archives of Dermatology*, **111**, 1312–16.
10. Tempest, Cancrum oris.
11. Morley and Woodland, *See How They Grow*, pp. 71–2.
12. J. J. M. Sauter (1976). *Xerophthalmia and Measles in Kenya*, Drukkerij va Denderden, Groningen, pp. 73, 150.
13. Morley and Woodland, *See How They Grow*, p. 91; P. Aaby, J. Bukh, A. Smits and I. Lisse, *Child Mortality in Guinea-Bissau: Malnutrition or Overcrowding?*, Institute of Anthropology, Copenhagen University.
14. Morley, *Paediatric Priorities in the Developing World*, p. 233.
15. *Ibid*., p. 232.
16. *Ibid*., p. 259.
17. Thomas McKeown (1976). *The Role of Medicine: Dream, Mirage or Nemesis?* Nuffield Provincial Hospitals Trust, p. 40.
18. *Health of Towns Magazine and Journal of Medical Jurisprudence* (1847–8), pp. 152–3.
19. E. P. Thompson (1968). *The Making of the English Working Class*, Pelican, London, pp. 359, 366.
20. McKeown, *The Role of Medicine: Dream, Mirage or Nemesis?*, p. 52.
21. W. P. D. Logan (1950). 'Mortality in England and Wales from 1848 to 1947,' in *Population Studies*, Vol **IV**, No. 2, September, p. 135.
22. McKeown, *The Role of Medicine: Dream, Mirage or Nemesis?* pp. 57–61.
23. *Ibid*.
24. *Ibid*.
25. David Morley, Protein–calorie deficiency, in TALC slide series.
26. W. A. Marshall, Growth, in TALC slide series.
27. *Ibid*.

28. *See* J. Habicht, R. Martorell, C. Yarborough, R. M. Malina and R. E. Klein (1974). Height and weight standards for the pre-school children, *Lancet*, **i**, 611.
29. McKeown, *The Role of Medicine: Dream, Mirage or Nemesis?*, p. 65.
30. *Ibid*.
31. *See* G. D. H. Cole and Raymond Postgate (1961). *The Common People*, Methuen, London, pp. 77–85, 351; E. J. Hobsbawm (1969), *Industry and Empire*, Pelican, pp. 28, 97; Lawrence Stone (1967), Introduction to R. H. Tawney, *The Agrarian Problem in the Sixteenth Century*, Harper Torchbooks.
32. W. H. Scott (1966). *Eastern Horizon*, Vol V, No 6, June.
33. Cited in Charles C. Hughes and John M. Hunter (1971). Disease and 'Development' in Africa. In *Recent Sociology No 3, The Social Organization of Health*, ed. Hans Peter Dreitzel, Macmillan, New York, p. 181.
34. *New Internationalist*, August 1976, pp. 6, 12.
35. *General Household Survey*, HMSO 1973, cited in Frank Field (1974), *Unequal Britain*, Arrow, London.
36. Peter Schnall (1977). Economic and social causes of cancer; Peter Schnall, An analysis of coronary heart disease using historical materialist epidemiology; Hila Shere (1977), Hypertension; all in *The Social Etiology of Disease*, HMO, New York.

3 Health, Population and Underdevelopment

THE DEVELOPED WORLD – A HISTORICAL PERSPECTIVE

To discover what needs to be done today in the underdeveloped world to *promote the health* of the people, it is worth looking at why nutrition and general living conditions have improved in England over the past 200 years.

Agricultural Revolution

The long, slow improvement in English living standards began with a revolution in agricultural production. This made possible two vital features of the industrial revolution: adequate food supplies and an increasingly urban population.

There are few statistics for agricultural production. But between 1750 and 1830 the British population more than doubled while the number of people engaged in agriculture declined. Yet more than 90 per cent of food was home produced. From an overwhelmingly rural society a few decades earlier, Britain in 1800 had become one where only about a third of the population was engaged in agriculture. That figure fell further as the century wore on (*Fig. 3.1*).

The revolutionary Parliament of the 1640s abolished the last legal remnants of the old feudal tenures, clearing the way for a more dynamic, capitalist, profit-oriented agriculture. The 'Glorious Revolution' of 1688 confirmed the political power of these landed capitalists.

The end of feudal rights and obligations speeded up the enclosure of the common land, which had begun as far back as the fourteenth century. This meant that areas that had long been used for semi-communal pasture and cultivation were fenced in and taken over by big private landlords. Between 1761 and 1801 over 3 million acres were enclosed and the land used for crops, particularly corn.[1]

Enclosure was only the most dramatic and unpopular example of a general concentration of agriculture into larger units. Sometimes the cultivation of waste land by 'improving' landlords brought more employment to an area. But the

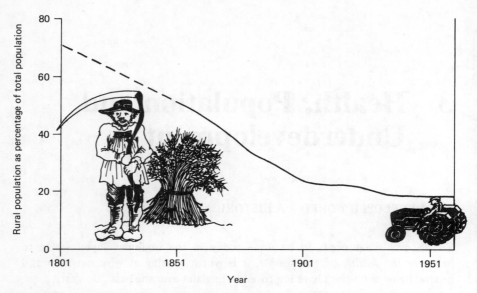

Figure 3.1 Urbanization of the English population. (From chapter 2, reference
            31. Courtesy Pelican.)

main effect of this concentration was to bring mass poverty to rural England at
the very moment when output was increasing.

Dispossessed peasants and cottagers made up an enormous reservoir of potential
waged labour. Some became farm labourers, some relied on the miserable poor
law relief. By far the largest part became the factory fodder for the industrial
revolution.

This agrarian revolution had dire social consequences for many, but it undoubtedly brought about a qualitative rise in efficiency. Market gardening and
intensive fruit farming date from the mid-seventeenth century and 'brought
about a minor revolution in the diet of ordinary citizens'.[2] One historian explains
the massive increase in food output in the eighteenth century. By 1780:

English wheat land produced nearly 40 per cent more per acre than French.
Despite the bounty on corn export, white bread was beginning to become
the staple diet even for the poor. From the mid-century new land was
coming into cultivation as agricultural prices rose. Since the seventeenth
century Agricultural Revolution, cattle could be kept alive throughout the
winter. This, together with improved communications, meant that fresh
meat and more corn were marketed all the year round: the consequent
decline in consumption of salted meat must have had a good effect on
health.

Reformation to Industrial Revolution[3]

Industrial Revolution[4]

The *technological* innovations of the 'industrial revolution' were not dramatic for the most part. The reason industrialization was genuinely revolutionary was that it included a radical transformation of the way production was organized — leading to a massive expansion of output. Steam power was used to effect a transition from workshop to factory production. Previously most production was done at home in 'cottage industries'. Now centralization of production was much more efficient and cheaper. Domestic, self-employed spinners and weavers, like small farmers, were unable to compete with large capitalist industries and were forced into factories in the towns.

The human resources for industrialization had been freed by the revolution in agriculture. Much of the necessary capital came from the same source, especially from smaller freeholders and farmers, who ploughed their profits back into their enterprise.

The other important source of capital was overseas trade. One historian has remarked that, 'The early iron industry of South Wales was largely the creation of tea-dealers and other traders of London and Bristol, and the Clyde Valley owed much of its industrial equipment to the tobacco merchants of Glasgow.' The single most important source of English trade revenue was the barbarous traffic in human beings from Africa to the Americas. Hardly a voice was raised in protest against the slave trade until English merchants had ceased to profit by it.

Without the exploitation of the non-European world, the industrial revolution could not have happened in the form or in the place that it did. For decades cotton was the spearhead of industrialization. Until 1770 more than 90 per cent of British cotton exports went to colonial markets. Even much later, in the second quarter of the nineteenth century, cotton products accounted for about half of all British exports.

This cotton industry based on colonial exports stimulated other sectors in turn. The mill owners paid such low wages that the industry made a major contribution to the further accumulation of capital.

The period 1830–50 was the era of railways and steamships which were the stimulus for the development of the iron and steel industries. This in turn stimulated a vast expansion of the coal-mining sector. Engineering and the industries devoted to making machines were still small scale, but after 1848 with the progress in engineering techniques, a large engineering and machine-tool industry arose. England was becoming 'the workshop of the world' and the average Englishman an urban industrial worker. During the nineteenth century and particularly the period 1850–71 Britain's total wealth grew tremendously.

The effects of the agricultural and industrial revolutions were profound. The rapid movement of dispossessed country people to towns with limited facilities gave rise to the horrors of such areas as Snow's Rents in London and many similar settings in all the major British towns. Overcrowding, filth and squalor existed on a scale seen today only in the towns of the underdeveloped world

(*Fig. 3.2*). Massive unemployment of the urban poor allowed employers to exploit workers cruelly. Even young children were forced to perform heavy manual work for 14–15 hours a day and were whipped if they faltered.

Popular Pressure

There was widespread discontent among the masses of people who had been dispossessed of land or displaced from individual domestic production and forced into industry, particularly when it was so difficult to get jobs. This discontent caused riots and strikes which often provoked brutal repression — such as the 'massacre of Peterloo' in Lancashire in 1819 — and gave birth to Sir Robert Peel's police force in 1829. However, it also resulted in the formation of trade unions and other workers' movements which, together with social reformers such as Owen and Shaftesbury, forced certain concessions and reforms.

WATER SUPPLY,—NO SUPPLY.   FRYINGPAN ALLEY, CLERKENWELL.

(a)

(b)

Figure 3.2 (a) Water supply in London, 1862 (by courtesy of the Wellcome Trustees); and (b) in Ethiopia, 1973 (courtesy of the World Bank.)

Pressure from labour organizations and reformers resulted in better wages and improvements in the appalling working conditions. The high death rates from infectious disease and particularly four major cholera epidemics between 1830 and 1866 created public unrest, illustrated by a broadside of 1832 (*Fig. 3.3*). Since these epidemics affected the middle class (who had the vote) as well as the working class (who did not), Parliament was reluctantly obliged to pass the 1848 Public Health Act. This provided for a General Board of Health and Local Boards of Health, though these remained within the penal Poor Law outlook towards health care. Even this was too much for Parliament, which first reduced the powers of the General Board and then dissolved it altogether. However, the local Boards remained and new reforming legislation in the 1870s finally meant that every area was covered by some sort of body responsible for sanitary measures. It was a decade that saw a number of important environmental provisions — water supply, sewage disposal, control of slaughtering of animals, parks and open spaces, isolation hospitals and the beginning of housing control — as well as the beginning of compulsory education.[5]

The Great Depression which began in the 1870s meant, ironically, an improvement in some working-class living standards as the value of real wages rose. Eating habits underwent a further important transformation. Meat and tea consumption rose significantly and the working class began to eat fruit. The decade even saw the first appearance of that great British institution, the fish and chip shop.

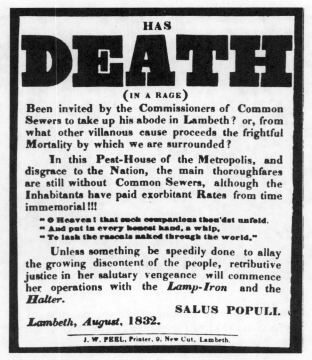

HAS

DEATH

(IN A RAGE)

Been invited by the Commissioners of Common
Sewers to take up his abode in Lambeth? or, from
what other villanous cause proceeds the frightful
Mortality by which we are surrounded?

In this Pest-House of the Metropolis, and
disgrace to the Nation, the main thoroughfares
are still without Common Sewers, although the
Inhabitants have paid exorbitant Rates from time
immemorial!!!

" O Heaven! that such companions thou'dst unfold.
" And put in every honest hand, a whip,
" To lash the rascals naked through the world."

Unless something be speedily done to allay
the growing discontent of the people, retributive
justice in her salutary vengeance will commence
her operations with the *Lamp-Iron* and the
Halter.

SALUS POPULI.

Lambeth, August, 1832.

J. W. PEEL, Printer, 9, New Cut, Lambeth.

Figure 3.3 An 1832 broadside on sanitary conditions. (By courtesy of the
Wellcome Trustees.)

But even though the working class was now enjoying fish and chips, music
halls and association football, this was far from the 'golden age' of legend.
Public expenditure on social aims other than education was minimal. In 1884,
when figures began, spending on housing was only about £200 000. Indeed, it
was the apparently increasing polarization of wealth and living standards that led
to a revival of militant trade unionism in the 1880s and the formation of a mass
independent working-class party, the Labour Party, at the turn of the century.[6]

In short, *health promotion* was the result of improvements in living conditions.
These did not always come about *automatically* with economic progress. *Often
people had to fight for them*. Health promotion was by far the most important
component in the major improvements in the health of the population of Britain
and in other industrialized countries, since the eighteenth century.

Even today living standards in the developed countries are not uniformly
good. A comprehensive recent survey, *Poverty in the United Kingdom* by
Professor Peter Townsend, shows that *more than half* the British population will
experience poverty at some time in their lives. At any one time 23 per cent live
in poverty.

This situation is only getting worse. Unemployment is increasing and the State's
measures to relieve poverty are ineffective at best. Many people simply do not

realize that they are eligible for benefits, especially when these are means-tested. Incredibly, less than 2 per cent of those eligible for free welfare milk actually claim it. Similarly, and tragically, some 9000 old people die in Britain each year from hypothermia. Although many pensioners at risk are eligible for financial assistance with heating bills many do not receive it because the system for claiming is so complex, or the means test that is imposed is often considered an indignity. Subsidies and social services that are widely believed to redistribute income in fact reinforce the existing inequalities. The richest 20 per cent of Townsend's sample received four times as much in social service benefits each year as the poorest 20 per cent.[7]

'The Medical Contribution'

What then about the 'medical contribution' — that is, specific measures to prevent or cure disease?

Before the twentieth century it is unlikely that immunization or therapy had a significant effect on mortality from infectious disease, apart from smallpox vaccination, compulsorily enforced in 1871.

Between 1900 and 1935 the following measures contributed in some diseases: antitoxin in treatment of diphtheria; surgery in appendicitis, peritonitis and ear infections; salvarsan in treatment of syphilis; intravenous therapy in diarrhoea; immunization against tetanus; and improved obstetric care resulting in prevention of puerperal fever.

After 1935 the first powerful chemotherapeutic agents, sulphonamides and later antibiotics, were used, as well as improved vaccines. Clearly the continuing improvements in living conditions continued to promote health and so it is difficult to assess precisely the 'medical contribution', but it is clear that it has been small. Of course the Schools Medical Service introduced in 1907 has played a positive role in the provision of cheap or free food, medical inspections, detection of handicaps and treatment of minor conditions. Similarly maternity and child welfare services established after the First World War have provided useful advice to mothers and immunization and screening of children for disease.[8]

A Ministry of Health was first set up in 1919 but in the 1920s and 1930s there was little progress towards free universal health care. The Second World War accelerated demands for a health service from two directions. On the one hand, the 'Committee on Social Insurance and Allied Services' headed by Lord Beveridge envisaged such a service as part of a package of social reforms aimed at 'the adequate continuance of the British Race and British Ideals in the World'. A 1944 government white paper proposed a 'comprehensive health service for everybody in this country', which should offer 'the best medical and other facilities available'.

On the other hand, the war transformed the expectations of workers, at home or in uniform, and in 1945 the Labour Party was swept to power to carry out massive social reforms. Many younger doctors also favoured a full-time salaried service, but the government met stiff resistance from the institutions of the

medical profession. In the event the Labour government and its Health Minister
Aneurin Bevan proved less radical than their supporters, conceding many points
to the medical profession without a fight. The National Health Service (NHS)
was set up in 1948.[9]

All hospital and consultant services were brought under 'public control'
although the Regional Hospital Boards set up to administer the National Health
Service were composed mainly of businessmen, local dignitaries and doctors,
while GPs became private contractors to the health service. That there was a
considerable latent demand for health care is revealed by the fact that visits to
GPs by the working class increased by 20 per cent after 1948.

Although the NHS has been important in making good medical care available
to everyone, instead of only to those who can afford it, the persistence of major
differences in disease and death only reinforces the conclusion that *it is living
and working conditions that are most important in determining the health of
populations.*

Population

Britain in the nineteenth century also gives an insight into the 'population
problem' which will be considered later in this chapter in relation to the underdeveloped world. When it was first recorded in 1086 in the Doomsday Book, the
population of England and Wales was 1½ millions. It more than trebled in the
next six centuries, again trebled in the next 150 years and more than doubled in
the following 100 years (*Fig. 3.4*).[10] So it seems that the English too have
experienced a 'population explosion'!

It has been possible to interpret the causes of the rise in the population using
the information available since 1838 when births and deaths were first registered.

Mortality remained fairly constant between 1838 and 1870 and then began
to decline. The continuous growth of population since 1838 and the particularly
rapid rate of growth between 1840 and 1910 was because of the excess of births
over deaths. The birth rate started to fall soon after the death rate, which itself
continued to fall. Both have now levelled off and the population is virtually
stable.[11] Most of the decline in the death rate was due to a decrease in deaths
from infectious disease (*Fig. 3.5*).

Most of the improvement in the health of the English population came about
through social changes. One of the first effects was a fall in the death rate and
thus a rapid increase in population, followed by a drop in the birth rate and a
levelling-off of population growth. This occurred even though there was no very
reliable contraception at this time. A similar process occurred in all the now
developed countries.

The age structure or age distribution (sometimes referred to as the 'population
pyramid') of populations of England and other developed countries has changed
substantially since the mid-nineteenth century.

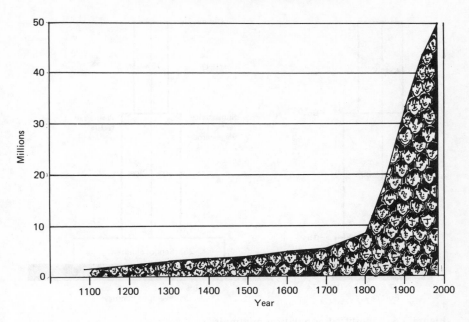

Figure 3.4 Growth of population of England and Wales. (From reference 5.
Courtesy Blackwell Scientific Publications.)

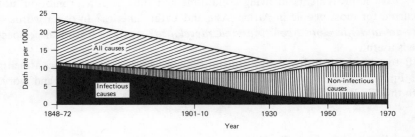

Figure 3.5 Mean annual death rates (males), England and Wales. (From reference
5. Courtesy Blackwell Scientific Publications.)

Whereas in 1841 approximately half the population were under 20 years old,
today more than half are over 45. We now have what is known as 'an ageing
population' (*Fig. 3.6*). The change in age distribution has come about through
two influences: (1) the reduction in the death rate, particularly in the young;
and following this (2) the decline of the birth rate.

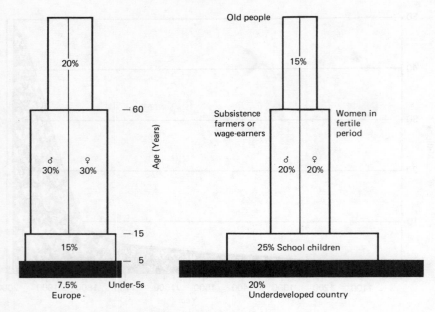

Figure 3.6 Simplified population pyramids.

THE UNDERDEVELOPED WORLD – A HISTORICAL PERSPECTIVE

Why have improvements in living conditions and thus 'health promotion' not occurred for most people in Africa, Asia and Latin America? In other words – *why are underdeveloped countries underdeveloped?* Again, a historical perspective is useful.

Before the sixteenth century contact between Europe and other continents was limited mostly to trade in such goods as spices, precious metals and ivory, with the Middle and Far East and to a lesser extent Africa.

Colonialism and the Slave Trade

Soon after Columbus accidentally 'discovered' North America for the Spanish Crown, Spain and Portugal colonized Central and South America. Treasure, usually gold and silver, was plundered and sent to Europe.

Later, mining centres were established in Mexico and Peru, and farms and ranches sprang up to supply them with raw materials and food. The precious metals were channelled to Spain to pay for manufactured goods made in Europe.

The impact on the native Indian population was disastrous. Millions died as they fought to resist the forced labour imposed on them. Or they were struck down by diseases introduced from Europe to which they had no resistance — smallpox, measles and typhus. Similar conquests of parts of Africa and the East occurred with similar effects on the native populations.[12]

In the late sixteenth century trade in people began. Over the next 200 years, the slave trade flourished. One hundred million people captured in West Africa were transported under the most inhuman conditions to the Americas where they were forced to work on English- and French-owned sugar, cotton and tobacco plantations (*Fig. 3.7*). Not only did many slaves die as a result of the brutal exploitation they suffered, but communicable diseases such as yellow fever, hookworm, leprosy and yaws were carried to the Americas.[13]

By the end of the sixteenth century Britain, France and Holland had started to develop their industries and needed the raw materials and mineral wealth that Spanish America could provide. At the same time the colonies had begun to struggle for freedom from ruthless Spanish domination. Wars broke out and, with help from Britain, Spanish America grabbed its independence. As the British Prime Minister, Canning, said in 1824: 'Spanish America is free, and if we do not mismanage our affairs she is English'.[14]

During the next 50 years Latin America supplied Europe and North America with raw materials at very low prices, the profits from the sales being distributed among the new rulers, the local capitalists. The majority of the people did not benefit at all. At the same time surplus goods produced in Europe were marketed

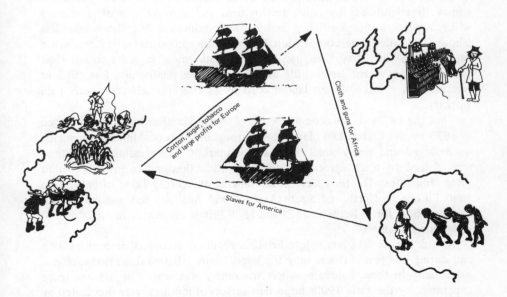

Figure 3.7 The triangular trade. (Adapted from Johnsson *et al.* (1974). *The History Book*. Courtesy Peace Press.)

in Latin America enabling a small group of European capitalists, who by now dominated agriculture and industry in their own countries, to accumulate further wealth.

A similar process took place in the Far East where spices, tea and rubber were the main spoils of the East India Company, whose exploitative operations were ended after the Indian Mutiny of 1857–8. Trade, however, continued with the colonies of the East. Some industry was even developed — as in China, where the very low wages paid to workers in the textile mills made such foreign operations exceedingly profitable. More often, though, indigenous industry was destroyed. This happened in India where the British used a combination of administrative and economic measures to snuff out the prosperous cotton textiles industry.

Imperialism

Large-scale industrial production replaced individual agricultural and domestic industry in the nineteenth century, first in Britain and then in Europe and North America. Raw materials for industry were easily available from colonies and former colonies in Asia and the Americas, and *capitalism*, the economic system that marked off the nineteenth century from earlier times, had become widespread in the industrial countries.

By the 1860s 'free competition' on which capitalism is based had reached a climax. It stimulated the rapid development and improvement of machinery which resulted in more efficient and greater production, but also needed less labour. Unbridled free competition led competing industrialists to produce a surplus of goods. They then had to lower their prices in order to sell their products. This meant less profits and many of the smaller and less efficient industries were forced to cut labour costs by sacking their already poorly paid workers.

Thus the 1870s saw an economic crisis of overproduction which was followed in 1873 by the first serious 'depression' throughout Europe. Millions were made unemployed and many small firms went bankrupt. The remaining companies were forced to reach agreements to limit production and to prevent further price reductions. The final wave in the nineteenth century flood of emigration from Europe to North and South America and Australia was swelled by this surplus labour force. Between 1853 and 1880 Britain alone sent about 2 466 000 emigrants abroad.[15]

It took almost 20 years before Britain's economy recovered from this slump and during this period it was only the larger, more efficient firms that survived, particularly in those industries where machinery was more complex and more expensive. By the early 1900s important sectors of industry were dominated by a few large firms owned by a very small number of people. In other words, *free competition* was being transformed into *monopoly*.

In the United States by the 1970s, 500 companies were responsible for nearly 70 per cent of industrial output. The top 50 had sales revenue amounting to nearly \$350 billion a year, or nearly a quarter of America's gross national product. General Motors alone has an annual sales revenue of more than \$35 billion — that is more than the total GNP of countries like South Africa, Denmark, Austria, Yugoslavia, Turkey and Norway.

This same process took place in Europe. *Figure 3.8* shows how the turnover of the top ten European companies compares with the annual budget of one of the poorer European countries. The same happened in all the countries that had industrialized rapidly since the first half of the nineteenth century. So whereas at the beginning of the twentieth century in England and the USA there were 100 or more firms in the motor-car industry, there are now only four or five or six such companies.[16]

For the underdeveloped world the consequence of this change has been very important. Because increased investment in the same branch of industry led to increased production and therefore lowering of prices, further expansion of home industry was not possible in the early 1900s. The surplus capital that could not be reinvested in industry could have been used to raise the standard of living of the working population by improving public services. However, this

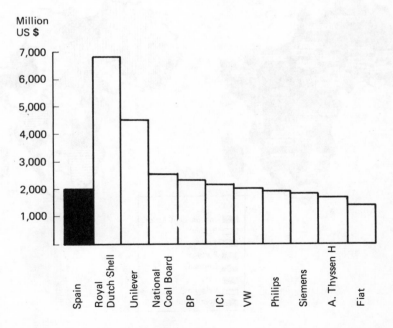

Figure 3.8 1964 turnover of top ten European companies compared with total 1964 budget of Spain. (From Sampedro (1967). *Decisive Forces in World Economics*. Courtesy Weidenfeld and Nicolson.)

would not have been a profitable investment and so export of capital to the non-industrialized world began.

This enabled capitalist enterprises to be set up in countries where monopolies had not yet entrenched themselves and in fact in countries where capitalism had not yet emerged. This is how *colonialism* in all its varieties managed to spread like wildfire at the turn of the century, starting from the small part of the world where capitalism existed, and eventually embracing the whole world. Every country on the map was transformed into a 'sphere of influence' and a field of investment for capital (*Fig. 3.9*).

This 'capturing' of most of the world's population was not because the imperialists were particularly inherently malicious, although the methods they used were often extremely brutal. It was because the concentration of capital which had resulted from unrestrained free competition forced them to invest abroad to maintain their profits. This is the stage of capitalism known as *imperialism*.

Frequently competition reached its natural conclusion in wars. In the eighteenth century Britain launched a series of wars for export markets. With the colonial division of the world such pressures were exacerbated and reached their ultimate in the horrors of the First World War.

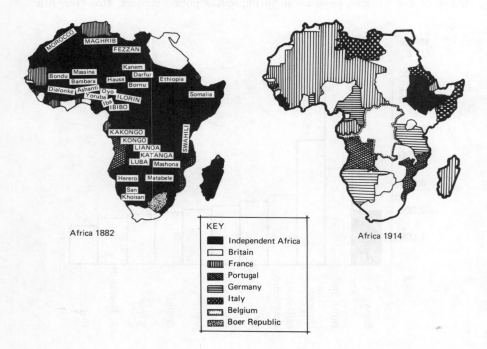

Figure 3.9   Africa divided. (Adapted from Johnsson *et al.* (1974). *The History Book*. Courtesy Peace Press.)

Multinational Companies

Monopolies in the second half of the twentieth century are the multinational companies (MNCs). The MNCs, whose influence continues to grow, currently control almost one-quarter of all production in the capitalist world. At their present rate of expansion 300 corporations will control 90% of the world market by the end of this century. They include such names as Pepsico with operations in 114 countries, Nestlé in 60, Ford in 29 and Rio Tinto-Zinc in 23.[17]

While MNCs are often the result of mergers of companies based in different countries, most of them are controlled in one country — usually the USA. Out of the ten largest companies eight are American and two — Shell and Unilever — are Anglo-Dutch. About two-thirds of their business is in the developed world — mainly in manufacturing — and one-third is in Asia, Africa and Latin America — mainly in mining and agribusiness.

The size of the MNCs is immense. More than 200 have annual sales over $1000 million a year and the 10 largest have incomes greater than any of 80 different countries.[18] Not only are they immensely wealthy and increasingly dominant in the economies of disparate countries but the biggest MNCs have also diversified and invested in industries very different from their original lines of business.

This set-up allows them to juggle their profit and loss figures between subsidiaries and so declare minimal profits. This enables them to avoid taxation by local governments. In 1970 Rio Tinto-Zinc paid only 2 per cent of its total tax bill in Britain. British Petroleum paid none at all. Both are 'British' MNCs.[19]

In this and other ways — such as raising much of the initial capital from the local economy and destroying local productive activities by their superior 'competitiveness' — they exploit and prevent the development of local industry.

Lastly, much of the finance for MNCs comes from foreign shareholders who continue to receive dividend payments, often for long periods. Between 1960–8 for MNCs operating in Latin America, each dollar of net profit generated was based on investment 83 per cent financed from local sources. But only 21 per cent of this profit remained in the country (*Fig. 3.10*).[20]

Governments are neither willing nor able to curb the activities of the multinationals. Evidently frustrated that the governments of most developed countries still have to provide a modicum of public accountability, the big American companies have set up a series of secret 'think tanks' involving all major Western leaders and cabinet ministers of whatever party. These are called the Trilateral Commission, the Bilderberg Conference and so on — and increasingly it is there rather than in the cabinet office that decisions are made.

Often, of course, there are personal links between multinationals and governments in ways that directly determine policy. For example, Lord Carrington, the British Foreign Secretary who negotiated the Zimbabwe independence settlement, was a former director of Rio Tinto-Zinc, Cadbury Schweppes and Barclays Bank — all British-based multinationals with substantial interests in Zimbabwe and the region as a whole.

New investment by the USA: $2300 million (£1340 million)

Profit on total USA investment returned to USA $6000 million (£4000 million)

Figure 3.10 US and Latin America: new investment and profit, 1960–7. (From Ward, *The Widening Gap*. Courtesy Columbia University Press.)

Ultimately conservative and social democratic governments feel themselves powerless before the multinationals. The British Cabinet Minister Richard Crossman wrote in his diary for 16 March 1969: '. . .this week was disastrous. The Ford strike continues. . . . There is a real danger now that Ford's will move all their European activity to their French and German factories. We feel totally impotent. . . .'[21]

An even more striking example of the contempt that multinationals display towards supposedly sovereign governments comes from the drugs industry. In 1973 the British government ordered large cuts in the price paid by the NHS for Valium and Librium – both tranquillizers produced by the Swiss-based company Hoffman-La Roche. It also demanded repayment of more than £2 million of past excess profits. Hoffman-La Roche would not pay back the money and said that if there were any attempt to cut its prices it would block the export of products made or finished in Britain, transfer manufacturing facilities out of the country and move planned research investment elsewhere.[22]

Many MNCs have found it more profitable to transfer operations to areas where wages are lowest – and that means the underdeveloped world. Much foreign-controlled manufacturing, especially in the electronics trade, is done in Hong Kong, Taiwan, South Korea and Malaysia. For the USA the Mexican border area is especially profitable, since wages are approximately one-eighth of the American average.

Creating a Labour Force

Earlier it was shown that two of the conditions for agricultural and industrial capitalism to evolve in Britain were:

(1) Dispossession of the smallholders and their replacement by more efficient farming of consolidated areas.
(2) Displacement of the individual producers of manufactured goods by mechanized industry concentrated in factories.

Thus a *permanent workforce* was created in the towns and agricultural and industrial production were concentrated in the hands of a few. This process was repeated in those underdeveloped countries that were colonized. It was especially stark in Africa in the nineteenth and early twentieth centuries. In Africa most people were stock breeders and primitive cultivators but always had a relative abundance of land. The agricultural yield was mediocre because of the crude implements and farming methods, and the standard of living in general was poor, but nothing forced this population to work in the mines, plantations or factories of the colonialists. Without a transformation in land administration both a labour force and a market in which manufactured goods could be sold were unrealizable. So:

(1) Large areas of what was often the best land were taken over by foreign companies or the colonizing State and used for production of cash crops — tea, coffee, cotton, sugar, cocoa, tobacco, jute, rubber, etc. — rather than food. The native populations were resettled in 'reserves' which were often small.
(2) A head-tax — and often a hut tax and cattle tax — was imposed. People had to produce crops for sale in order to be able to pay this.

Thus people were forced to work for money.

Imperialism has only been able to carry out this process with the help of local rulers. In the early colonial days a class of local agents was created which owed its wealth to the foreign colonizer and could be trusted to defend its interests. In Bengal, for example, the *zamindari* were transformed from mere tax collectors for the Mogul emperors into landlords with a vested interest in British rule.

As colonial countries gained independence a new alliance emerged between foreign capitalists, the small class of local industrial capitalists and the top bureaucrats of the newly independent State. This neo-colonial State could be relied upon to protect the interests of foreign capital. Often, of course, it has been the army that has formed the government.

But the capitalist economic system is unstable. Contractions and expansions follow each other periodically, so a *reserve work-force* is necessary to keep wages stable. In some countries the 'reserves' have literally become labour reserves: the 'bantustans' serving South Africa's needs, North Yemen serving Saudi Arabia,

Figure 3.11 Algerian workers' shanty town in Paris: the underdeveloped serve the developed. (Courtesy ILO.)

Mexico for the USA, Turkey serving primarily West Germany, Portugal and North Africa mostly serving France, Ireland serving England (*Fig. 3.11*).

Even *within* certain countries underdeveloped regions supply developed regions with labour — southern Italy supplies the north, south-western France provides the north-west, the southern States in the USA supply the north-eastern. And in underdeveloped countries the countryside supplies the towns.

The creation of a work-force has only been achieved at the most appalling cost to the health of the workers. For example, sleeping sickness is on the increase because the growth of roads in Africa helps spread the tsetse fly which carries the disease. Food production has dropped because of the concentration on export of raw materials and production of irrelevant manufactured goods. Africa, once self-sufficient in food, now imports some 11 million tonnes a year and still starvation is on the increase.

Pre-colonial life was no idyll but it did not compare with the perils of the modern neo-colonial world. The Tonga people in Zimbabwe have been displaced from their home in the Bumi River area to make way for the artifical Lake Kariba. This forced removal has destroyed their traditional sources of food and created widespread malnutrition. When the government provided a grain store it was sited in such a place that it became a transmission site for sleeping sickness. Such is the effect of colonialism.[23]

The colonizers also brought their 'social diseases'. In the Transvaal in the 1890s it was 'a common thing', said one contemporary observer, 'to find "boys" lying dead on the veld from exposure and the effects of the vile liquids sold them by unscrupulous dealers.' The number of black miners 'disabled by drink' each day was put at 15 per cent by the mine-owners. Others put it as high as 25 per cent.[24]

UNDERDEVELOPMENT

To return to the question posed earlier: *why are underdeveloped countries under-developed?* The question can be extended and made more precise: *why are all countries unevenly developed and why is this uneven development most stark in the Third World?*

Competition between enterprises in the advanced capitalist countries — the developed world — results in large monopolies which need to expand abroad if they are to maintain profits. They impose themselves on countries that have not yet evolved their own capitalism.

In the countries dominated by imperialism — and today that means the whole of Africa, and most of Latin America and Asia — *full development of the capitalist system as occurred in nineteenth-century Europe is prevented*. Giant monopolies with their advanced technology and sophisticated marketing systems penetrate countries where subsistence agriculture predominates. They promote cash-crop production and mining, and sometimes industries such as electronics or plastics.

These highly developed sectors cater for the wealthier minority *within* the underdeveloped country — especially in Latin America and Asia — but mostly for the *external market* — Europe, North America and Japan. The underdeveloped, pre-capitalist sector is *subsidizing* capitalist production by providing it with a ready-made worker.

Much of what little he earns is spent on the various taxes imposed by the government, on educating his children in the hope that better qualifications will enable *them* to succeed in the competition for employment, and on buying the new foodstuffs, clothes and the much-coveted radio — the radio which broadcasts persuasive advertisements for luxury goods and might itself be manufactured by the same giant monopoly that owns the industry he works in.

There has thus been created in every underdeveloped country, and on a world scale, a system of dominant and dominated economies. The term 'dual economy' has been used to indicate the great differences between the 'developed' (dominant) and underdeveloped (dominated) sectors of a particular country. While this term is useful in that it conveys the stark differences within one national boundary, the term 'dual' does tend to suggest a separation between the two sectors. Yet the overdevelopment of the one depends on and creates the underdevelopment of the other (*Fig. 3.12*).

Figure 3.12   Bombay: the overdevelopment of one sector depends on the underdevelopment of the other. (Courtesy Christian Aid.)

The impact of capitalism on traditional societies has been greatest in terms of land ownership and food production. The dispossession of smallholders and replacement by capitalist farmers which occurred during England's agricultural revolution has been repeated in an exaggerated way in the Third World. In *Latin America* 17 per cent of the landowners control 90 per cent of the land and over one-third of the rural population uses only 1 per cent of the cropland. In *Asia* although there are more small farmers than in Latin America, 20 per cent of the landowners control 60 per cent of the arable land and their portion is increasing. In *Africa* three-quarters of the people have access to 4 per cent of the land. And in 22 underdeveloped countries one-third of the active agricultural population has no land at all.[25]

In the developed world this tendency is just as clearly seen. In the United States, where there were 6.8 million farms 40 years ago, there are now 2.8 million, involving 4 per cent of the population. More significantly, however, *under 4 per cent* of these farms produce half of all the food in the USA.[26]

And here in Britain too the number of farms has halved over the past 20 years to about 200 000. Of these, the top 10 per cent account for half the food produced.[27]

Vast areas of the world are potentially able to produce food crops. It has been calculated that the potentially cultivatable area is 2.3 times the present and could support 38–48 billion people, 10–13 times the present world population. The developed countries alone could feed 11.2 billion people. *As it is, even in the worst famine years of the early 1970s, there was enough being produced to give everyone in the world 3000–4000 kilocalories (12.5–16.7 mJ) a day in grain alone.*[28]

However, average calorie intakes in the underdeveloped world range from 1500 to 3000 kcal per day, while undoubtedly the landless and poorer people receive much less than even these low national averages.

Most agricultural production in the underdeveloped world is by peasant farmers. With their small plots of land they are economically vulnerable to large-scale producers who control productive technology (*Fig. 3.13*), storage and marketing facilities. This threatens the very survival of the peasants. *Studies in North India in 1969 discovered that only 14 per cent of the peasants managed to feed themselves and their families for the whole year, 36 per cent for 7–9 months, 29 per cent for 4–6 months and 21 per cent for only 1–3 months of the year.*[29] This pattern is more or less universal in the underdeveloped world.

Before the Second World War the underdeveloped countries as a whole were net exporters of cereals but have since become net importers, while coffee, cocoa, tea and sugar are being exported to the developed world in increasing amounts.[30] In Senegal, desert has been irrigated so that multinational firms can grow eggplant and mangoes for Europe's wealthy while some Senegalese starve. In Costa Rica the beef export business expands as local consumption of meat and dairy products declines. In Colombia wheat production is discontinued since

Figure 3.13 Large-scale producers control productive technology. (Courtesy Alan Hutchison Library; Oxfam.)

carnations for North America bring 80 per cent greater returns per acre.[31] And there are many equally sordid examples.

So we have a situation where hunger abounds in the underdeveloped world while grain, beef and butter mountains as well as milk and wine lakes accumulate in the developed world. And just to complete this incredible picture, the US Bureau of Census stated in 1972 that at least 10-12 million Americans are starving or sick, because they have too little to spend on food.[32] That is to say nothing of the estimate that at least 12 per cent of the British population receive diets so inadequate as to cause serious risks to health (*Fig. 3.14*).[33]

Figure 3.14 London: a pensioner in a supermarket. (Courtesy Peter Harrap, *Report.*)

Urbanization

People who are no longer able to subsist on the land and forced to participate in a cash economy often try to get a job in the nearest town. Thus the 'urban drift' of nineteenth-century England is repeated in the underdeveloped world today.

In 1975 there were 90 towns in the underdeveloped world with more than a million inhabitants, and it is estimated that in 2000 there will be nearly 300. In the same period the urban population of these countries is expected to grow from 28 per cent to 42 per cent of the total population. But the high-technology industry exported to these countries can only provide jobs for relatively few.

The wages paid are usually exceedingly low, since the competition for jobs is, to say the least, brisk.

For every one job created in the towns of the underdeveloped world there are as many as three people leaving the countryside. When the promise of factory work is unfulfilled, the job-seeker often remains in town. Success depends on being 'on the spot' for any chance vacancy. This has resulted in the rapid growth of urban and periurban shanty towns in every underdeveloped country. Here survival requires resourcefulness, and people's meagre earnings come from basket-making and vegetable-hawking, refuse-collection and shoe-making, water-selling and guiding tourists – and of course begging.

Surveys from Bombay, Nairobi, Sao Paulo, Abidjan, Jakarta and cities in Peru say that this 'informal sector' accounts for between 40 and 60 per cent of total employment in the city. In Lima, Peru, it was found that three-quarters of street vendors were earning below the government's minimum wage; 13 per cent were actually making a loss. This informal sector (*Fig. 3.15*) subsidizes the capitalist sector by providing services such as urban transport which might otherwise prove costly.[34]

Figure 3.15 The informal sector. (Courtesy Oxfam.)

Industry

Even when there are jobs in industry, standards of health and safety almost always compare badly with conditions in the developed world. For example, many multinationals produce cheap manufactured goods and electronics in countries like South Korea, Hong Kong and the Philippines where pro-Western governments have an open-door policy. There are tough anti-trade union legislation, lax safety laws, and low wages because of the pressure for jobs. There is a strong preference for hiring young women, who are seen by employers as more docile and obedient and easier to sack.

In the electronics industry there is usually a three-shift system. Several countries have dispensed with the prohibition on night work for women so that these factories can maximize production. Sometimes married women are permanently hired on the late-night shift so that they can do housework and care for their families during the day.

The fast pace, rigid discipline and repetitiveness of this work aggravates nervousness and stomach complaints. Forced overtime and increased productivity increases fatigue and the danger of accidents. Health and safety precautions are often overlooked.

The Occupational Health and Safety Administration in the United States has placed electronics on its list of high health risk industries using the greatest number of hazardous substances. Workers are continually exposed to carcinogenic substances such as acids, solvents and gases. There are frequent complaints of acid burns, rashes, nausea, dizziness, lung trouble, swollen eyes and urinary tract infections. In addition there is the problem of deteriorating eyesight.

In the Malaysian electronics industry it is estimated that workers have a working life of only 4 years. Either they are worn out physically or their eyesight has deteriorated so much that they cannot carry on working.[35]

Companies export industrial processes that are illegal or unprofitable in their own countries to the underdeveloped world. For example, in recent years there has been considerable concern over the use of asbestos in the developed world. Its needle-like fibres can cause a variety of diseases, including lung cancer. In West Germany the Deutsche Kap Asbest Werke was hit by tighter safety regulations. From 1969 up to one-third of the investment in the factory was spent on dust extraction, pushing costs up to an unprofitable level. So the owners dismantled the plant and sold it lock, stock and barrel to a South African company, Kapasit Asbestos (Pty). In South Africa, it can be safely assumed, the welfare of workers will not be allowed to get in the way of profits. Reportedly, the South African company will still use the German trade name for its exports.[36]

The problem in South Africa and the Far Eastern countries is government collaboration in dangerous practices. But the case of the Asbesco plant in Dar es Salaam, Tanzania, shows how management negligence can combine with ignorance on the part of government. 'Poor countries like Tanzania just don't have access to the latest medical and scientific information so they easily fall prey to unscrupulous multinationals', according to a researcher at the University of Dar es Salaam.

Management claims that the only dangerous stage of production at the Asbesco plant is at the beginning where workers open bags of dry asbestos and dump them into a mill to be mixed with water and cement. But where in Europe workers would wear protective clothing and specially designed masks, here they wear their own clothes, no gloves and sometimes thin cotton masks. These are a waste of time because the needle-like fibres can pass through cotton.

The process is supposed to be 'totally enclosed' but in fact the door is left open so that the machine can be fed more quickly. Puffs of asbestos–cement dust billow out of a silo. Management claims that the air is fibre free but it has no machine for measuring the fibre level. There is no safe disposal of waste from the plant. It is simply shovelled into mounds in the factory compound. Sludge and contaminated water from the plant runs on to common land where people and cattle often pass, turning it into a bog laced with asbestos. Local people do not drink the water because they know it is poisonous. But cattle do drink from the bog and some have died.

The government's reaction is typical of the dilemma of Third World governments. Initially it knew nothing of conditions at the Asbesco plant. When told of them by a journalist, the Minister of Industries ordered an investigation. But he concluded: 'At present we need the asbestos factory. We can try to clean it up, but we can't close it down until an alternative is found.'[37]

POPULATION

'Overpopulation' has traditionally been identified as the major obstacle to world development. The last President of the World Bank, Robert McNamara, recently said: '. . . the greatest single obstacle to the economic and social advancement of the peoples in the underdeveloped world is rampant population growth. . . .'[38]

The Cause of Underdevelopment?

This view gave rise in the 1960s to the rapid spread of 'family planning' programmes in the underdeveloped world. Massive resources were — and still are — pumped into such programmes by the Western countries, in particular the USA.

American President Lyndon Johnson once remarked that $5 invested in population control was worth $100 invested in other kinds of overseas aid.[39] This peculiar set of priorities is reflected in recent figures for US aid to Latin America. Population projects get 50 per cent more than health ones.[40] The media took up the message and the general public were told that Asians, Africans and Latin Americans are poor because they have too many children and therefore we needed to help them 'to plan small families'.

The originator of this view of population was Thomas Malthus (1766-1834). He asserted that the poor insist on indulging in large families. Population, he said, increases in a geometrical way: 2, 4, 8, 16, 32, 64, etc. But food production, Malthus believed, can only grow arithmetically: 2, 3, 4, 5, 6, etc. Therefore, the number of people will always exceed the amount of food available. The 'natural' result, said Malthus, was poverty and starvation. He advocated 'sexual restraint' as the only escape from this threat of overpopulation of the earth by the poor.

The more sophisticated modern argument for 'family planning' is an extension of this. For it sees the 'population explosion' – the emotive term used – as the *cause* of disasters, famine, depletion of resources and disease. Development is too slow to keep up with population increase. Hence the need for 'family planning'.

It is easy enough to show that Malthus was quite wrong in terms of his predictions about inevitable food shortage. Comparing 1830 with 1750, *less* food producers were producing *more* food for *more than double* the population. Already by 1850, four farmers could produce enough food for five persons, and by 1940 one farmer could produce enough for ten persons. By 1960 one farmer could produce enough food for 24 persons![41]

The real problem is *not* inadequate food production. It is *inappropriate production* and *inequitable distribution*. As we have seen, underdeveloped countries are unable to develop their agricultural potential because of grossly unfair land distribution. A tiny number of foreign and local capitalists control the best land, most productive methods and marketing facilities. The Third World therefore relies on meagre payment for its cash crops (and other industrial products) to *buy* the excess grain that the developed countries produce.

Of the food on the world market, more than half of all wheat, more than three-quarters of all maize and three-fifths of soybeans move into or within the Western world. The dominant country is the USA, where just five companies control all sugar and cereal exports. Two of these handle more than half of all grain shipments.

The chairman of Booker McConnell, one of the largest food multinationals, brought home how hunger is fostered by greed and not by scarcity:

> 'The quantities of grain needed for the Sahelian relief were trifling in relation to available supplies. The supplies could have been purchased and freight was readily available for shipment. Money and organisation – not available grain supply, seem to have been the problem in the Sahel zone.'
>
> *Profits of Doom*[42]

And *within* the underdeveloped countries the distribution is inequitable; the great majority are therefore undernourished.

An additional nail in the coffin of the Malthusian argument is the fact that the people of the underdeveloped world – the poor who are so 'dangerous' – consume only one-tenth of the world's resources. On the other hand, USA, with

6 per cent of the world's population, consumes about 35 per cent of the world's total resources. It accounts for over 25 per cent of the consumption of oil and minerals and for over 40 per cent of the world's coal and natural gas.[43] This does not mean that all Europeans and Americans are benefiting from this ravage of the world's resources (*Fig. 3.16*).

Figure 3.16 Not all Europeans and Americans are benefiting from the ravage of the world's resources. (Courtesy Child Poverty Action Group.)

Growth and Composition

Before discussing the 'population problem' of the underdeveloped world it is worth returning for a moment to the 'population explosion' in the now developed world.

The population of England and Wales increased from 9 million in 1801 to 33 million in 1901. This rapid increase after 1838 was due to a fall in the very high death rate, while the birth rate remained high. At first the decline in the death rate was very small and up to 1900 only significantly dropped in the 2–34 age group. After 1900 death rates in the very young and old also fell.

As we saw, the decline in mortality was overwhelmingly due to a reduction in the prevalence and the effects of communicable diseases. Most of this was achieved through an improvement in living standards and hygiene – *health promotion* – while considerably less was due to specific preventive and curative measures – the *medical contribution*.

The fall in the very high birth rate only started in about 1880. It was in the period between 1840 and 1880 that the most rapid population growth occurred. For when both death rates and birth rates are high, only a small fall in the death rate is necessary to cause rapid population increase. Death rates in all age groups, particularly in young children, continued to fall until the mid-twentieth century, but there was a parallel fall in the birth rate. This meant that the rate of population growth began to slow down and now Britain's population growth rate is one of the lowest in the world (*Fig. 3.17*). *Six European countries today experience zero population growth*.[44] This change from high death rates matched by high birth rates to low death rates with still high birth rates, then finally to low death rates with low birth rates, is termed the *demographic transition*. Different countries are in different phases of this demographic transition. On the whole, underdeveloped countries are in the early, and developed countries in the late phases.

Typically, therefore, there is a decline in the high mortality followed after a *lag period* by a slower decline in the high fertility. The length of this lag period varies from country to country, although in a World Health Organization study of 53 countries, 43 experienced a lag period of between 6 and 19 years.[45]

Another important factor in the growth of populations is their *structure*. Underdeveloped countries are in the relatively early phases of demographic transition. Their populations, which have been growing fast, have a far higher proportion of young people. They consequently have a considerable *potential* for further population growth since a high proportion of their populations are potentially fertile. This means that even *after* the lag period between the fall in mortality and the fall in fertility, there will still be a period of rapid population growth.

Eventually, however, the population stabilizes and, in the late phase of demographic transition, becomes an ageing population – as in Northern Europe today.

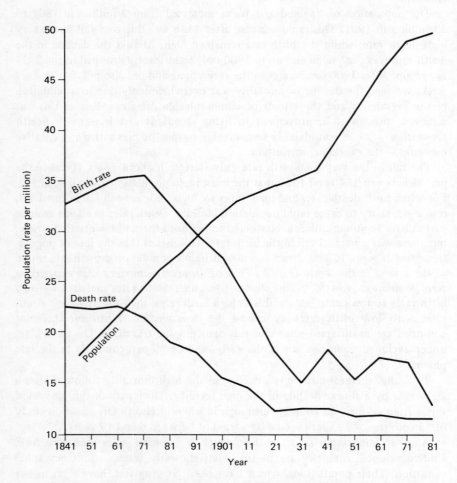

Figure 3.17 Birth rates, death rates and population: England and Wales. (From reference 5. Courtesy Office of Population, Censuses and Surveys.)

Population Growth, Mortality and Underdevelopment

What is it about the population growth of underdeveloped countries that has provoked the Malthusian revival and the huge expenditure on 'family planning' – which we shall more accurately term *population control?*

The world's population doubled from about 500 million in 1630 to 1000 million in 1830. It doubled again over the next 100 years to about 2000 million in 1930. The total world population in 1980 was about 4364 million (*Fig. 3.18*).[46]

In the nineteenth century a disproportionate share of the population growth occurred in the now developed countries (Table 3.1). Today most of the increase

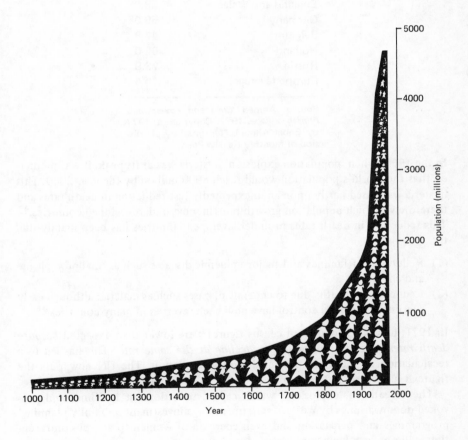

Figure 3.18 The modern rise of world population. (From McKeown, *The Modern Rise of World Population*. Courtesy Edward Arnold.)

in population is occurring in the underdeveloped world. Population growth rates — the difference between birth rates and death rates — in 1973 were as follows:

(1) Europe, 0.7 per cent.
(2) North America, 0.8 per cent.
(3) Asia, 2.3 per cent.
(4) Africa, 2.5 per cent.
(5) Latin America, 2.8 per cent.

Table 3.1 **Percentage Increase in Population 1870–1910**

India	18.9
England and Wales	58.0
Germany	59.0
Belgium	47.8
Holland	62.0
Russia	73.9
Europe (average)	45.4

Source: Ahmad, *Class and Power in a Punjab Village*, 1977. Copyright © 1977 by Eqbal Ahmad. Reprinted by permission of Monthly Review Press.

In the 1960s when 'population explosion' hysteria was at its peak, it was predicted that the world's population would reach 8000 million by the year 2000. This hysteria was based partly upon an unexpectedly fast reduction in death rates and therefore very high population growth rates in most underdeveloped countries.[47] This reduction in death rates in underdeveloped countries has been mainly due to:

(1) Reduction of famines and major epidemic diseases such as smallpox, plague and cholera.
(2) Reduction in deaths due to endemic diseases such as malaria, although early successes in malaria control have now been reversed in many countries.[48]

In 1971, however, population census figures were lower than expected *because death rates have not continued to decline at the same rate*. This has led to a recalculation of the 1961 projected world population. The UN now puts the figure at just over 6250 million by 2000.[49]

The threatened 'explosion', which caused sensationalist headlines and provoked doomwarnings by Western statesmen, huge investment in 'family planning' programmes and persuasion and even coercion of women to accept contraception, will *not even happen* as forecast!

Why is it that death rates have not *continued* to fall in underdeveloped countries as they did in England and Wales after 1838? Why do they still remain tragically high, especially in the young, who constitute a large segment of their populations?

In Asia — especially India — infant and child mortality remain high and communicable diseases are the most frequently recorded causes of adult deaths. In Bangladesh there has been no improvement in mortality rates in the past 10 years.

In Africa little impact has been made on infant and child mortality which accounts for a high proportion of deaths on the continent.

In Latin America, in the high-mortality countries of the Caribbean and Latin America, infant mortality stopped falling in the late 1960s — it even rose for a period in a few countries. In some cities such as Sao Paulo mortality is increasing because of accelerating urbanization and impoverishment. A contradictory new phenomenon is now being seen in certain countries such as Chile under authoritarian rule. Here even during a period of economic hardship for the majority, infant mortality rates have fallen. However, morbidity or *disease* rates have increased markedly. We have here a situation where people are surviving but almost certainly in a sicker condition.

In nineteenth-century England and Wales improved nutrition and later widespread environmental improvements led to a sustained drop in mortality from communicable disease. This was followed by a sustained decline in fertility. The overall effect was a *sustained but decelerating* growth of population for 120 years, a growth that has only recently ceased.

But it is precisely because the relatively small decline in mortality in underdeveloped countries has *not* been *sustained* that continued rapid growth of population is fading. Specific medical measures — control of epidemic and endemic diseases — have largely been responsible for these small drops in death rates while fertility has remained high. This has allowed the rapid, short-lived population growth.

These specific medical measures have been transferred to the underdeveloped world. But the nutritional and environmental improvements that accompanied them in nineteenth-century England have *not* occurred. It is for this reason that no further great impact on mortality can be made. *And the problem of health promotion cannot be approached without tackling the problems of underdevelopment.*

Population Growth, Fertility and Underdevelopment

It is important to know something about the factors that determine fertility, because 'family planning' or population control is really *fertility control*. Why then does fertility remain high in underdeveloped countries (Table 3.2)? In short, as the latter day Malthusians would have it, why do the world's poor insist on having so many children?

One of the most important factors influencing fertility is *infant and child mortality*. This is because, as many surveys have not surprisingly shown, parents want *surviving* offspring. Even today, poor families in India must produce an average of 6.5 children to be 95 per cent sure of having one surviving son.[51]

Table 3.2 **Live births per thousand of female population**

US	59.1
Japan	57.6
Sweden	53.3
UK	52.9
USSR	55.5
Benin	226.9
Congo	143.3
Libya	311.9
Togo	229.7
El Salvador	194.5
Pakistan	174.8
Sri Lanka	143.5

Source: *UN Demographic Year-book* (1978)

Moreover, if the infant survives and the mother breast feeds, the likelihood of conception is reduced during lactation. In many cultures this effect is reinforced by social practices such as sexual abstention during the early months following a birth. Both these factors which tend to reduce fertility will be cut short if the infant dies. So mortality decline is virtually a pre-condition for fertility decline.

Economic motivation is perhaps an equally important factor. It is very difficult to calculate whether children are 'economically beneficial' or otherwise in families living in underdeveloped countries. But it *is* clear from various studies done in Africa and India that poor parents strongly believe that their children are economically useful in several ways.

In some areas land holdings are allocated on the basis of the number of sons in each family; the more sons the more land allotted.

In many underdeveloped countries children can become producers as early as 7 or 8 years old when they participate in nearly all the 'subsistence work' of the family – in agricultural work, in cooking and cleaning, in collecting fuel and water, in looking after animals. The important role children play in this 'subsistence work' is obvious. Many of the men travel to the urban areas – the developed sectors – leaving the women in the underdeveloped sectors with the exhausting tasks of caring for the young and old – with no household labour-saving devices (*Fig. 3.19*)!

Moreover, with numerous children there is an increased possibility that one or some of them will later be lucky enough to get a paid job in town and send money back to the family. This is usually the reasoning behind the high priority poor parents give to their children's education, for the better educated stand

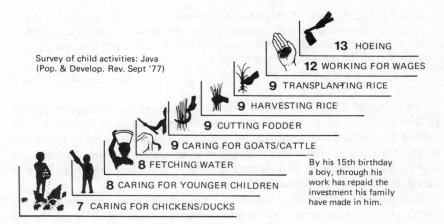

Survey of child activities: Java
(Pop. & Develop. Rev. Sept '77)

13 HOEING
12 WORKING FOR WAGES
9 TRANSPLANTING RICE
9 HARVESTING RICE
9 CUTTING FODDER
9 CARING FOR GOATS/CATTLE
8 FETCHING WATER
8 CARING FOR YOUNGER CHILDREN
7 CARING FOR CHICKENS/DUCKS

By his 15th birthday a boy, through his work has repaid the investment his family have made in him.

Figure 3.19 Age of child when activity is started. (Courtesy TALC, Institute of Child Health, London.)

more chance of gaining employment. Finally, children are often the only 'insurance' for the poor, for without them there is no help or support in illness or old age.[52]

Other important factors influencing fertility are status and employment of women as well as levels of education and literacy, especially among women. However, simply bringing more girls into school without improving employment opportunities may have very little effect on fertility. Improved educational status and greater female employment — both necessarily associated with development — usually are accompanied by increased age of marriage and increased use of modern methods of contraception.[53] These will mean a lowering of fertility.

This is why large families and hence high fertility are 'part of the culture' in underdeveloped countries. It is because for centuries high mortality has prevailed and has not substantially changed. Also, economic factors continue to dictate the need for many children. It is not until there is a *sustained* improvement in the child's chances of survival and social changes that reduce the economic need for children that fertility will decline and stay low.

Clearly there *is* a role for contraceptive usage. Women's need to control their own bodies is shown by extremely high abortion rates and even infanticide. In underdeveloped countries there is all too often a conflict between the economic needs of a family and the wishes of the women. While the man may want a child — often a son — sometimes his wife will feel unable to cope with an extra pregnancy and another child. She will often be forced to resort to primitive and dangerous methods of contraception or abortion and occasionally even infanticide — particularly of girls. As one account says:

'The Bible story of the baby in the bullrushes and the fairytale of the orphan on the doorstep are the acceptable, sentimental faces of practices as old as society itself. Today's less cosy versions are about the Asian baby sold to a lucrative American adoption racket, the small corpse on a rubbish tip in a South American city slum, and the little Indian girl neglected and underfed in the hope that she may die'.

New Internationalist[54]

An estimated 150 000 women a year die from the effects of illegal abortions. In Bolivia it costs 50 per cent of the maternity care budget to treat the complications from illegal abortions. In one region of Colombia a survey found that abortion was the leading cause of death in women aged between 15 and 35.[55] One survey conducted in 87 countries discovered that there are more than four abortions for every ten live births.[56]

Infanticide is a horror that has only recently disappeared from the developed world. In the eighteenth and nineteenth centuries it was commonly practised in England. Disraeli is reported as saying that infanticide 'was hardly less prevalent in England than on the banks of the Ganges. . .'.

The situation is fortunately changing in the developed world largely as a result of popular pressure — particularly by the women's movement. Whereas in 1971 only 38 per cent of the world's people lived in areas where safe, legalized abortion was freely available, by 1976 it was 64 per cent.[57]

So for the individual woman the existence of contraceptive technology is a great step forward. But what about the use of contraception as a technology for population control? European fertility declined to its present level with little reliance on modern contraceptive methods. What effect have these had on fertility and population growth in the underdeveloped world?

Officially sponsored 'family planning' programmes cover 75 per cent of the population of underdeveloped countries and a further 16 per cent of this population is in countries that give official support to 'family planning' activities.[58]

Pakistan and India have two of the largest and oldest 'family planning' programmes. In Pakistan the fertility rate in the 1972 census was not significantly lower than in 1961 — despite a programme that absorbed 1.4 per cent of total development expenditure. In India, where massive resources have been diverted to this field, 'family planning' has had little success, despite widespread coercion. In Bihar, one of the most underdeveloped States, it has had no impact, while in Kerala, where over 50 per cent of the women are educated and nutritional standards are much higher, fertility has declined.

The countries with the greatest and fastest declines in fertility have mostly been small, many of them islands and typically with levels of socioeconomic development above average among underdeveloped countries.[59] Thus the successes of 'family planning' are greatly outnumbered by the failures.

But one country stands out, a vast country that contains about one-fifth of the world's population — *China*. All reports indicate that China's birth rate has dropped from approximately 43 per 1000 in the 1940s to 32 in 1970 and to 19 in 1975 and is still falling![60] What has been responsible for this change? In Chapter 2 there was a description of China in the 1930s when the death rate was over 30 per 1000 and the infant mortality rate approximately 200 per 1000.[61] But now in China:

(1) *The infant mortality rate is 28 per 1000 (1972 estimate).* [62]
(2) *There is full employment both of men and of women and everybody is satisfactorily fed, clothed and housed.*
(3) *Old-age security for all people is provided by the 'five guarantees' – food, clothing, shelter, medical care and decent burial.*
(4) *Secondary schooling is universal and illiteracy has virtually been eliminated.*
(5) *Late marriages are the rule.*
(6) *Disease prevention and cure services are widespread and free.*[63]

It must also be acknowledged that from 1970 the above socioeconomic measures were accompanied by a sustained campaign to make contraceptive methods available and accessible to the reproductive population, and free of charge.

Although all the above measures led to a significant fall in birth rate (from about 44 births per 1000 population in 1963, to 18 per 1000 population in 1979), further population projections presented at the Second session of the Fifth National People's Congress in June 1979 indicated that China's future population growth would still be enormous. These projections showed that, even if the number of children born were reduced dramatically to one child per couple by 1985 and thereafter maintained at that level, China's population would still continue to grow for another 25 years and peak at just over 1 billion in 2004. It would then begin to fall. The reason for this projected continuing rise in population over the next 25 years is due to the age structure of China's population. For example, in 1978 it was estimated that 39 per cent of the population was under the age of 15 years, and thus had yet to reach childbearing age. Faced with these projections, the National People's Congress decided to launch a massive campaign to promote the one-child family. This was not only an ideological campaign but also linked to policies giving material incentives to couples with one child and loss of certain benefits for those not conforming to this norm.[64]

Recent estimates suggest that this campaign has been effective in enforcing the one-child family. Criticisms have been raised about certain aspects of this campaign, notably the resultant increase in female infanticide, and selective induced abortion of female fetuses due to the preference for male children. On the other hand, it can also be argued that the social and economic measures in China outlined above have removed many of the social and economic imperatives to have many children and have made smaller families more desirable. It would be instructive to know how much popular support this campaign has had or whether it has been viewed as a coercive measure. It may only be possible to answer such questions in the future.

This then is a concrete example of a country where the interrelated features of underdevelopment that have been looked at – *disease* and *population growth*

— have been tackled at their roots and substantially overcome. This tremendous achievement carries some profound lessons for all those millions who suffer the effects of underdevelopment.

References

1. Much of the above draws on Hobsbawm (1969). *Industry and Empire*. Pelican, London.
2. Christopher Hill (1967). *Reformation to Industrial Revolution*, Weidenfeld and Nicolson, p. 118.
3. *Ibid.*, pp. 221-2.
4. The following discussion is drawn from the works already cited by Hobsbawm, Thompson, Hill, and Cole and Postgate, and from David Thomson (1950). *England in the Nineteenth Century*, Pelican.
5. Thomas McKeown and C. R. Lowe (1974). *An Introduction to Social Medicine*, Blackwell, Oxford, p. 237.
6. Hobsbawm, *Industry and Empire*, pp. 162, 166; Cole and Postgate, *Common People*, pp. 351, 442.
7. Peter Townsend (1979). *Poverty in the United Kingdom. A Survey of Household Resources and Standards of Living*, Pelican; *The Sunday Times*, 27 January 1985.
8. McKeown (1976). *The Role of Medicine: Dream, Mirage or Nemesis?* Nuffield Provincial Hospitals Trust, p. 109.
9. *See* John Robson, *Quality, Inequality and Health Care, Medicine in Society* special edition; Asa Briggs in *New Society*, 16 November 1978.
10. McKeown and Lowe, *An Introduction to Social Medicine*, p. 5.
11. *Ibid.*, p. 6.
12. Lesley Doyal and Imogen Pennell (1976). 'Pox Britannica': health, medicine and underdevelopment. *Race and Class*, **XVIII**, 159.
13. *Ibid.*
14. Christian Aid Latin America pack.
15. Thomson, *England in the Nineteenth Century*, p. 164.
16. Ernest Mandel (1976). *An Introduction to Marxist Economic Theory*, Pathfinder Press, New York, p. 45.
17. Multinationals: Global Menace or Just Good Business? Part of *Latin America: A Study Course for Small Groups*, published by the United Society for the Propagation of the Gospel and the Methodist Missionary Society, London.
18. *Ibid.*
19. Peter Donaldson (1978). *Economics of the Real World*, BBC/Pelican, pp. 227-8.
20. *Review of African Political Economy*, No. 2, Jan–April 1975, p. 4.
21. Richard Crossman (1977). *The Diaries of a Cabinet Minister*, Vol. **III**, Hamish Hamilton and Jonathan Cape, p. 417.
22. Donaldson, *Economics of the Real World*, p. 217.

23. Hughes and Hunter (1971). Disease and 'Development' in Africa. In *Recent Sociology No 3, The Social Organization of Health*, ed. Hans Peter Dreitzel. Macmillan, New York, p. 169.
24. Charles van Onselen (1976). Randlords and rotgut, *History Workshop Journal*, 2, Autumn.
25. George (1976). *How the Other Half Dies*, Pelican, London, p. 35.
26. *Ibid.*, p. 25.
27. *The Guardian*, 30 June and 1 July 1980.
28. Cited in *Profits of Doom*, War on Want, London (1976). p. 4.
29. George (1976). *How the Other Half Dies*, p. 42.
30. *Ibid.*, p. 36.
31. *New Internationalist*, August 1976, p. 7.
32. George (1976). *How the Other Half Dies*, p. 31.
33. *New Internationalist*, August 1976, p. 22.
34. Paul Harrison (1979). *Inside the Third World*, Pelican.
35. *Trade Unions and the Transnationals Information Bulletin*, Issue No 3, ICFTU, Brussels (1983).
36. Killer asbestos moves south, *Africa Now*, June 1981.
37. Deadly dust threatens workers, *Africa Now*, February 1983.
38. Quoted in *New Internationalist*, May 1974, p. 11.
39. Quoted in *New Internationalist*, May 1974, p. 31.
40. International Health Program (1972), Before Subcommittee on International Health, Education and Labor Programs Committee on Labor and Public Welfare, US Senate, 92nd Congress, 2nd Sessions, June 1972, p. 162.
41. Quoted in Joseph Hansen (1970). *The Population Explosion*, Pathfinder Press, New York, p. 18.
42. *Profits of Doom*, p. 5.
43. George (1976). *How the Other Half Dies*, p. 55.
44. *New Internationalist*, June 1977, p. 5.
45. World Bank (1975). *Health Sector Policy Paper*, March, p. 16.
46. McKeown and Lowe (1981). *Social Medicine*, p. 77; World Bank, *World Development Report*.
47. *New Internationalist*, June 1977, p. 5.
48. Robert H. Cassen (1976). Population and Development: A Survey. *World Development*, Vol. IV, Pergamon Press, Oxford, 800–801.
49. *New Internationalist*, June 1977, p. 5.
50. Cassen (1976). Population and Development: A Survey, p. 800; UNICEF, *The State of the World's Children* (1984), p. 34; Solimans, G. and Haignere, C. (1984), *'Free-Market' Politics and Nutrition in Chile; A grim future after a short-lived success*, Working papers, Columbia University, New York.
51. *New Internationalist*, May 1974, p. 8.
52. *New Internationalist*, June 1977, pp. 16–17.
53. *Ibid.*, p. 22.
54. *Ibid.*, p. 24.
55. *Ibid.*, p. 22.

56. *Ibid.*, p. 23.
57. Cassen (1976). Population and Development: A Survey. p. 786.
58. *New Internationalist*, June 1977, p. 7.
59. Cassen (1976). Population and Development: A Survey. p. 796.
60. H. T. J. Chabot (1976). The Chinese system of health care. *Tropical and Geographical Medicine*, **28**, p. 5113.
61. *Ibid.*, p. S113.
62. *Ibid.*, p. S114.
63. All the above achievements are cited in J. D. Wray, *Health and Nutritional Factors in Early Childhood Development in the People's Republic of China*, prepared for the report of the Early Childhood Development Delegation visit to the People's Republic of China, Nov.-Dec. 1973.
64. V. Sidel and R. Sidel (1983). *The Health of China*, Zed, London, pp. 79–89.

4 The Medical Contribution

Chapter 3 showed how resources for health promotion are very inequitably distributed. It seems that little improvement is occurring for most of the world's people — in fact the situation is worsening. What then about the medical contribution? What about disease prevention and disease cure? Does the 'medical contribution' significantly counteract the imbalance in the spread of 'health promoting' resources?

It would be useful first to look at the history of medical services in those societies dominated by imperialism. Colonial medical services are the foundations of present-day health services. The discussion will again concentrate on Britain and its 'sphere of influence' although the general pattern is applicable to all underdeveloped countries.

HEALTH SERVICES IN THE UNDERDEVELOPED WORLD

Before, during and after the colonial period traditional healers — variously described as herbalists or witchdoctors — have provided an alternative to Western scientific medicine, often for the majority of people. Before the nineteenth century, medical facilities in the colonial territories were provided by doctors attached to companies trading throughout the Empire almost exclusively for their European employees. They were joined by physicians and surgeons serving in the armed forces overseas and in the nineteenth century medical missionary work expanded rapidly.[1]

In the later part of the century, economic depression resulted in major emigration to the colonies. The number of fatal epidemics among Britons abroad and the simultaneous improvement in health conditions at home highlighted the inadequacies of colonial medicine. The Colonial Secretary, Chamberlain, according to the *British Medical Journal* in 1900:

'. . . grasped the truth that the question of successful combatting of tropical disease lies at the bottom of the problem of colonisation.'[2]

This was the basis for the creation of the colonial medical services. In 1903 medical administrators were instructed first to preserve the health of the European community; secondly, to keep the African and Asian labour force in good working condition; and lastly, to prevent the spread of epidemics.[3] According to one administrator:

> 'As we want to have a healthy white nation we have got to tackle infectious disease in the native. The native is the reservoir of these infectious diseases.'
>
> *National Archives of Rhodesia*[4]

This policy resulted in some minimal medical facilities for plantation workers, miners and railway builders. The medical problems of the majority were neglected unless they threatened the health of the administration.

Missions generally served remote rural areas and provided only rudimentary curative medicine. In addition to promoting evangelism this work was recognized as 'most helpful to the Government in their endeavour of opening up tropical Africa.'[5] Consequently, permanent subsidies from the British administration were soon granted to medical missions.[6] What little medical care there was generally came from the missions (*Fig. 4.1*). The London Missionary Society, for

Figure 4.1 Medical care from the missions. (Courtesy Oxfam.)

example, expanded from 11 hospitals in China in 1898 to 31 in 1910. In India, the Society's training of local personnel provided the core of the future nursing service.[7]

Any public health activities were initiated to combat diseases that affected the European populations (e.g. malaria and sleeping sickness) or as attempts to maintain a healthier work-force and so ensure greater profits. For example, the Colonial Development Advisory Committee in 1939 noted that:

'If the productivity of the East African territories is to be fully developed, and with it, the potential capacity of those territories to absorb manufact-ured goods from the United Kingdom, it is essential that the standard of life of the native should be raised and to this end the eradication of disease is one of the most important measures.'

Economic History Review[8]

Traditional Healers (*Fig. 4.2*)[9]

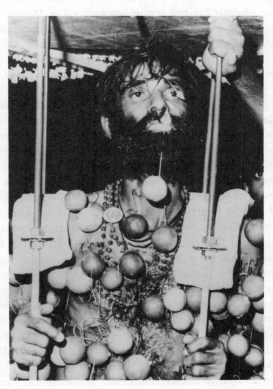

Figure 4.2 Traditional medicine is still very popular. (Courtesy World Health Organization.)

Traditional medicine in underdeveloped countries predated the colonial medical services, co-existed with them and still survives, often in an uneasy relationship with the Western-style medical hierarchy. Some governments, for example in Zimbabwe and Mozambique, have tried to register traditional practitioners or bring them into the national health effort in some other way. This approach has often revealed the wide popularity of traditional methods. The Zimbabwe National Traditional Healers Association (Zinatha) has some 11 000 members which is probably less than half the number of traditional practitioners in the country.

Zinatha's president, Gordon Chavunduka, has made a study of the choice of medical treatment by 200 people in Highfield, a township of the capital, Harare. He found that 22 per cent first consulted a traditional healer when they became ill and 55.2 per cent of those who received Western medical care later consulted a traditional healer.

Karl Peltzer, a West German researcher, made a study of Nyabanga village in the east of the country which suggests that rural people have the same level-headed approach as their urban counterparts. Since both Western and traditional approaches have obvious failings people are inclined to try both. Many people attend the local clinic because drug-based Western medicine can clear up the symptoms of their illness. But they go to the spiritual healer, the *n'anga*, to deal with the cause. The two main causes of illness are seen as the ancestral spirits or *vadzimu* and witchcraft. A foreign or alien spirit, *shave* or *ngozi*, can also play a part.

The Nyabanga study also gives some idea of what sort of person becomes a traditional healer. The village has 19 traditional practitioners — more than most villages — 13 of them registered with Zinatha. Fourteen are women. On average they have been in practice about 9 years. Less than 20 per cent of them are literate. Fifteen of them practise part-time, heal less than 10 different illnesses and have less than five patients a week.

A recent survey of *n'angas* in a number of Harare townships reveals a different picture. Of the 50 interviewed only 16 were women. The vast majority of both sexes were full-time healers: 73 per cent of men and 94 per cent of women.

The social status of the traditional practitioner varies widely. In Mozambique many of the traditional *curandeiros* in remote areas remain well-integrated in their local communities, perhaps accepting a chicken or another gift for their services. Others grew fat in the colonial period, when the government health services were weak and accessible to only a few. *Curandeiros* were forced into the money economy like other peasants and had to market their only commodity for cash. The fees charged by some *curandeiros* in urban areas were comparable with those charged by Portuguese doctors, enabling them to adopt a far from 'traditional' life-style.

In international health circles traditional medicine has recently become fashionable, with particular emphasis on its achievements in the area of mental health. For example, the *aladura*, the faith healers of the Yoruba areas of Nigeria, have a particular reputation in this regard.

But the recent survey of *n'angas* in townships of Harare showed that they were not primarily consulted on questions of mental illness. The *n'angas* were asked to name the illnesses they treated most often. The researchers then divided these illnesses into four categories: traditional, Western (those potentially treated by Western medical services), medical and gynaecological. There was some overlap between the four. The results were surprising: 81 per cent were Western illnesses, 28 per cent traditional and 15 per cent gynaecological, with mental cases, supposedly the *n'anga*'s speciality, accounting for only 13 per cent.

In many places traditional midwives or birth attendants play an important role in pregnancy, delivery and childcare. It is estimated that between 60 and 70 per cent of deliveries in Zimbabwe are attended by traditional midwives.

There is no easy answer to the question of how effective are the remedies offered by traditional healers. This is partly because there is such a variety of practitioners: spirit mediums, herbalists, bone-setters, midwives and so on. A large number of herbal remedies clearly do work though others may be dangerous. (The same, of course, can be said of Western drugs.) Ultimately the only way of judging the effectiveness of traditional medicine is to do what the Mozambican Government is doing — and the Chinese have done already — which is to collect and test the remedies. We will return to the problem of integrating traditional healing in Chapter 6.

Medical Services

Most developed countries devote 5–8 per cent of their gross national product (GNP) to direct health service expenditure. Underdeveloped countries today seldom devote more than 2 per cent of their much smaller GNPs to health services (Table 4.1).[10] For the 65 underdeveloped countries for which data are

Table 4.1 **Comparative health service expenditure**

Country	Health budget as % of GNP	Government health expenditure per capita (US$)
Brazil	1.2	13
Algeria	1.3	13
Turkey	0.6	6
Kenya	1.8	4
Tanzania	1.9	3
USSR	2.7	90
UK	5.2	204

Source: World Bank (1980)

available, about 40 spend less than $3.00 per year per person on health care with 27 spending $2.00 or less.[11]

'Expenditure per capita' is calculated by dividing the total expenditure by the number in the population. It is a rather misleading statistic for a number of reasons. First, health budgets (like any other) include capital and recurrent expenditures. This means that any buildings or expensive equipment (capital) are likely to consume an appreciable proportion of this meagre budget and yet be available to only a very limited section of the population. Also, the running costs of health care institutions (recurrent budget) are usually at least one-third of the capital cost. Thus a teaching hospital built in the early 1970s might well have cost £8 million. To run such a complex will cost £2-3 million a year. This, in most underdeveloped countries, is about 25 per cent of the total health budget and in some exceeds 50 per cent.[12] Therefore, even the small 'per capita' expenditures are exaggerations of the amount spent on the health care of most individuals.

For example, the cost of financing one bed in the Parirenyatwa hospital in Zimbabwe's capital is equal to the cost of running a rural health centre. And the capital — £5 million — involved in the construction of the new teaching hospital in Lusaka, Zambia, could have financed the construction of 250 health centres, which, if each served 20 000 people, could cover the entire population (*Fig. 4.3*).[13] Most of the small health budget of an underdeveloped country is spent on curative services, with only a small proportion being allocated to environmental and preventive services.

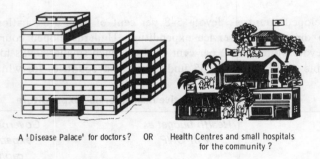

A 'Disease Palace' for doctors?   OR   Health Centres and small hospitals for the community?

Figure 4.3 Capital expenditure: which option? (TALC, courtesy Institute of Child Health, London.)

Organization

The organization of health services in underdeveloped countries is based on a modified version of the same 'referral system' that evolved in the West. This system is developed to different degrees in different countries. It is based on the ideal that patients are to be treated as close to their homes as possible in the cheapest, smallest, most simply equipped and most humbly staffed unit that will look after them adequately.[14] It is only when a particular unit cannot care adequately for a patient that he or she is referred higher up the chain. The chain starts with *aid stations* and *dispensaries* and then moves up through *health centres, rural* or *district hospitals*, and finally ends with the *regional, central* or *teaching hospital*.

Both the capital and the running costs of these different units in the health care system differ enormously (Table 4.2). The higher running costs of the larger, more expensive hospitals are not simply due to size. A major expense is the higher

Table 4.2   **Health care facility treatment costs ($US) 1972**

Facility	Cost of treatment per case	
	Tanzania	Kenya
National hospital	77.20	54.40
Regional hospital	33.80	25.00
District hospital	25.30	12.35
Health centre	0.73	0.58
Dispensaries	0.33	0.30

Source: M. Segall (1972). The politics of health in Tanzania. *Development and Change*, Vol. 4. Sage, London

proportion of specialist doctors, general duty doctors and nurses than in district hospitals. District hospitals in turn have more qualified staff than rural hospitals.

Is it a reasonably efficient way of providing medical care for the majority? What proportion of the population does it reach and how well does referral work *in practice?*

Coverage

The few surveys that have been done indicate that most patients visiting health care facilities come from the immediate vicinity. In Kenya, 40 per cent of the outpatients attending a health centre lived within 8 km (5 miles); 30 per cent lived 8-16 km (5-10 miles) away, and only 30 per cent lived more than 16 km (10 miles) away.[15] And in Tanzania two separate studies showed that 80 per cent of attending outpatients came from within 15 km (9.3 miles) of rural health centres (*Fig. 4.4*).[16] An Indian study revealed that for every additional half-mile (0.8 km) between the community and a dispensary, the number of people attending decreased by 50 per cent.[17] Another study showed that over 60 per cent of patients came from within a mile (1.6 km) of the primary health centre.[18]

The decline in inpatient use of health facilities is less sharp but still dramatic. In Uganda outpatient attendances halved for every 2 miles (3.2 km) while the use of inpatient facilities halved for every 5 miles (8 km). A survey in Ghana

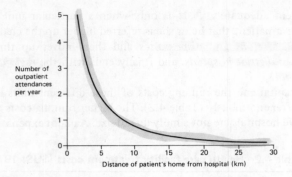

Figure 4.4 Average number of outpatient attendances per year, Tanzania. (From reference 14. Courtesy Oxford University Press.)

showed that 80 per cent of the inpatients at the five major hospitals came from surrounding urban districts.[19] It is possible to calculate roughly the proportion of a country's population without access to government health coverage. On this basis, in Ghana for example, only about half the population is covered.[20]

The inadequacy of the referral system is illustrated by some data from Kampala, Uganda. In 1964, of all admissions to the 'national referral' hospital, 93 per cent came from the surrounding district. And in Ghana, although the central hospital absorbed 149 of the 298 doctors in the official health service, only about 1 per cent of the patients in this hospital had been referred by outside health workers. Another 7 per cent had independently come into the Accra region for treatment.[21]

These and other studies clearly show that so-called 'referral hospitals' are actually serving as very expensive district hospitals for their local communities, who are often the élite who least need the facilities.

Personnel

The development of the early health services in the colonial world was modelled on the system 'at home'. The pattern was one of expensive, high-technology, urban-based curative care in large hospitals with Western-trained doctors as the main providers of medical care – almost totally confined to the towns.

This pattern still dominates today and is remarkably uniform throughout the underdeveloped world although the era of classic colonialism has now passed.

A hospital-based system inevitably requires doctors and so the skewed distribution of facilities is accompanied by the maldistribution of medical personnel.

The considerable disparities between the developed and underdeveloped countries in resources available for medical care were clear enough from the health budgets. They are equally obvious in the case of medical personnel (Table 4.3). But again these ratios understate the case because they take no account of

Table 4.3 **Disparities in medical personnel**

Nation	Population per:	
	Physician	Nursing person
Bangladesh	10 940	24 450
Nigeria	12 550	3010
Guatemala	8600	1620
Ivory Coast	21 040	1590
Iran	2320	2520
USA	520	150

Source: World Bank (1983), *World Development Report*

the great variation in distribution of health workers. Doctors especially are concentrated in towns — particularly the capital cities — while few practise in the countryside where the majority of the population lives. In Colombia 74 per cent of all doctors and 86 per cent of all nurses practise in the State capitals where only 31 per cent of the population lives.[22] In India 80 per cent of all doctors work in the cities while 80 per cent of the people live on the land.[23] In 11 African French-speaking countries in 1965 about 60 per cent of the indigenous and 50 per cent of the foreign doctors were located in the capital cities.[24]

Chapter 3 looked at the drain of resources from the poor to the richer sectors of underdeveloped countries and thence to the developed world. The situation with respect to medical personnel is much the same. For not only do health workers congregate in the major cities, but a significant proportion actually leave their countries for Europe, North America and Australasia.

International Migration — the 'Brain Drain'

About 140 000 doctors work in countries other than the one where they were trained. Of these 120 000 work in just five countries: USA (77 000), Britain (21 000), Canada (11 000), West Germany (6000) and Australia (4000).

Some 95 per cent of migrant doctors from Latin America go to the USA and 5 per cent to Europe. About 40 per cent from Africa go to Europe, 40 per cent to North America and the rest to other underdeveloped countries. Medical 'aid' does nothing to redress the balance: there are more Togolese doctors in France than there are French doctors in Togo under the assistance programmes. Ireland and Haiti have more of their doctors abroad than in their own countries.[25] Fifteen thousand Indian doctors are working abroad. It costs India $9600 to train each one — a total loss of some $144 million. Between 1962 and 1967

Pakistan lost over 2000 doctors and currently loses over 50 per cent of each year's output immediately after they graduate from medical school.[26] Similarly, despite attempts to restrict emigration of doctors, Sri Lanka loses half of its new graduates each year while Iran loses a quarter.[27] *And in the Philippines some years ago a football stadium had to be hired to send all the doctors taking the qualifying examination to work in the USA (Fig. 4.5).*[28] The Philippines has lost 9500 doctors — 68 per cent of its total.

Figure 4.5   The 'brain drain'. (Courtesy Chris Welch.)

This export of health personnel is not confined to doctors. It includes vast numbers of nurses, midwives and unskilled hospital workers. A survey showed that four out of every seven newly trained West Indian midwives were working in Britain while only three remained in the Caribbean.[29] South Korea has an official programme for 'exporting' nurses and nursing aides to Austria, West Germany, Japan and Switzerland. The Philippines has similar programmes in Europe and North America.[30]

Given the costs of medical education, migration of medical personnel is a great drain on resources — not just on brains. In fact, the transfer of resources to the USA by the immigration of professionals from the underdeveloped world in 1970 alone was calculated as $3700 million.[31] And at UK training costs the foreign doctors working there represent about £150 million of investment made by some of the world's most underdeveloped countries.

The Auxiliary

Professional health staff are costly to train and employ and tend to congregate in urban areas and from there often migrate abroad. The pattern of disease in under-developed countries is one of nutritional and communicable diseases. This means that the number of different conditions seen and the major causes of death — particularly among children — are limited.

Therefore the number of actions needed to prevent or cure the bulk of diseases is relatively small. A sophisticated and extensive knowledge of modern medical methods is unnecessary for these interventions which can be simple yet effective.

These are some of the important factors behind the development of the category *'auxiliary'*. Auxiliaries have been used to extend the effectiveness of professional and paramedical care into the rural areas where most of the population lives. They have traditionally been considered as people with less education and less developed skills than professionals doing part of the work of professionals and under their direction. They are an integral part of the *health team*.

The *health team* is conceived of as a group of different health workers who work together and whose collective efforts cover the medical need. Its composition varies in different countries and different situations but the *primary health worker* — the health worker who has first direct contact with the recipient of health care — is obviously most important. And, in underdeveloped countries, it is the auxiliary who has been developed to provide primary health care.

Late in the nineteenth century auxiliaries were used to combat single diseases — especially as smallpox vaccinators. After 1920, auxiliaries were used for treating yaws, yellow fever, sleeping sickness, leprosy, tuberculosis, venereal disease and more recently malaria eradication campaigns. These single-purpose auxiliaries were uneducated and often illiterate and their training was informal and inexpensive.

The need to improve quality and coverage of health services prompted the training of *multi-purpose auxiliaries*, the earliest of these being the dispensary auxiliary or dresser. But most categories of auxiliaries were developed to correspond to categories of professional and para-medical personnel: nursing, midwifery, health-visiting, environmental health, laboratory technology, pharmacy, radiography, entomology and in some places medical care.[32]

While originally candidates for auxiliary training were illiterate, gradually the educational requirements increased so that now there exist many categories of auxiliary with different educational levels. So for example, in Kenya, where the auxiliary concept has been carefully studied and developed, there were in 1966 five categories of auxiliary (Table 4.4). Since that time new *categories* have been added and the original categories have been expanded to include additional levels so that, for example, by 1969 the environmental health category included three levels. The lowest level auxiliary was the health worker whose only requirements

Table 4.4 **Categories of auxiliary**

Categories	Levels
Curative medicine and paediatrics	The medical assistant
Nursing	The enrolled nurse and the graded dresser
Midwifery	The enrolled midwife
Health visiting	The assistant health visitor
Environmental health	The assistant health inspector and the health assistant[33]

were interest, intelligence and an ill-defined apprenticeship. Next was the health assistant with 8 years of schooling and 2 years of formal training. Most senior was the assistant health inspector with 12 years of schooling and a 3-year technical course.

While this remains the basic scheme in underdeveloped countries, in some the categories have been further subdivided, so that for example in Indonesia no less than 44 categories of health auxiliaries existed by 1960! However, in most areas where auxiliaries are used the underlying principles guiding their training and function remain.[34]

Because of the population structure and distribution in most underdeveloped countries, health problems affecting pregnant and nursing mothers and small children constitute the majority of the health needs. For this reason one category of auxiliary — the auxiliary for maternal and child care or auxiliary nurse midwife (ANM) — has become almost universal. These workers, usually women, have had around 2 years' training both in preventive and in curative care. They operate from 'under-5s clinics' which have come to be integral parts of hospitals, health centres or sub-centres. Under-5s clinics aim to extend low-cost curative and preventive care to as large a proportion of the population as possible through the ANM.[35] Some of the specific duties of such a health worker will be considered along with the role of the *village health worker* (vhw) in Chapter 6, although the role of the vhw differs from that of the auxiliary in several very important ways.

The need for improved coverage by official health services lay behind the creation of the auxiliary grade. An obvious advantage in the use of these primary health workers is their cost, both of training and of employment. It is expensive to train doctors both in developed and in underdeveloped countries. In 1971 the estimated cost of training a doctor in the UK was £15 000 and in the USA £22 000. Costs in the underdeveloped world are comparable with those in the USA. In Tanzania, for example, in 1974/5 the cost of educating and training one medical graduate was £14 700, for a rural medical assistant £880, and for a rural medical aide £425. So for the price of one qualified doctor there could be eight medical assistants plus 16 aides![36] *The World Health Organization reckons on average that for the cost of training a doctor, a country could get five nurses, 24 medical assistants or 50 sanitary inspectors.*

Similarly, the salary paid to an auxiliary after training is a fraction of the doctor's. So. . .even in Tanzania, where efforts have been made to reduce differentials, the yearly earnings of a doctor are more than four times those of a rural medical aide. The *financial* advantages of auxiliaries over doctors are clear enough. Another frequently cited advantage of auxiliaries over doctors is that they are more closely in touch with local inhabitants and are also more content to remain in the rural areas.

It is difficult to prove such assertions. But there is some evidence to suggest that although auxiliaries often originate in the communities they are trained to serve, they may not be all that closely in touch after they have become auxiliaries. A survey of health officers in Ethiopia showed that 83 per cent did not want to work in health centres for long and 78 per cent wished to study for a medical degree.[37] Auxiliaries of all categories both in Ethiopia and in Tanzania almost always reveal in discussions their desire to become doctors.[38] In Thailand it was noted by an American delegation studying the country's health services that 'another problem has to do with the reluctance of government health personnel to carry health services to the surrounding communities. They tend to stay close to their posts, even though the work there may not keep them busy'.[39] And in other countries there are frequent reports of rural-based auxiliaries catering for the health needs of 'important' people such as local teachers and shop-owners rather than the lower status, 'ordinary' members of the community.

Has the use of auxiliaries, supposedly closer both geographically and culturally to their communities, significantly increased the utilization of health services in underdeveloped countries?

In Cali, Colombia, where the doctor to population ratio is 1:910, 17.3 per cent of children who die are not seen by a doctor and another 19 per cent have no medical attention at all during the 48 hours preceding death. In the rural areas around Cali the 17.3 per cent figure rises to 50 per cent. Similar figures apply to Colombia as a whole. Moreover probably considerably less than 50 per cent of the population is reached by health services. In other words, *more than half the population has no contact with anyone in the health team.*

Health and the Developing World[40]

For a sick person living in a remote area the obstacles to attending a distant health centre are obviously substantial. But many people decide against visiting even *nearby* health centres — as in Cali. A survey of families living in the area served by one of the newest and best-staffed health centres in this city showed that 40 per cent used the health centre, 28 per cent knew of it but did not use it and 32 per cent did not know anything about it.[41] Three studies in India confirm these findings:

(1) In rural Punjab for every 100 of the population there were 89 contacts per year with health team staff of the primary health centre, as against 221 with registered indigenous medical practitioners.

(2) A recent study in a village close to New Delhi showed that only 7 per cent of illness came to the attention of the health services.
(3) In another study of over 8000 episodes of illness the health needs were related to the facilities available and the unmet need measured (*Fig. 4.6*).

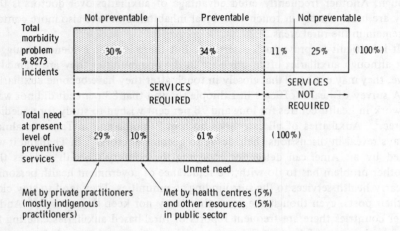

Figure 4.6 Distribution of 8273 morbidity problems identified by household visits in Punjab villages. (From chapter 1, reference 7. Courtesy Butterworths.)

Figure 4.6 shows that 36 per cent or 3000 of these episodes did not require the attention of medical services. Of the remaining 5000, 29 per cent were dealt with by mostly indigenous practitioners, only 10 per cent by official health services while over 60 per cent received no treatment from either source! These figures, it is stressed, come from an economically well-off area of a State in which peripheral services are better planned than in most underdeveloped countries.

Lastly, in Egypt, which has a more widely distributed health service than India, one study revealed that only 20–25 per cent of families used national child health centres, and up to 80 per cent of mothers depended on traditional midwives for delivery.[42]

Conclusion

Morely's 'three-quarters rule' describes the allocation of health-care resources in underdeveloped countries:

> 'Although three-quarters of the population in most countries in the tropics and sub-tropics live in rural areas, three-quarters of the spending on medical care is in urban areas, and also three-quarters of the doctors (and other

health workers) live there. Three-quarters of the deaths are due to conditions that can be prevented at low cost, but three-quarters of the medical budget is spent on curative services, many of them provided at high cost.'

Paediatric Priorities[43] (*see* also *Fig. 4.7*)

Figure 4.7 Part of the problem, not part of the solution: two views of a hospital in South Africa.

HEALTH SERVICES IN THE DEVELOPED WORLD

The 'medical contribution' played a very minor part in the improvement in the health of the British population which began in the second half of the nineteenth century.

A quite different population structure and disease pattern has come into existence both in the developed world and among the privileged groups living in the developed sectors of underdeveloped countries. In Britain for instance, a country in the late phase of the demographic transition, the proportion of old people in the population has been increasing rapidly. Between 1949 and 1974 the number over 75 increased by 55 per cent and is expected to rise by 2 per cent per year.[44] Certain conditions become the new 'epidemic diseases'. Degenerative diseases of the skeleton and blood vessels, cancer and mental illness have supplanted the diseases of undernutrition and poor hygiene as the major causes of illness and death.

But differences in living and working conditions in different sections of the population are still reflected in quite marked differences in health. While overall the health of the British population has improved, differences in standards of health between social classes have actually *increased* in recent years (*Fig. 4.8*).

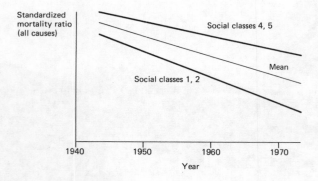

Figure 4.8 Standardized mortality ratio (all causes), Britain. (From Registrar General's Occupational Mortality Tables, 1959–63.)

We have already seen how factors like industrial disease and accidents, poor environment, inadequate housing, stress and cigarette smoking disproportionately affect the working class. But what about the allocation of health care? Does the medical contribution counteract this imbalance in health promoting resources in the developed world?

Facilities

It was not investment in health care that improved levels of health in the developed world. So greater investment in health care does not necessarily have much impact on the statistics of disease and death.

Health services are indispensable not so much for the small number of 'cures' they effect, but for the care they provide for the seriously ill and many others with disabling and uncomfortable conditions. Personal social services are important in providing help and care for the especially vulnerable members of society – the elderly, mentally ill and mentally and physically handicapped, and children. Yet spending on health and personal social services in Britain has fallen dramatically in recent years. Of this continually declining health service spending, only 0.38 per cent of the total[45] is devoted to specifically preventive work, while the health education budget of the NHS accounts for 0.01 per cent of the total.[46] And these figures are falling.

The hospitals take 63 per cent of the inadequate health care budget, with acute hospitals claiming nearly half of the total expenditure – and many of these hospitals are in a state of decay (Table 4.5). Teaching hospitals, which

Table 4.5 **Percentages of NHS gross expenditure**

Year	Hospital services	GP services	Community health
1951	55.7	9.5	8.5
1961	57.0	9.6	9.3
1971	66.6	8.3	7.1
1980	62.7	6.2	6.2

Source: Office of Health Economics, *Compendium of Health Statistics* (1981)

cater for a disproportionately high number of middle- and upper-class patients, consume more than a quarter of the total NHS capital budget and this adds to their recurrent budget too.

It is not possible to examine all areas of the NHS. But a brief examination of one of the most important sectors – care of the elderly – reveals its inappropriate development. *Over 37 per cent of all hospital beds are occupied by patients over 65, about half of these being in psychiatric hospitals.*[47] Because of the small number of geriatric day hospitals in Britain, the elderly account for around 30 per cent of admissions to acute wards of general hospitals.[48]

This is not surprising when community services for the elderly fall pitifully short of the national requirements (Table 4.6). With the cuts in capital expenditure for building programmes (from £96m in 1974 to £44m in 1980 for the elderly)[48] and the paltry projected growth rate of 2 per cent it will take a long time before services for the elderly achieve the standards proposed by the

Table 4.6   **Shortfall in services for the elderly**

Service	1974 level of service	National requirement	Shortfall as % of requirement
Home helps per 1000	6	12	50
Meals on wheels served weekly	600 000	1 300 000	54
Day centre places per 1000	2	3–4	33.50
Local authority residential places per 1000	18.5	25	26
Geriatric hospital beds per 1000	8.57	10	14

Source: Radical Statistics Health Group[45]

Department of Health and Social Security (DHSS) -- 35 years to reach the target for the number of home helps, 39 years for the meals on wheels service and 15 years for the number of places in local authority residential care.[49] These estimates assume a constant number of old people. The targets are even more remote in view of the inevitable and rapid growth of this age group.

It is not just by sector, but also by geographical region that NHS facilities are unfairly distributed. Whereas London spends 24 per cent above the national average on its hospitals, Birmingham spends 15 per cent less, East Anglia 17 per cent less and Sheffield 22 per cent less.[50] This unevenness occurs not just between regions but also within regions. For example, in East Anglia spending in the urban teaching district of Cambridge falls only 13 per cent below the national average, while King's Lynn and Great Yarmouth districts are each more than 51 per cent below.

Likewise, in the 'rich' Metropolitan London region there are gross local discrepancies. There are a large number of teaching hospitals in London. This inflates the budget and gives the impression that the region is overprovided with services. East London, for example, is an area of particular need, with an infant mortality rate 20 per cent above the national average and hospital admissions nearly 30 per cent higher than the national figure. Yet, as part of a 'rationalization of services', 21 hospitals in this area are being closed and six partially closed.

Personnel

The geographical distribution of doctors -- and other health workers -- follows the distribution of other resources. Two studies in 1964 and 1965 found that:

'. . . in predominantly working-class areas 80% of the doctors' surgeries were built before 1900, and only 5% since 1945 — in middle-class areas less than 50% were built before 1900, and 25% since 1945 . . . more middle-class area GPs had lists under 2000 than did working-class area GPs and few had lists over 2500; nearly twice as many had higher qualifications; more had access to physiotherapy, four times as many had been to Oxford or Cambridge, five times as many had been to a London medical school, twice as many held hospital appointments or hospital beds in which they could care for their own patients, and nearly three times as many some-times visited their patients when they were in hospital under a specialist.'

Lancet[51]

Medical education concentrates on the super-technological specialities. Medical students thus aspire to become specialists in those areas which are most presti-gious and which also attract the lion's share of health-service resources. A survey of 25 British medical schools showed that only seven schools allocated 6 or more hours to the subject of occupational medicine and 10 schools (including eight in London) totally neglected it.[52] The Royal Commission on Medical Education recommended that departments of community medicine should be established. Four years later a survey found that only four of 12 London medical schools had done so.[53] Similar gaps exist in the teaching of psychiatry, geriatrics and even in training for primary care. This emphasis on technological specialization is reflected in the career preferences of medical students (Table 4.7).

Table 4.7 **Career preferences of medical students: first choices (as percentages of total)**

Career choice	Royal Commission 1968	Manchester and Sheffield Enquiry	
		1971	1972
Medicine	26.5	24.0	23.8
Surgery	17.8	19.9	13.5
Obstetrics and gynaecology	12.4	5.5	4.0
General practice	23.5	32.2	46.8
Psychiatry	5.2	1.4	2.4
Community medicine	1.6	2.0	1.6
Pathology	2.1	3.4	4.7
Anaesthetics	2.0	8.2	3.2
Radiology	0.8	0.7	—
Other	8.1	2.7	—

Source: quoted in Tom Heller (1978), *Restructuring the Health Service*, Croom Helm, p. 39

Technological specialities receive the vast majority of 'merit awards'. These are awards given predominantly to private part-time consultants and in 1974 ranged from about £4500 to £20 000 *in addition* to NHS salaries. The identity of the recipients as well as the criteria employed for assessment are secret although it *is* known that there are no specialists in community medicine on the awarding committee. Not surprisingly, only 2.9 per cent of community physicians and 23 per cent of geriatricians receive awards, while 73 per cent of thoracic surgeons and 70 per cent of cardiologists are so favoured (*Fig. 4.9*)![54]

Approximately half of the 10 600 consultants are full-timers in the NHS with no private practice, although a significant proportion of them *are* recipients of merit awards. The salary scale for these full-time hospital consultants ranged from £18 900 to £24 260 in 1984. Of course, those 5000–6000 who have private practices are able to augment their incomes substantially. The average for GPs, nearly all of whom are full-time 'contractors' to the NHS, was £20 670 in 1984, excluding the additional payment from the contraceptive services.[55]

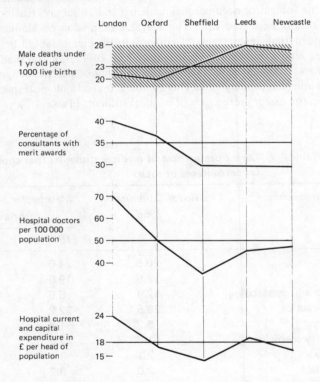

Figure 4.9 Infant mortality, merit awards, hospital doctors and resources by region. (From Robson (1977). *Quality, Inequality and Health Care*. Marxists in Medicine, p. 39. Available Central Books, 37 Gray's Inn Road, London WC1.)

But though those salaries put doctors among the highest earners, these financial rewards are evidently insufficient for some. When the possibilities offered by private practice are exhausted, *international migration* can be resorted to. Rather than work in the under-resourced and unpopular specialities of geriatrics, psychiatry and community medicine – all incidentally sectors with limited possibilities for private practice – or as GPs in underprovided areas, some migrate abroad. Each year, about 300 doctors from Britain emigrate, especially to North America where medical practice is considerably more lucrative.[56]

The wages of one large section of health personnel, ancillary workers – porters, cleaners, domestics, kitchen and laundry staff – who are vital to the running of any health care institution, are about one-sixth of the salaries paid to consultants.[57]

One of the important factors influencing wage levels is the *reserve work-force* – that is, the existence of a significant number of unemployed. This allows employers to pay low wages because there are always 'replacement workers' easily recruited from this reserve pool. *Female labour* has mostly been used. But British women were not the only source of additional labour in the long post-war boom from the 1950s to the 1970s. It was in this period that immigration to Britain from the West Indies, India, Pakistan and East Africa was encouraged (*Fig. 4.10*). In the medical and dental services not only were 76 per cent of

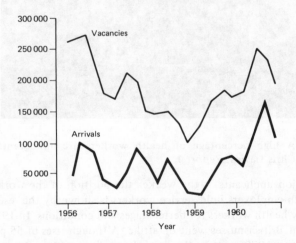

Figure 4.10 Employment vacancies and West Indian arrivals 1956–60. (Courtesy *New Internationalist*.)

workers in 1977 *women*, but of these a disproportionately high percentage were *immigrants* (*Fig. 4.11*).

So most health workers have been drawn from the reserve pool of unemployed, a pool that extends beyond national boundaries. The size of this pool determines not only wage levels but also job security. The bigger the pool – or the number

Figure 4.11   A high percentage of health workers are immigrants. (Courtesy Chris Davies, *Report*.)

of potential job applicants — the weaker the position of the worker. The low value in which employers hold service workers is shown by the results of industrial action by health workers for better wages and conditions. In 1974 traditionally compliant British nurses went on strike. Although rises of 55 per cent were needed to regain 1970 wage levels, the only grade to achieve this was the senior administrative grade nurse. A student nurse of 21 in her first year only received 4.8 per cent, in her second year 10.3 per cent and in her third 14.8 per cent.[58]

Also, although the number of health-service personnel has increased, the number of patients has *doubled* since 1949.[59] This has placed greater demands and responsibilities on all health workers, many of whom continue to work extremely long hours in poor conditions. *One of the major health service unions estimates a shortage of 70 000 nurses in the NHS.*[60] Yet at the same time we find that the official number of unemployed nurses has risen from 3418 in September 1975 to 6496 in September 1976 and stood at 8574 in June 1980.[61]

Health Team

In the underdeveloped world primary health workers — auxiliaries — are seen as part of a health team. There is no exact equivalent of the auxiliary in the British health service, but the concept of a 'health team' does exist.

People in developed societies often need advice and care and not a super-technological intervention or the attention of a doctor. This has been acknow-ledged by the development of various workers whose operations are part of local authority health and welfare services. They include *health visitors, district nurses* and *home helps*. Their functions include simple curative care, ante- and postnatal care and occasional home deliveries, rehabilitation, preventive measures and a certain amount of health education and domestic help for the ill and elderly.

The traditional approach of doctors, and hence all health workers, has been to respond to demands from patients when they feel themselves to be ill. This approach ignores the people in the community with diseases who do not or can-not present themselves for treatment. It includes those who delay until their illnesses are so severe that treatment is expensive, dramatic and often futile. Also, there are a large number of symptomless conditions that could be diag-nosed using available techniques. The latent demand for health care that was revealed in the early years of the NHS has already been mentioned. More recently though, community surveys have indicated that:

'. . . for every case of diabetes, rheumatism or epilepsy known to the GP there appears to be another undiagnosed case. In the case of psychiatric illness, bronchitis, blood pressure, glaucoma and urinary infections there are likely to be another five cases undiscovered, etc. . . .'

Evidence[62]

A community survey in Southwark, London, using simple screening techniques, found that 52 per cent of persons screened would need further investigation and possible treatment.[63] Contrary to popular belief, the tendency of patients *not* to consult their doctors with painful or disabling symptoms is much more of a problem than consultation for 'trivial' reasons. A study in Glasgow showed that 23 per cent of adults had at least one symptom that was causing disability or pain or was thought by them to be serious but for which they had not consulted their GP. In contrast, only 9 per cent had seen their doctors with symptoms that they did not consider serious.[64]

The allegation that a free service from GPs leads to infinite demand is not supported by the facts. Between 1955-6 and 1970-1 the number of patients who visited their GPs remained constant, while the number of visits per patient per year actually fell from 3.4 to 2.6 for males and 4.1 to 3.4 for females.[65] However, in the USA where medical care is largely private, this rate increased from 4.0 to 4.3 for men and from 5.1 to 5.6 for women.[66]

Conclusion

Even in developed countries only a small proportion of the ill health present in the community comes to the attention of the health and social services. This is particularly marked among the elderly, the mentally ill, the mentally and physically handicapped and the chronically sick. The most deprived are areas with predominantly working-class populations. Most ill health is dealt with within *the family* and also by friends and neighbours. This is largely done by women, many of whom are likely to be service workers or even health-service employees during their 'working' hours!

The medical contribution in the developed world is effectively summed up by the 'Inverse Care Law': 'The availability of good medical care tends to vary inversely with the need of the population served.'[67]

References

1. Doyal and Pennell (1976). 'Pox Britannica': health, medicine and under-development. *Race and Class*, **XVIII**, 161.
2. *British Medical Journal* (1900), **ii**, 1041; cited in T. Johnson, (1973), Imperialism and the professions, in P. Halmos (ed.), *Professionalisation and Social Change*, Keele.
3. A. Beck (1970). *A History of the British Medical Administration of East Africa, 1900–1950*, Harvard; cited in Doyal and Pennell, 'Pox Britannica'.
4. National Archives of Rhodesia, S1173 & 337, notes by Dr Askins, 6 December 1930; Medical Director Salisbury to Director of Native Development, 10 December 1930.
5. Beck, *British Medical Administration*, p. 55.
6. *Ibid.*, p. 82.
7. Norman Goodall (1954). *A History of the London Missionary Society, 1895–1945*. Oxford University Press, pp. 514–15.
8. Quoted in D. Meredith, The British Government and colonial economic policy 1919–39, in *Economic History Review*, **XXVIII**, 493.
9. Richard Carver (1983), 'integrating traditional healing' and Carol Barker, 'a long-term check', *Africa Now*, January.
10. World Bank (1975). *Health Sector Policy Paper*, p. 32.
11. *Ibid.*, p. 33.

12. D. C. Morley (1975). The large teaching hospital – a disaster? In *British Health Care Planning and Technology*, British Hospitals Export Council Year Book, pp. 119–22.
13. M. King. *A Teaching Hospital for a Developing Country*, mimeo.
14. M. King. *Medical Care in Developing Countries*, Oxford University Press, pp. 2, 5.
15. N. R. E. Fendall (1965). Medical Planning and the Training of Personnel in Kenya. *Journal of Tropical Medicine and Hygiene*, **68**, 12.
16. O. Gish (1973). Resource allocation, equality of access and health. *World Development*, **I**, December.
17. H. Frederiksen (1964). *Maintenance of Malaria Eradication*, duplicated report WHO/Mal/429. World Health Organization, Geneva, pp. 2, 6.
18. Milton I. Roemer (1972). *Evaluation of Community Health Centres*. World Health Organization, Geneva, p. 25.
19. Study by Saakwa-Mante, cited in M. J. Sharpston (1972), Uneven geographic distribution of medical care: a Ghanaian case study, *Journal of Development Studies*, **8**, 210.
20. World Bank (1975). *Health Sector Policy Paper*, p. 36.
21. Study by Saakwa-Mante, cited in Sharpston, *Journal of Development Studies*, **8**, 209–11.
22. Culture, disease and health services in Colombia, special issue of *The Milbank Memorial Fund Quarterly*, (1968), **XLVI**, p. 223.
23. C. Whittemore (1976). *The Doctor-Go-Round*, Oxfam, p. 7.
24. O. Gish (1970). Health planning in developing countries. *Journal of Development Studies,* **6**, 71.
25. *Le Monde*, 11 June 1980.
26. T. Heller (undated). Patterns of medical practice in England and the Third World. *Contact*, No. 33, Christian Medical Commission, Geneva.
27. B. Senewiratne (1975). Emigration of doctors, *British Medical Journal,* **i**, 618, 669, 687; H. A. Ronaghy (1974). Physician Migration to the USA, *Journal of the American Medical Association,* **227**, 538.
28. Editorial (1973). How Many Doctors? *Lancet*, December, 1367.
29. O. Gish (1971). *Doctor Migration and World Health*, London, p. 139.
30. O. Gish and M. Godfrey (1977). Why did the doctor cross the road? *New Society*, 17 March.
31. *Ibid.*
32. J. Bryant (1969). *Health and the Developing World*, Cornell University Press, Ithaca and London, p. 164.
33. King, *Medical Care in Developing Countries*, pp. 3, 4.
34. Bryant, *Health and the Developing World*, p. 165.
35. Morley, *Paediatric Priorities*, p. 317.
36. Whittemore, *The Doctor-Go-Round*, p. 10.
37. M. Segall. Theoretical problems of 'middle-level' rural health centres and of rural health in the countries of East Africa (with special reference to Ethiopia and Tanzania), mimeo, p. 9.

38. *Ibid.*, p. 10.
39. Bryant, *Health and the Developing World*, p. 78.
40. *Ibid.*, pp. 87-8.
41. *Ibid.*, p. 88.
42. Morley (1973). *Paediatric Priorities in the Developing World*. Butterworths, London, pp. 57-9.
43. *Ibid.*, p. 4.
44. Robson, *Quality, Inequality and Health Care. Medicine in Society*, special edition, p. 48.
45. Radical Statistics Health Group. *Whose Priorities?* p. 2.
46. *Ibid.*, p. 2.
47. Robson, *Quality, Inequality and Health Care*. p. 38.
48. National Co-ordinating Committee Against the Cuts, publication No. 1, p. 13.
49. Radical Statistics Health Group. *Whose Priorities?* p. 13.
50. T. Heller and D. Jenkins (1976). *Evidence for the Royal Commission on the National Health Service*, the William Temple Foundation.
51. J. T. Hart (1971). The inverse care law. *Lancet*, **i**, 405-12.
52. Heller. Patterns of Medical Practice in England and the Third World. *Contact*, No. 33.
53. *Ibid.*
54. *Ibid., British Medical Journal*, (1983) 21 May, 1667.
55. *British Medical Journal*, (1983) 21 May, 1667.
56. Whittemore, *The Doctor-Go-Round*.
57. *Revolutionary Communist*, No. **5**, p. 24.
58. International Marxist Group, 'Struggle for Health' pamphlet.
59. Estimate from Confederation of Health Service Employees.
60. Quoted in *Women's Voice*.
61. Heller and Jenkins. *Evidence for the Royal Commission on the National Health Service*, p. 66.
62. *Ibid.*, p. 66.
63. D. R. Hannay and E. J. Maddox (1975). Incongruous referrals. *Lancet*, **ii**, 1195-7.
64. W. P. D. Logan and A. A. Cushion (1958). *Morbidity Statistics from General Practice*, Vol. **1**, *Studies on Medical and Population Subjects*, No. 14, HMSO, London.
65. Physician visits: volume and interval since last visit, *United States Vital and Health Statistics Series* (1975) **10**, 97.
66. Study quoted in Heller and Jenkins, *Evidence for the Royal Commission on the National Health Service*, pp. 67-9.
67. Hart. *The Inverse Care Law*, p. 405.

5 Medicine, Business and the State

Chapter 3 looked at the reasons for the inequitable distribution of the resources necessary to promote health both in underdeveloped countries and in the developed ones that dominate them.

Chapter 4 showed that the medical contribution does little to alter the effects of social conditions on the health of most people. It also raised certain questions which will be looked at here:

(1) *Why are health services inappropriate in nature and inequitably distributed?*
(2) *What part have doctors played in creating and maintaining this set-up?*
(3) *What other functions might health care systems have in society?*

THE PART PLAYED BY THE HEALTH PROFESSIONS

History

The medical profession in Britain originated as one of the 'status occupations' of the leisured gentry. They possessed no specialized knowledge or skills, but derived their position from title and tradition supported by inherited wealth.[1]

Their theoretical training was restricted largely to the works of the ancient Roman physician Galen. No experimentation was taught and patients were rarely seen. Thus the university-trained physician, when confronted with a sick person, had to resort largely to superstition and quasi-religious rituals.[2]

The Crown recognized the first professional body – the Royal College of Physicians – in 1518. The Surgeons, because of their blood-spilling, were disapproved of by the Church and therefore in 1540 had to ally with the Barbers in a craft guild. The Royal College of Surgeons was recognized only in 1880. Apothecaries, of much lower social status, were reviled both by physicians and by surgeons and were disallowed from charging for medical advice or their potions until 1815.[3]

The profession that was to emerge under capitalism grew out of these three groupings: the physicians from the 'status occupations', the surgeons from the craftsmen and artisans and the apothecaries from the tradesmen.

Women in Health Care

Women had been involved in health care from early times — mainly as midwives but also as healers. In contrast to doctors, they practised especially amongst the peasant classes. It was they who discovered and administered herbal remedies still important today such as ergot for labour pains, belladonna to inhibit uterine contractions during threatened miscarriage and digitalis for treating heart ailments.[4]

These wise women, or *witches* as they came to be called, believed in trial and error, cause and effect, relying on their senses rather than doctrine or faith. Their methods and results consequently posed a great threat to the Church which discredited material values and profoundly distrusted the senses. But they also threatened the emerging medical profession, who early on ensured their exclusion from the universities. English doctors petitioned Parliament concerning the 'worthless and presumptuous women who usurped the profession', and requested that fines and 'long imprisonment' be imposed on any woman who attempted to 'use the practyse of Fisyk'.[5]

However, the great majority of female healers — the 'witches' — remained. This 'problem' was resolved by the witch-hunts of the fourteenth to seventeenth centuries when many thousands were tortured and burnt to death.[6]

The assault on the last preserve of female healing — *midwifery* — was led by non-professionals — barber–surgeons — who claimed technical superiority based on their use of the obstetrical forceps. (The forceps were classed as a surgical instrument and women were legally barred from surgical practice.) So began the rapid transformation of neighbourly midwifery into lucrative obstetrics, a business that was entered by doctors in the eighteenth century.

By the middle of the nineteenth century the only remaining occupation for women in health care was *nursing*. In the early nineteenth century some nurses were employed to provide token care in the hospitals which served mainly as squalid refuges for the dying poor. But most nurses were simply women who happened to be nursing someone — usually a sick relative.[7]

In order to be acceptable to doctors and women of 'good character' nursing had to be reformed. Florence Nightingale with her team of sober, disciplined, middle-aged Victorian women in the battle-front hospitals of Crimea led the movement, and was soon emulated by Dorothea Dix in the Union hospitals of the American Civil War. This pursuit was deemed 'natural' and acceptable for women of their class (*Fig. 5.1*).

But nursing was largely low-paid, heavy-duty housework and soon began attracting fewer upper-class women. However, the educators continued to impose

Figure 5.1 Florence Nightingale at Scutari — nursing for women of 'good character'. (Courtesy Mansell Collection.)

their values on trainees. Until recently the teaching of upper-class graces was integral to nursing training.

Nightingale further strengthened the prevailing attitudes in society and confirmed the dominance of the male medical profession by reinforcing women's subservient role. When some English nurses proposed that nursing be modelled on the medical profession with examinations and licensing, Nightingale responded that 'nurses cannot be registered and examined any more than mothers'. She also said of the few female doctors of her time: 'They have only tried to be men, and they have succeeded only in being third-rate men'.[8] Indeed, in the late nineteenth century as the number of nursing students rose, the number of female medical students started to decline. Woman had been prescribed her place in the health care system.

The Modern Doctor

Many of the fundamental characteristics of today's medical profession can be traced to the period of the industrial revolution when the capitalist system became dominant and created an impoverished and urbanized working class — whose only source of wealth was its labour — and also the middle classes. Those gentlemen doctors without private means were now forced to seek payment for their services among these people. Public examinations replaced personal patronage as the qualification for membership of the medical profession.

Doctors also found it necessary to unify to preserve their privilege and status. So in 1834 the British Medical Association (BMA) was formed, which was initially a militant body representing those providing services under the Poor Law. In 1858 the Medical Act recognized all educational and licensing bodies and placed them under the supervision of the General Medical Council (GMC) which contained representatives of government, the universities and the profession. Medicine was thus formally linked with the State.[9]

Through the BMA and GMC a 'code of practice' was formulated whereby activities that might be detrimental to the profession as a whole — such as advertising and 'patient snatching' — were legislated against. Nothwithstanding these controls, GPs continued to minister largely to working people and thus remained poor. Around the turn of the century a character in one of Bernard Shaw's plays said:

'When you are so poor that you cannot refuse eighteen-pence from a man who is too poor to pay you any more, it is useless to tell him that what he and his sick child needs is not medicine but more leisure, better food and a better drained and ventilated house. It is kinder to give him a bottle of something almost as cheap as water and tell him to come again with another eighteen-pence if it does not cure him. When you have done this over and over again every day for a week, how much scientific conscience have you got left?'

The Doctor's Dilemma[10]

However, the specialists, physicians and surgeons, because of their long-established connection with the upper classes and the selfishly guarded knowledge, maintained their wealth and power.

Perhaps an even better example than the protracted British industrial revolution is the French Revolution when all areas of society, including medical institutions, came under close scrutiny. Two great ideas were born: first, that health care was a function of the State; and secondly, that social change could eradicate disease and return humanity to a state of original health. For a while the faculties were closed and doctors' societies and associations abolished: they were to be employed by the State. Sickness was to be dealt with at home with State-administered public assistance. Indeed, the first task of the doctor was seen as a political one; the struggle against disease was to be a fight against bad government.[11] In the words of one French revolutionary:

'Who then should denounce tyrants to mankind if not the doctors who make man their sole study and who each day in the homes of poor and rich, among ordinary citizens and among the highest in the land, in cottage and mansion, contemplates the human miseries that have no other origin but tyranny and slavery.'

Quality, Inequality and Health Care[12]

However, these ideals — and many others — did not materialize. Throughout Europe the medical profession developed and strengthened — a profession that still today insists on the *separation* of 'medicine' and 'politics', and which in its practice and education promotes this belief. The main causes of this reverse did not lie solely in the area of medicine. *All kinds* of libertarian ideals thrown up in the popular struggles that swept Europe in this period soon became dreams of the past, as the previous ruling class of feudal lords and monarchs was replaced by the capitalists.

The most important way in which this new system differed from pre-capitalist societies was in the area of production. All kinds of commodities necessary for a reasonable standard of living were now being produced on a large and much more efficient scale in factories and on farms.

In theory such ideals as 'Liberty, Equality and Fraternity' could have been realized. But in this system the means whereby these commodities were produced were owned by a very few people. The competitive nature of capitalism further accentuated this and eventually resulted in today's monopoly ownership. In practice, therefore, the ideals born in the overthrow of the old order inevitably foundered on new class divisions and inequalities.

Doctors had already secured a privileged position by an alliance with the wealthy and powerful who had helped them in defeating competition from lay healers. But with the emergence of capitalism status was no longer sufficient. In order to survive, it was necessary to possess a commodity that both satisfied a human want and could be exchanged for money. The new capitalists had their products and the workers their commodity — capacity for labour. The doctors too now needed a commodity. At this time a greater understanding of the body's structure and function — anatomy, physiology and pathology — was being gained through observation of corpses and ill patients. The invention of the microscope, one of the most advanced pieces of nineteenth-century technology,[13] gave birth to microbiology which in turn gave rise to the germ theory of disease. For the first time in history a rational basis for disease prevention and cure was established.[14]

These advances were timely since they constituted for doctors a body of knowledge which they appropriated for themselves and which became the basis for their commodity — modern health care.[15] The monopoly ownership of this commodity, health care, was consolidated by the establishment of professional associations, colleges and hospitals. Doctors now determined the entry, training, numbers and employment of graduates. In short, they controlled the production of their commodity. Similarly, they increasingly controlled its character and distribution.

But why should health care have become so *inappropriate in character and inequitable in distribution?* Is it because doctors — and other health workers whom they dominate — are innately insensitive? This question strikes a familiar note. When capitalism spread internationally, the 'capturing' of most of the world's population was not because the imperialists were particularly inherently malicious but because they were merely obeying a law of the economic system: the result was the brutal exploitation of the colonized. By the same token, although some health workers are often insensitive and even inconsiderate, their actions can only be understood as a result of the commodity nature of health care.

Why is Health Care so Inappropriate?

Under capitalism all production is geared to the manufacture of commodities. Commodities are produced in order to be sold for the highest price possible. The concern of the owner of the enterprise is not the usefulness of the product but the financial gain to be realized by its sale. Many expensive commodities may have little social utility. This applies also to health care as presently practised. Both in the underdeveloped and in the developed world the medical contribution is largely inappropriate to health needs and does not cope with the health problems of the vast majority.

The germ theory of disease and advances in medical science created the basis for what has been termed 'the bio-engineering approach' to illness. This approach persists today where a patient is regarded as a set of systems, one or more of which go wrong in illness, and which health workers attempt to put right with drugs and high technology. But most illness in the developed and underdeveloped world has its origins in social conditions. This information is widely available. Indeed some of it is even taught — albeit in an abstract way — in medical schools. In the social medicine 'part' of the course, medical students learn of the similarity between the disease pattern of nineteenth-century Europe and today's underdeveloped countries. But even social medicine books do not attempt to dissect the *social roots* of the new physical and psychological 'illnesses' of twentieth-century industrialized societies. For example, it is accepted that cigarette smoking is an important factor in the development of different cancers and vascular and lung disease, but few doctors question why smoking has become such a widespread habit with such a marked social-class distribution (*Fig. 5.2*).

Nevertheless, it is widely and increasingly acknowledged that living and working conditions and the social organization of developed societies underlie these new 'epidemics'. However, this awareness is *in practice* negated by concentration on a high-technology, individual-oriented, after-the-event curative approach, and the half-understood lessons of social medicine and epidemiology are largely ignored. This is illustrated by the following advertisement:

'Lack of space, lack of privacy, breeds unhappy people. But while society can offer little in the material sense, help is forthcoming where the effects of bad conditions are measured in human distress.

'Victims of overcrowding are familiar anxious faces in some surgeries. Yet their presence is often prompted by insomnia, headache, rash or other symptoms rather than their cause; anxiety or depression.

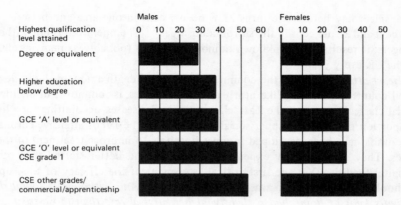

Figure 5.2 Cigarette-smoking status of current smokers aged 15 or over, by highest qualification level obtained. Results are given in percentages.

'The anxiety depression syndrome responds well to Limbitrol: swift anxiolytic action preceding gradual but sure elevation of mood.'

The inappropriateness of this approach is even starker in underdeveloped countries where the social origins of disease are so obvious. This is because the *fundamental* causes of ill health are out of the control of doctors. Indeed, any open recognition of the real causes would call into question the very system that allows doctors to own and market their commodity. In short, it is not in the interests of the medical profession to examine, and still less to confront, the fundamental social roots of illness.

It is not only this overwhelmingly important area of health promotion that is minimized and ignored. The medical contribution itself has been distorted in accordance with the demands of the market. Cure has become overdeveloped at the expense of care and prevention. Certain conditions susceptible to cure are highly researched and resourced. This is especially the case with those conditions that disproportionately affect the wealthy and powerful. The research goes into, say, coronary artery disease rather than a more 'class-conscious' disease like bronchitis, or, especially, a tropical one, like malaria. The most profitable sectors of the market are catered for.

The anomalies inherent in this 'free market' system are particularly clear in the fields of acute medicine and surgery, especially in countries where the market is 'free-est'. *For example, the disease pattern in Britain and the USA is very similar, yet the probability of a person in America undergoing surgery is twice as high as in Britain.*[16] The following examples emphasize this point.

Tonsillectomy is one of the most common surgical procedures. The frequency with which it is performed varies so much that it is unlikely that the operation has any major beneficial (or harmful) effects. And though there are no known differences in the rates of tonsillitis, in Vermont, USA, the probability of having a tonsillectomy before one turns 21 is 66 per cent in one area and between 16 per cent and 22 per cent in the surrounding areas.[17] The operation is not without dangers; it results in an unknown number of deaths (possibly as many as eight) in the UK every year.[18]

Heart attack is one of the commonest causes of death among males in developed countries. While it, like nearly all other illnesses, is commoner in the lower social classes it is one of the least 'class-conscious' diseases, accounting for a high proportion of deaths in upper social classes. Since the 1960s intensive coronary care units have been developed in most hospitals to improve treatment of these cases. They are invariably expensively equipped and better staffed than other hospital facilities. Yet the first critical assessment of the efficacy of this super-technological intervention was published in 1976. *And, although it found that patients kept at home had a slightly higher survival rate than those treated in intensive coronary care units,*[19] *the latter continue to be built!*

At the same time State spending on all public services has been cut back. The caring services for the elderly, handicapped and chronic sick are becoming increasingly inadequate. Waiting lists for many beneficial but not dramatically life-saving surgical operations, like hip replacement and gynaecological operations, have increased greatly. This has mainly affected working people for the wealthier can afford to go 'privately'.

Victim Blaming

As part of the general economic crisis, inflation has affected the health sector too and cost increases are worrying economic planners. For example, General Motors claims it spent more money in 1975 with Blue Cross and Blue Shield (the major USA health insurance companies) than it did with United States steel, its principal supplier of steel. Indeed General Motors added $175 to the price of every car and truck in passing on its employee health benefits costs![20]

So a newer and more 'radical' approach is being advanced by those who yesterday were advocating the most costly, sophisticated curative techniques. The essence of this new approach — aptly termed 'victim blaming' by some Americans — is that if individuals take appropriate action, if they avoid unhealthy behaviour, then they may prevent most diseases produced by social conditions. Life-style and environmental factors are combined and the message is that individuals are the primary agents in shaping or modifying the effects of their environment. It is implied that little can be done about the living and working conditions of modern industrial technological society but we can do much for ourselves as individuals.[21] It is reminiscent of earlier attitudes to disease sufferers and all-too-prevalent attitudes towards the poor and ill in underdeveloped countries. Remember the Victorian account of Snow's Rents in Westminster:

'There is an ease in the man's appearance which shows that his calling and his residence for many years among filth, have rendered him familiar with such scenes; it has almost made him love filth. His little girl has in one hand a bloater and in the other *the Gin Bottle*, the God chiefly worshipped among such people.

Health of Towns Magazine[22]

The patent hollowness of this argument is best demonstrated for the developed world by a consideration of occupational disease. In the USA for example, 114 000 people are killed and more than 2½ million disabled by occupational accidents and diseases each year.[23] In the new 'radical' health ideology this is explained not by the hazards of work speed, the pollution of working environments or the danger of machinery, but by the lack of sufficient caution by the workers or even by their 'genetic susceptibilities'! And in Britain about 17 million working days are lost each year as a result of industrial injuries and diseases — considerably more than as a result of strikes — and over 500 000 reportable accidents with 1000 deaths occur annually. Yet the Health and Safety at Work Act puts responsibility for safety jointly on employers and workers — assuming that their interests in this regard are the same! It, like the American legislation, emphasizes *individual* initiative — the wearing of protective clothing etc. — rather than control of industrial processes. The general responsibilities of management under this Act are qualified by the phrase 'as far as is reasonably practicable'. In the current economic crisis, when safer working conditions would be 'economically unviable' and with fines for infringement ludicrously small, this loophole is likely to be eagerly used.

The unhealthy addictive habits of cigarette smoking and alcohol consumption are approached similarly. Health education attempts to persuade people to adopt healthier life-styles. Yet neither the social stresses nor advertising pressures that induce the habits are effectively confronted. In comparison with the £65 million budget spent in 1974 on alcohol and tobacco advertising, the total expenditure in Britain on health education, vaccination, immunization, water fluoridation and other specific preventive measures was £15 million.[24]

This same 'victim blaming' argument is used in relation to the underdeveloped world's 'problems' of high population growth (solution: 'family planning') and undernutrition (solution: 'health education') — rather than tackling underdevelopment.

So most people accept the proposition that illness caused by social conditions can and should be *individually* solved by *'professional'* medical intervention or *individual* preventive action. Consequently any thoughts of a collective assault on the roots of illness — which are social — are undermined. This is one of the important ways in which the medical profession serves the interests of those in power and strengthens the status quo.

Why is Health Care so Inequitably Distributed?

The value of a commodity is roughly set by the amount of labour — mental and physical — expended in producing it. Ever since products first began to be exchanged, there has had to be a common, socially acceptable measure of their value — something that establishes an equivalence between items with different uses and characteristics. This measure is labour. Thus a manufactured product acquires its value from a combination of the labour time need to produce it and the previous labour time embodied in the tools or capital goods that are used.

In the case of health care this includes the labour expended by the student, the skilled labour performed by the teachers and the labour embodied in the various commodities consumed in the process of training.[25] When health care became a commodity there was therefore an incentive for the producers and owners — the doctors — to obtain as long and as complex an education as possible to *raise the value of the commodity*.

Despite the fact that much medical practice was not only unscientific but positively dangerous, the training period was very lengthy. Nowadays several years are spent on the 'preclinical' biomedical sciences although much of the detail learned is unnecessary for the sort of health care most doctors do most of the time, and is in any case rapidly forgotten by the student. So after at least 5 years of university training and 1 year's compulsory internship a 'jack of all trades and master of none' is produced. But, before this highly educated graduate can actually provide even a primary care service proficiently, several further years of experience and often specialist training are needed. The effect of such an educational system is to increase the value of the doctors' commodity and allow them a wide choice of specialization whereby their earning power can be even further increased. However, the useful skills that doctors eventually acquire can be learned in a much shorter time and far less expensively by non-professionals.

The usual arguments for this 'professional' training cite the necessity of preserving 'standards of excellence' and 'equipping doctors with the education necessary to enable them to make the weighty decisions demanded of them'.

However, these assertions are unrealistic. Most doctors, because of their class backgrounds, will have had a different social experience from most of the population. Partly for this reason, but more importantly because of the inappropriate approach to health care already discussed, they will be unable to approach health problems sensitively and realistically. Similarly, they will be unable rationally to plan services that cater for the real health care needs of most people. Doctors want to *market* their commodity profitably. Therefore, those in private practice in developed countries will work predominantly in those localities that house the rich and will perform that sort of care — mostly high-technology cure — that can be easily sold to buyers who can afford it. *In underdeveloped countries this means that doctors are concentrated in the towns and offer a service both inappropriate to and inaccessible to most people.*

Nor does 'nationalization' of the health sector substantially overcome these problems. For doctors employed by the State medical service increase their income by climbing up the career ladder and especially by gaining a specialist qualification. Since medical skills are acquired through practice, there is an incentive for doctors to work both in the most technologically sophisticated institutions and in those specialities that provide the best possibilities for profits. Hence, even in a nationalized health service, GPs tend to work in richer localities where possibilities exist for private practice, and hospital doctors in the most technologically advanced hospitals in those centres where prospects for private practice are greatest.

Because doctors are so dominant in influencing the shape of the health sector, together with the wealthy and powerful whose diseases are most susceptible to high-technology individualized care, health services remain both inappropriate and inequitably distributed.

Summary

Doctors have not only appropriated health care as *their* commodity but have also determined its value. This they have done by various guild mechanisms which are by now accepted as 'natural' both by health workers and by the general public. These have ensured the profession's near-monopoly of knowledge about health. This has allowed *it* to pose the main questions about health in terms of *itself*. This prevents *people* learning about and acting confidently on their health problems – although most health care is in fact done by 'unqualified' people.

The other features of professionalism have resulted from the necessity for doctors to regulate the price of their commodity. This has been achieved by the guild mechanisms of controlling competition and monopoly price-fixing. Rules about advertising, under-bidding and patient-snatching are examples of this within the profession.

To avoid competition from non-guild health workers the profession strictly defines what is a 'doctor' and determines all the privileges that go with it. The work of other health workers is then defined in relation to that of doctors – to whom they are subordinated. The scope of their knowledge and skills is regulated and they are categorized as 'para-medical' or 'auxiliary' – to doctors. These are important ways in which the profession can regulate the supply of their commodity on the market, fix prices in private practice, and negotiate with governments their terms in any nationalized health service. And this is done not only at a national level by licensing bodies such as the General Medical Council in Britain, but on an international scale. For, still today, delegations from these registration bodies in developed countries visit medical schools in underdeveloped countries to assess the 'quality' of their medical education and determine whether their graduates will be competent to practise in the developed country.

The international value of doctors' health care – as with all other commodities – is regulated by the most powerful monopolies.

Reproduction of the Profession

Another important way in which the price of the commodity is indirectly regulated is through *selection* of medical students and thus the control of the standard and supply of graduates. In Britain, despite widespread myths to the contrary, in recent years the social gap between doctor and patient has, if anything, actually widened. The profile of the profession has not changed greatly since Shaftesbury referred to 'flash and fashionable doctors' of the mid-nineteenth century (*Fig. 5.3* and Table 5.1).

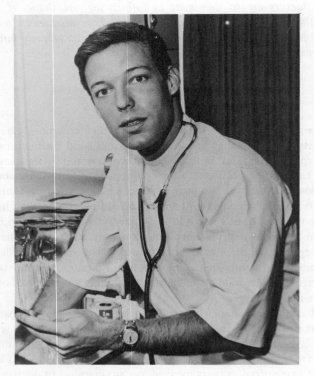

Figure 5.3 The 'flash and fashionable' doctor in the 1960s.

Table 5.1 **Social class of medical students, 1961–6**

Social class	General population	Final-year students 1961	First-year students 1966
1 and 2	18.3	68.9	75.7
3, 4 and 5	81.7	31.1	24.2

Source: Robson, *Quality, Inequality and Health Care* (Chapter 3, reference 9)

Figures for the nursing profession in 1972 showed that 52 per cent chosen for State Registered Nurse training came from professional or managerial homes while only 12 per cent were from the families of semi-skilled or unskilled workers.

Once selected, medical students and nurses are effectively isolated not only from the community they will eventually serve but even from other students, for entry to medical or nursing school means virtually exclusive contact with professionals. Consequently many attitudes, often already present because of social class, are reinforced by the inappropriate approach to health care that is taught, and by the organization of teaching and the example of 'superiors' — doctors and qualified nurses.

An indication of how open medical students are to being influenced by 'professional' ideas was revealed by a study in the USA which showed that one-third of junior medical students already considered themselves primarily as doctors.[26] An expression of this aspiration is seen in the way medical students often dress and talk. Not surprisingly, therefore, the scorn that most consultants pour on social medicine is readily echoed by medical students. Even when social factors *are* taken into account they are considered in *individual* terms. Illness is attributed to unhealthy life-style — 'diseases of affluence' in the developed countries or ignorance and 'overbreeding' in the underdeveloped world.

Social-class differences in health are blandly ascribed to 'more unhealthy life-styles' or 'greater ignorance'. (It is indeed difficult to ascribe worse statistics for all diseases in the lower social classes to 'more affluence!') The assumption is that disparities in living standards and inequality of access to education are 'natural' and can be surmounted by individual effort.

Having been socialized in the 'professional approach' to health and health care, medical — and to a lesser extent nursing — students are taught a 'professional approach' to patients. Patients are regarded as passive objects of care. Most training is done in hospitals where patients are either so ill or too intimidated by the hospital environment to be anything but passive. Patients who ask questions about their illnesses are often regarded as 'troublesome'. In fact, certain sociological studies have revealed that in the doctor's eyes the ideal patient is completely compliant, submissive, obedient and non-assertive.[27] An 'interesting' patient is one with a rare, complex and often fatal disease. The average patient with a common degenerative disease or psychological illness may be disdained. Given the social gap that we have referred to and the complex socialization process, it is hardly surprising that class distinctions are seen here too. It has been shown that patients from social classes 1 and 2 are given more time by doctors in consultation, receiving different treatment and more explanation.[28] Working-class patients are often given no explanation for their treatment — or given one that is simplistic and patronizing.

In the past when neither doctors nor patients possessed much knowledge about the causes of and cures for disease, practitioners relied on mystification to maintain their livelihood. However, with the knowledge of disease that is currently available, most of which could be quite easily transmitted to patients, mystification becomes quite unproductive. It prevents patients, that is all non-medical people, from learning about their own bodies and understanding and dealing with their illnesses.

Doctors are reluctant to offer knowledge for fear of jeopardizing their authority and threatening their monopoly hold over health care. Also doctors find it difficult to talk to patients from quite different social backgrounds and with quite different vocabularies. This problem is considerably magnified when doctors trained in the West, or in medical schools modelled on those in the West, work in underdeveloped countries.

For here most patients not only do not understand medical terminology but do not even conceive of the disease process in terms that are familiar to most non-medical people in the developed world. For example, the notion that 'germs cause (infectious) disease' is commonplace in twentieth-century Europe and North America, whereas in much of the underdeveloped world it is literally a foreign concept.

Women and Health

Chapter 3 showed how underdeveloped countries and even underdeveloped areas in developed countries provide labour for the more developed regions. But there is *in all countries* an ever-present potential reserve work-force. Women are drawn in and out of employment when needed, not only on a large scale during times of boom and crisis, but also continually on a small scale when labour is required for short intervals, such as in harvesting or piece-work.

Like any other reserve work-force, because they are often temporary and therefore poorly organized and frequently unskilled, they are badly paid for long hours in bad working conditions. And immigrant workers, many of whom are female, have the same experience. Additionally, because in our societies a woman's place is seen as 'in the home', her primary task is as homemaker, not just cleaning and cooking but as nurse. Much responsibility in caring for the elderly and sick is, even today, thrust on to women. A job is therefore often regarded as less important for her than for a man and looked on as merely a part-time pursuit or a way of earning 'pin-money'.

It is for all these reasons that women are poorly paid (Table 5.2). In short, the common denominator of 'women's work' is low pay for less skilled work. This is why the earnings of the vast majority of health workers, most of whom are women and immigrants, are so very low.

It is by now clear that there is a specific oppression of women as a sex, that is *sexism*. With the advent of private property and inheritance, a division of labour occurred according to sex. From that time assumptions about women changed fundamentally. They came to be regarded as 'natural' homemakers and 'natural' servants although in reality this had not always been the case. In short, attitudes to women were and are still determined *primarily* by the role they play in pro-

Table 5.2 **Women's average weekly earnings as percentage of men's full-time manual earnings**

1950	1955	1965	1970	1974	1975
58.7	51.7	49.0	49.9	55.5	57.4

Source: quoted in *Revolutionary Communist* No. 5 (*see* Chapter 4, reference 57)

duction for society. The situation today confirms this. The dominant attitude towards women in developed societies remains *fundamentally* unchanged, yet the rapid increase in the number of women in employment during the post-war boom — and the corresponding decline in the proportion in the homes — has been the basis for the development of a powerful women's movement. Many women have started to *challenge* the assumptions about their 'natural' role.

Although most health workers are female, the vast majority of doctors are male. In the USA, only 7 per cent of doctors are female, in Britain 24 per cent, though in the USSR 75 per cent are female.[29] While in recent years in Britain the intake of women medical students has risen to approximately 30 per cent, it is already clear that women doctors are channelled into unpopular specialities and many are restricted in their careers by the demands of their families and absence of child-care facilities. But discriminatory practices against women in medicine are not merely institutional — such as poor child-care facilities. They are enforced within medical schools by the 'men's club' atmosphere (*Fig. 5.4*).

Figure 5.4 A woman's place?

Indeed, until recent years, in one London teaching hospital, nurses (female) were not permitted to walk along the same (main) corridor as doctors and medical students (predominantly male)!

As well as most non-professional health workers being female, a disproportionate number are foreign, and the proportion of immigrants and ethnic minorities increase the lower down the scale of technical expertise one proceeds. Most doctors, particularly in the super-technological specialities, are male, white and upper class while many other health workers, especially unskilled personnel, are female, black and lower middle class or working class, apart from a percentage of State Registered Nurses (SRNs). The composition of the health work-force reflects in a concentrated form the hierarchical arrangement of capitalist societies.

Women and the Family

In a more subtle way the medical profession helps to reinforce the sexual division of labour and hence the oppression of women. This it does by emphasizing that the family is the foundation of society. This sentiment is sometimes explicit, as in the way in which unmarried mothers are often regarded. More often, however, it is implicit. This is particularly so in such sectors as geriatrics and mental handicap. In both of these cases, medical staff often condemn families who are no longer willing or able to continue to look after aged or mentally handicapped relatives. Rather than insist that society as a whole shoulder its responsibilities for these people through the State, the health professions pressure the families — and that usually means the *women* — to shoulder 'their responsibilities'.

In underdeveloped countries the demands made on women are often even greater. They often have other tasks such as fetching water and growing food for the family to eat (*Fig. 5.5*).

Women as Patients

The medical profession's perception of the *ideal patient* undoubtedly overlaps with the predominant male perception — and even more with the medical perception — of the *ideal woman*. Blatantly sexist assumptions are quite explicit in many medical textbooks, particularly those dealing with obstetrics and gynaecology. One such widely used work, published as recently as 1975, asserted: 'The traits that compose the core of female personality are feminine narcissism, masochism and passivity.'[30]

The strength of such attitudes justifies the particularly unsympathetic way women patients are treated by the health profession. Women who manifest the illnesses of developed societies are dismissed as inherently neurotic. Their complaints are assumed to be 'psychosomatic' even when they may not be (*Fig. 5.6*). Seldom is the isolation that many women (and some men) experience implicated in their depressions. It is seldom that better housing or nursery schools are provided, but almost invariably an anti-depressant is! In 1972, tranquillizers,

Figure 5.5 In underdeveloped countries the demands made on women are even greater. (Courtesy Oxfam.)

Figure 5.6 (Courtesy *Science for People*.)

hypnotics and anti-depressants accounted for about 17 per cent of GPs' pharmaceutical expenditure and twice as many women as men are receiving prescriptions of this kind.

A more recent survey by *Woman's Own* also found that one in four women were taking tranquillizers or sedatives, usually Valium (diazepam) or Librium (chlordiazepoxide). According to one woman, 'My new doctor has signed a prescription for sleeping tablets every time I ask the receptionist, but not once has he asked to see me'.[31] Similarly, the medicalization of childbirth has resulted in 'planned delivery' — that is, planned by and for the medical staff, and is a lonely dehumanizing, conveyor-belt type experience for women. These medical instances of women's oppression are experienced especially by the least powerful and least vocal social classes.

Racism

The sexist attitudes doctors have towards patients are not merely a reflection of the attitudes prevalent in society but are actually reinforced within their medical practice. Much the same can be said about racial attitudes. Doctors in developed countries may be racist because of their ethnic origins and the racial attitudes they are imbued with in society. These notions of racial supremacy are likely to be strengthened by the racial stratification within the health work-force, which is assumed to be because doctors, mostly white males, are innately intellectually and technically superior to black females. These attitudes are further fuelled by such widely promoted assumptions that 'overbreeding' is an 'inborn', 'natural' characteristic of blacks. Indeed, there is evidence that coercion has been employed in persuading black mothers in Britain both to have abortions and to be sterilized.

The injectable contraceptive drug Depo Provera (DP) has been widely dumped in the Third World, because it is well established that it has a number of dangerous and unpleasant side-effects. But it is also used on black women in the developed countries. For example, in 1977 in the London Hospital, Whitechapel, two-thirds of the women given DP were Asians. The medical profession is also complicit in racist 'virginity tests' carried out on black women at Britain's airports. This is the account of a 35-year-old Indian woman who arrived at Heathrow Airport to meet her fiancé:

'I was sent for a medical examination by immigration officials. A woman told me to take all my clothes off. I was given nothing to cover myself with — no dressing gown or blanket although I asked for one. I waited like that for 20 minutes.
'Then a man doctor came in. I asked to be seen by a lady doctor, but they said no. I was most reluctant to have the examination, but I didn't know whether it was normal practice here. So I signed the consent form. I was frightened that otherwise they would send me back.

'The doctor was wearing rubber gloves and took some medicine out of a tube and put it on some cotton and inserted it into me. He said he was deciding whether I was pregnant now or had been pregnant before. I said that he could see that without doing anything to me.
'I have been feeling very bad mentally ever since. I was very embarrassed and upset. I had never had a gynaecological examination before.'

This test took place at a time when the British Government claimed to have banned them. Such tests would be intolerable even if they achieved what they claimed. In fact they would not prove whether a woman was pregnant and might not even prove whether she was a virgin. Their purpose can only be to humiliate the woman.[32]

Conclusion

Because of its narrow class background and its material interest in preserving the status quo, the medical profession retains an unquestioning belief in the values set by the ruling class and institutionalized by the State. Indeed, in the way it relates both to workers and to patients, it reinforces both sexist and racist assumptions. This 'medical consciousness' is transmitted first to other health professionals and then generalized to the population.

The medical profession believes itself to have a monopoly of the knowledge necessary for the health of the people. The two words 'health' and 'medicine' have become virtually interchangeable in the popular consciousness. Thus people are actively discouraged from seeking non-medical causes – and therefore remedies – for their illnesses.

In short, one of the important effects of the health-care system is to support and reinforce the present arrangement of society. So, it is now possible to answer the earlier question: *What other functions might health care systems have in society?*

The health professions, under the dominance of doctors, have in large measure determined the nature of health care and the distribution of health care resources. But what of the other social forces that have participated in this historical process? The most important instances of popular pressure in stimulating certain improvements in health and health care in Britain were:

(1) The struggle over the institution of the First Public Health Act, where the medical establishment and water companies were greatly opposed to such legislation.
(2) The struggle for reforms in welfare legislation which resulted in the National Health Insurance Act of 1911, opposed only by medical interests.
(3) The struggle to set up the NHS, where a section of the medical profession, represented by the British Medical Association, was a consistent opposition force.

THE PART PLAYED BY BIG BUSINESS

In general business interests and their representatives in government have resisted pressure from the people for improvements in living and working conditions and provision of health services. However, in some situations, business interests have recognized it to be in their interests to support certain reforms and social provisions. The best demonstration of this is the 1911 British National Health Insurance Act. This Act gave, for the first time, a measure of health care free at the time of use. However, it applied only to working males, while unproductive sectors of the population such as wives, children and the unemployed were left to fend for themselves in the private sector.

The Act reflected not just the demands of the people but also the needs of big business, which required a healthy working population for the rapidly expanding industries, and also the needs of the State, which required a healthy fighting population for the wars of colonial expansion. For it was reported that the recruits for the Boer War manifested 'the gradual deterioration of the physique of the working classes from whom the bulk of recruits must always be drawn'.[33] And towards the end of the First World War it was revealed in a Ministry of National Service Report that only one man in three was medically fit for military service.[34] Not surprisingly, therefore, the representatives of business interests in the government — the Conservatives — voted unanimously in support of the Act. It was only medical interests that remained opposed.

However, medical interests have not, for the most part, been in conflict with the State and business interests. Indeed, they have helped create the conditions for the continued operation of business interests and have even linked up with business in opposing the struggles of the people for health. *This alliance between medical and business interests has existed for a long time but it has become increasingly prominent over the last few decades.*

The Private Health Sector

In Britain in 1948 *private health insurance schemes* catered mainly for a small section of the middle class. The growth of these schemes has depended on tax relief and especially on their access to NHS facilities at low cost. By 1978 nearly 2½ million people were covered by private health insurance, compared with just over ½ million in 1955.[35] They have fostered a corresponding increase in part-time private consultants. The board members and directors of these schemes are businessmen and eminent doctors. Many of the latter and most part-time private consultants receive 'merit awards' and also occupy influential positions in the Royal Colleges and on the staff of teaching hospitals. The already inappropriate development of the health service is further distorted by the influence of these powerful professionals who help decide siting of medical schools, plan medical training, and in the many other ways help to 'socialize' medical students and doctors.

In purely economic terms, it is well established that the private sector is a parasite on the NHS. The relationship between these sectors is analogous to that in the underdeveloped world between the developed sector of the economy, catering mostly for the external market, and the underdeveloped sector, where the majority lives.

A similar thing happens in the case of professional health workers. Doctors and nurses — trained at public expense — are increasingly being supplied to the NHS at double the cost of their counterparts in the NHS by locum agencies. The rapid growth of nursing agencies has been ensured by chronic understaffing and poor pay and the need for a mobile pool of trained nurses in the NHS.

Accompanying the cuts in the NHS referred to earlier there has been a rapid growth of the private health sector. This has included not only the building of large numbers of hospitals but even the 'privatization' of services — catering, cleaning, laundry — in NHS facilities.

The Drug and Medical Supplies Industry

Spending on drugs has increased rapidly over the past 20 years not only in the NHS but in all developed countries' health services (*Fig. 5.7*). More is being

Figure 5.7 British drug industry: expenditure. (Courtesy ABPI.)

spent now on drugs in the NHS than on the GP services. In 1970, profit from the sale of drugs to the NHS amounted to £70 million and it continues to increase.[36] The drugs industry has a vested interest in ill health, as the chairman of Beechams indicated in his 1972 annual report:

'The pharmaceutical side of the business, including proprietary medicines, was clearly not helped by the very low level of winter sickness throughout the Northern Hemisphere'.

Table 5.3 **Percentage return on capital employed in the pharmaceutical and comparable industries, 1963–5**

Year	Chemicals	Food	Drink	Pharmaceuticals
1963	13.2	15.9	13.8	16.1
1964	13.9	14.9	14.5	17.8
1965	13.5	14.7	14.7	19.9

Source: Quoted in Robson, *Quality, Inequality and Health Care* (Chapter 3, reference 9)

However, pharmaceutical companies still manage to make the highest profits when compared with other sectors (Table 5.3).

However, even these averages mask their exorbitant profits. For example, in Britain in 1973, Boots and Beechams showed 45 per cent and 41 per cent return respectively on capital employed. Similarly, Merck, Sharp and Dohme, the second largest drug manufacturer in the USA, enjoyed a 50 per cent return on capital in 1973.[37] One indicator of the driving concern of the drug industry is that it spends more on advertising than on research. The advertising budget of over £300 per year for every British doctor covers, in addition to mountains of mailed literature, such subtle promotional gambits as free gifts ranging from stethoscopes to bed-socks embroidered with the drug's name.[38]

The crucial role doctors play, sometimes unconsciously, in the current operations of the drug industry is revealed in the statement of a Geigy delegate at a 1970 seminar on marketing:

'All of us recognise the end purpose of our efforts in the area of physician technology. It is to identify those segments of the physician population which contain our best customer prospects. . . . By far the most important criteria is estimated or observed prescribing volume. Informal spot checks of local pharmacy files, plus conversational exchanges with pharmacists themselves afford the most direct evidence of high-level prescribing . . . the classifications of each physician are then coded into the company's promotion units and used to control the number of detail calls, sampling practices, direct mail advertisements and so forth. . . . Geigy categorises physicians primarily on the basis of judged overall "prescribing productivity".'

Take a Pill[39]

Those doctors with 'high prescribing productivity' – defended vigorously by many as their 'clinical freedom' – are those most susceptible to the persuasive power of drug representatives.

Table 5.4 **Promotional expenditure as percentage
of sales costs to retail pharmacist**

Antacids	13.9
Cough and cold preparations	12.9
Anti-obesity preparations	11.1
Sedatives and hypnotics	10.3
Cardiovascular preparations	4.3
Diabetic therapy	1.9

Source: Robson, *Take a Pill*[37]

A confirmation of the economic importance that drug companies attach to promotion is revealed by considering expenditure on advertising different preparations (Table 5.4).

Clearly those drugs used for the least easily definable conditions and whose effectiveness is questionable are most heavily promoted. And the 47 million prescriptions for psychotropic drugs alone in Britain in 1970 show that the drug companies are not being wholly unsuccessful![40]

But in this area too the link between business interests and medicine is not just informal. For, while most significant advances have been the result of research discoveries in publicly-financed institutions — hospitals, universities and research centres — subsequent commercial development has been by the drug companies, and the *profits* accrue to a few individuals with financial interests. In fact a body, the Medico-Pharmaceutical Forum, has been set up in Britain by the drug companies and the Royal Colleges to promote closer links between medical faculties and the drug industry. Some members of the medical profession even act as paid advisers to industrial concerns. In the USA the links between big business and the medical profession are even more overt.

Apart from the direct *economic* burden it imposes on any country's health services and thus on the taxpayer, the drug industry also shifts the focus of society and the research resources committed by it away from the fundamental causes of ill health. So, as cardiovascular disease in the developed world assumes frightening proportions, 'after the event' cardiovascular drugs constitute one of the fastest growing sectors of industry. Yet the root causes of this disease remain under-researched.

Moreover, these 'breakthrough' drugs are not without their risks. Practolol, one of the first of them, was withdrawn after severe side-effects, including blindness and even death. The Thalidomide disaster is even better known, while many of the barbiturate and non-barbiturate hypnotics (sleep-inducing drugs) encourage dependence and addiction. In fact it has been estimated that at least 400 000 people in Britain are on long-term treatment with dependence-producing barbiturates!

Conclusion

From all that has been said it becomes clear that the history of the medical contribution, like all history, is one of conflicts and relationships between certain social forces. In the case of health services these forces are medical interests, business interests and the State on the one hand, and the people on the other.

Business interests are the owners and controllers of finance, industry and property and specifically of the water companies in Britain in the past, and private health insurance schemes and the drug and supply industries nowadays.

Medical interests are that sector of the medical profession — historically the dominant sector — that has consistently allied with business interests.[41]

The State is broadly all those agencies, institutions and groupings through which the class dominating the economy assumes political power to become the ruling class. In the Western developed countries and in most underdeveloped ones, the State is a capitalist one. Because capitalism is fundamentally competitive there will be conflicts at different times between different sectors of the capitalist class. Then the State has to act as a mediator between these different groups. This is how, occasionally, the State has even intervened against the combined opposition of medical and business interests to promote measures that, in the long term, have turned out to be in capitalism's best interests. The most notable examples of such State interventions in Britain were during the cholera epidemics of the 1830–50s and again in 1948 with the introduction of the National Health Service.

THE MEDICAL CONTRIBUTION IN THE UNDERDEVELOPED WORLD

Chapter 4 showed that the early truncated health services provided by the colonial State were directed towards caring for the colonial administrators and their dependants and maintaining a healthy labour force. And, the mission health services, although their overriding motive was evangelical, did not differ substantially from those of the State.

In addition to the disastrous effects on large sections of the population of the importation of new communicable diseases, ill health was indirectly produced by the adverse effects of cash-cropping, the money economy and population movements on nutrition and environment.

One of the results of the advent of imperialist medicine was the discrediting and partial displacement of traditional practitioners, though this process was far more limited than the previous elimination of 'witches' in Europe. This was first because the medical services provided by the State were available to only a tiny minority — the settlers and urban, mining, and plantation work-force. The mass of the population who continued to rely on traditional healers were of little concern to the colonial administration. Secondly, Western-trained practitioners were few since in most colonies it was only the small European communities who could afford private medical care. Since Europeans were in any case unlikely to resort to traditional healers the competition offered by the latter did not constitute a great threat to the monopoly of private practice. However, it has already been seen how doctors have resisted the acquisition of skills by auxiliaries and it will be seen later how they have actively opposed the successful operation of non-professional village health workers in some areas.

The transplantation to the underdeveloped world of this Western medical contribution was part of the more general process of the extension of the capitalist system. Medicine was just one of many commodities now circulating in the dominant sectors of the economies of underdeveloped countries. This resulted in the neglect of health promotion, the stunting and individualization of preventive care and the overdevelopment of curative medicine – and also in the gross maldistribution of these inappropriate services.

Education

This approach to health and health care has been made possible through the transfer of medical curricula and attitudes from the developed to the underdeveloped world. This was initially effected through colonial educational institutions. In most independent countries that remain dominated by imperialism the same general and medical educational systems persist today. Thus in a comprehensive review of medical education in Latin America in 1973, it was shown that most medical curricula have been patterned on German, French, Spanish and now American models. All of these reflect the 'engineering' approach to understanding the body and its diseases and neglect the socioeconomic environment that caused the diseases. The emphasis is on hospital-based technologically-oriented medicine and especially on individual, acute-episodic care, which is typical of the medical education in developed countries. Rural, ambulatory, social and continuous care were under-represented in the curricula, if not non-existent.[42]

Indeed, many of the underdeveloped countries have gone to great lengths to obtain recognition for their medical educational standards from the professional registration bodies in the developed world. One negative and extremely costly product of this has been the international migration of health workers, particularly doctors, to developed countries or even to other underdeveloped countries where a larger market exists for private practice.

The attempt to offset these losses and to improve the spread of health service personnel by developing the auxiliary grade has met with only limited success. For here too the impact of the 'professional approach' on the practice and attitudes of auxiliaries has had negative effects.

The criterion for selection of medical auxiliaries is, invariably, academic attainment, which reflects social background even more than in developed countries. In Tanzania a recent investigation into the social and educational background of student medical auxiliaries found that over 30 per cent of students had received more than the minimum standard of education. They tended to come from more developed regions of the country. Between 20 and 40 per cent of students' fathers and between 50 and 70 per cent of their eldest brothers had a non-farming occupation.

The survey also looked at the attitudes that medical auxiliaries acquired in their training — which are strikingly similar to those found in health workers in developed countries. Both students and graduates identified the medical auxiliary with the clinical, and not with the public health hierarchy. Students saw the auxiliary primarily as a curative worker and often as a hospital worker. Male students regarded the medical assistant in the hospital as an assistant to the doctor, whereas the female students saw the assistant as a help to the nursing staff.[43] This comes from a country that has an unusually explicit commitment to a more equitable distribution of health care. So it is no surprise that similar findings on selection and training of auxiliaries come from Ethiopia and other underdeveloped countries.[44]

The Drugs Industry

It was noted earlier that pharmaceuticals in the developed world are exorbitantly priced. In underdeveloped countries prices are, as one British trade unionist has put it, 'near criminal'.[45] Whereas Britain in 1975 paid American firms $2.50 per kilogram for vitamin C, India paid nearly $10 per kilo. While a semi-synthetic penicillin, Bristol's Polycillin, has been sold for $41.85 per 100 tablets in Brazil, the price in the USA was $21.84. Similarly the tetracycline antibiotics, costing at that time $24–30 in Europe, were being sold to Pakistan, India and Colombia for between $100 and $270. Furthermore, the cost of well-established drugs whose patents expired years ago declines in the developed countries but continues to rise in the underdeveloped.[46]

Most of the overpricing of drugs both in the developed and in the underdeveloped world is achieved through a mechanism that was mentioned earlier: transfer pricing. The parent company sells the drug ingredient to a subsidiary at an artificially inflated price. The subsidiary then markets the drug at a price related to the cost of the ingredient from the parent company. In this way the subsidiary's declared profits are artificially low and the real profits accrue to the parent company. Thus an investigation of foreign drug firms in Colombia in the early 1970s revealed that their profit rate was not 6 per cent as had been declared to the Colombia Government, but was over 79 per cent. The average overpricing of imported intermediate ingredients was 155 per cent. For Valium (diazepam) and Librium (chlordiazepoxide), the two worst cases, overpricing was 6155 per cent and 6478 per cent respectively! It is hardly surprising that the world-wide profit on these two drugs alone was over $2000 million.[47]

Such profiteering is possible only in a situation of monopoly control. Competition is minimized by a patent system. After a patent is registered, whether or not it is being exploited by the patent holder, no competitor can enter the market. Thus in underdeveloped countries, even those that are relatively industrialized such as India, 90 per cent or more of drug patents are foreign-owned.[48] These patents are concentrated in very few hands: in Colombia in 1970, 60 per cent of drug patents were held by only 10 per cent of all foreign patent holders. So patents preserve secure import markets for foreign companies without necessitating investment and block any potential competition.

Qualitative improvements in health will come about through far-reaching social changes. But there has been a positive, if limited contribution made by medical technology in alleviating disease and suffering. Some obvious examples are: on the preventive side, certain vaccines; and on the curative side, antibiotics like penicillin, which has helped to reduce substantially diseases such as yaws, and anti-malarial drugs. The drug industry with its highly developed international research and productive facilities is ideally placed to develop effective drugs and vaccines for diseases prevalent in underdeveloped countries. Yet in 1976 total world expenditure on tropical disease research was about $30 million a year — just 2 per cent of the amount spent each year on cancer research.[49]

This low level of investment is undoubtedly related to 'poor market potential'. It is more profitable to develop yet another tranquillizer or analgesic for the already over-drugged but lucrative Western market. On the other hand, the people of underdeveloped countries are increasingly used in clinical trials. This has particularly been the case with women who have in recent years been used to determine whether oral and injectable contraceptives are effective or safe for women in the developed world. For example, Depo-Provera, an injectable hormonal contraceptive, has had its licence for general use in America withdrawn because of unpleasant and potentially serious side-effects. Yet its US manufacturer continues to export under 'clinical trial' status quantities sufficient for over 1 million women in 70 different countries.[50]

If the gap between expenditure on research and that on advertising and promotion is large in the developed world then in underdeveloped countries it is truly enormous. In a recently completed study in Tanzania it was revealed that there is one drug representative for every four doctors as opposed to one for every 30 in Britain. (In Mexico and much of South America there is one drug representative for every three doctors.) Three times as much as in Britain is spent by the drug companies on each doctor. The estimated £1 million which the companies spend on 'educating' doctors about which drugs to use is more than the £800 000 annual budget of the faculty of medicine![51]

A British doctor who studied this situation advanced three reasons for the drug companies' concern with the Tanzanian market — and no doubt similar reasons apply for other underdeveloped countries. First, each doctor in effect controls on average more than three times as much as a British doctor will spend on drugs. Secondly, the rate of increase in drug spending in Tanzania is 33 per cent per year as compared with 10 per cent in other countries – also, a rapid increase in the number of health workers ensures an ever-increasing market for the drug if doctors can be persuaded to advocate its use. Thirdly, drug company representatives are often the only source of information about drugs, little counter-information being available.[52]

The promotional methods used in underdeveloped countries are similar to those in developed countries. Apart from the familiar free gifts, drug company parties and free samples for doctors, there is the fact that drug advertisements in Tanzania (and most other underdeveloped countries) do not include prices, and drug representatives have easy access to government medical stores where they can influence ordering of stocks.

Taking advantage of the fact that in most underdeveloped countries the regulations governing advertising, packaging and labelling of drugs are weaker, representatives suggest hazardous drugs for the treatment of minor conditions. The risks or side-effects are minimized.

Yet given that many drugs, available only on prescription in developed countries, can be bought over the counter in much of the underdeveloped world (*Fig. 5.8*), the need for adequate labelling and warnings is even greater.

For example, in the USA the analgesic drugs dipyrone and aminopyrine can only be prescribed for patients with terminal cancer. Since 1964 the packages have had to carry a label: 'Warning – this drug may cause fatal agranulocytosis' (failure to produce the white blood cells which protect against infection). However, in the African *Monthly Index of Medical Specialities (MIMS)*, which

Figure 5.8 Penicillin on sale on a market stall in Upper Volta – exposure to heat destroys its effectiveness. (Courtesy Oxfam.)

includes information provided by drug companies about their products and is sent free of charge to all African doctors, there are drugs containing aminopyrine produced by Ciba-Geigy, Sandoz, Hoechst, Ravensberg and Polfa. While some preparations carry a mention of 'very rare' agranulocytosis, several are advertised as 'having a wide margin of safety' and their use suggested for such complaints as toothache, sprains, headache, gynaecological pain and 15 or 20 different indications. Furthermore, in many countries it is possible to buy these preparations without prescription.

In 1977, drug regulatory bodies in a number of countries including Switzerland, recommended the withdrawal of aminopyrine. Ciba-Geigy, the Swiss multinational, said that it would reformulate all aminopyrine products. Yet in 1979 a Ciba-Geigy representative was distributing samples of Cibalgin, an analgesic tablet containing aminopyrine, in Maputo in Mozambique. This case came to light when an English teacher bought some Cibalgin tablets without prescription in Beira. Within 4 days she was suffering from the symptoms of agranulocytosis and almost died. This case is known because she was a foreigner. It is not known how many Africans may have suffered and died from this condition.[53]

Similarly, use of the powerful antibiotic chloramphenicol which produces an infrequent but fatal blood disorder is restricted in the USA to patients with the life-threatening infections of meningitis and typhoid fever. In South and Central America, Africa and Asia the multinational corporation Parke-Davis promotes its use for a variety of minor infections and in many countries it is available without prescription and often there is no mention of side-effects. In 1972 the annual meeting of the Warner-Lambert Company's Parke-Davis division considered the following resolution: 'That the company should include the same details of the toxicity of chloromycetin in package inserts and advertisements for other countries as are required by US law for promotion in the USA'. Ninety-seven per cent of the shareholders voted against![54]

As these instances show, the foreign drug companies are responsible for the suffering of a large and unknown number of recipients of their irresponsibly marketed products. The following statistics for Tanzania – which are certainly not extreme – also show the debilitating impact of the drug multinationals on the health services of underdeveloped countries.

(1) In 1976 spending on drugs accounted for 22 per cent of the recurrent budget of the Ministry of Health: by 1980/1 the drugs bill was projected to have consumed 40 per cent.

(2) Over three-quarters of all money spent on drugs is used by hospitals although much of the expenditure, especially in large hospitals, is not on life-saving drugs, but on sedatives, tranquillizers and anti-depressants.

(3) The money spent at the country's university hospital each year on Avafortan and Baralgan (two aminopyrine/dipyrone analgesics), Valium (a relaxant) and Melleril (a mood-stabilizing drug) could be used to protect half a million children against malaria.[55]

The Baby-Foods Business

As in the developed world the pharmaceutical industry has had the greatest impact among medical business interests on the health services of underdeveloped countries.

However, it is the baby-foods industry that has probably attracted most attention. This has mainly been a result of the vigorous campaign in recent years to expose the milk companies' activities. These have been described in detail in a report entitled *The Baby Killer*.[56]

Human breast milk is nutritionally superior to artificial formulas (*Fig. 5.9*). It protects against infection. Breast feeding acts as a contraceptive, both directly through its hormonal effects and often indirectly for cultural reasons. Yet in the past few decades the practice has declined considerably both in the developed and in the underdeveloped world. In Chile where the fall has been extremely

Figure 5.9 Nutritionally superior and always available. (Courtesy UNICEF.)

Somewhat controversial

marked, 95 per cent of 1 year olds were being breast-fed 20 years ago. Now only 20 per cent of infants are being breast-fed at 2 months! In Jamaica a survey revealed that nearly 90 per cent of mothers started bottle feeding before 6 months. In Ibadan, Nigeria, where traditionally breast feeding continued for up to 4 years, over 70 per cent of mothers surveyed recently began bottle feeding their babies before they were 4 months old.[57] In Britain today breast feeding is practised very uncommonly. In 1946, 60 per cent of infants were breast fed to 1 month, in 1970–1 possibly as few as 8 per cent. A recent revival in breast feeding among some of the middle and upper classes is reversing this trend.[58]

A number of problems results from this decline in breast feeding. Diarrhoea — a water-related disease — is an important cause of illness and death among infants and children in underdeveloped countries. Breast-fed infants are not immune to bowel infections, but they are considerably protected not only by antiviral and antibacterial factors present in breast milk, but also by being spared exposure to infective organisms present on sometimes inadequately sterilized feeding bottles. Undernutrition can lead to more frequent and more severe diarrhoeal attacks and is aggravated if, as often happens, the powdered milk is over-diluted.

Research performed recently in Chile showed that babies who were bottle fed during the first 3 months of their lives suffered treble the mortality rate of their breast-fed brothers and sisters.[59] Similarly, in a recent study of 339 children admitted to hospital in Manchester, England, 79 per cent were under 12 months of age and only one was being breast fed.[60] This relationship between early weaning on to breast-milk substitutes and disease and death has been documented for India, Jamaica, Jordan and Arab communities in Israel.[61]

Access to reasonable quantities of safe water is extremely limited in Africa, Asia and Latin America. Very few mothers can carry out the instructions of the baby food companies 'to wash your hands thoroughly with soap each time you have to prepare a meal for baby'.[62] Nor is it possible for more than a small minority to follow the Cow & Gate *Babycare* booklet for West Africa and 'place bottle and lid in a saucepan of water with sufficient water to cover them. Bring to the boil and allow to boil for 10 minutes'. The vast majority of West African mothers have the use of one pot and a wood fire — a far cry from the gleaming aluminium saucepan and electric stove pictured in the brochure. Furthermore, although Nestlé's products have accompanying instructions leaflets in the main languages of the countries of sale, most mothers in underdeveloped countries are illiterate even in their native language. Finally, Cow & Gate's argument that their product '. . . is a complete food for babies under 6 months and can be used as a substitute for breast feeding. . .' takes no account of the widespread, often desperate poverty. For example, in Nigeria the cost of feeding a 3-month-old infant is approximately 30 per cent of the minium urban wage and for an infant aged 6 months it is 47 per cent.[63] There is no explicit indication on the labels of baby milk tins of how long a baby can be fed from the contents. Combined with illiteracy and poverty, this leads inevitably to the preparation of over-diluted feeds.

Here are all the ingredients for the fatal cycle of undernutrition and bowel infection. And in the developed world bottle feeding is increasingly being implicated in the development of childhood allergies and even in unexplained infant 'cot deaths' as well as obesity and its attendant problems in adulthood. Small wonder that the feeding bottle has been termed 'the baby killer'. Perhaps the most callous example of the exploitation of mothers and children comes from Nigeria. The government there recently took tough action against two firms who were selling custard powder — that is, corn starch, flavouring and colouring — as baby food. The food was packaged and labelled in Lagos after being exported to Nigeria by a British company, Bestoval. The label read: 'For strong growth of your baby insist on nothing but Daily Baby Food Custard Powder.' With none of the proteins, fats, minerals and vitamins needed for proper growth, 'nothing but' custard powder would soon starve any baby to death.[64]

Why is it then that breast feeding has declined so much and been replaced by bottle feeding which is clearly so inappropriate and even dangerous in under-developed countries? The impact of capitalism or rural pre-capitalist societies has been the underlying factor. It has resulted in a large increase in the propor-tion of women in waged employment who are discouraged from breast feeding. This situation has been reinforced by the attitude that regards the breast as a cosmetic sex symbol rather than a source of nourishment.

But in order to move from breast feeding it is necessary for an alternative form of infant feeding to exist. It is this 'alternative' that the baby-food com-panies have vigorously promoted. They justify their operations by asserting that a large proportion of mothers are unable to breast feed and therefore have to rely on breast-milk substitutes. Yet a survey in rural Nigeria found less than 1 per cent of mothers with serious breast-feeding problems, and 2–3 per cent who had temporary trouble because of illness still managed to breast feed for most of their babies' first 6 months.[65]

Also, contrary to popular belief, failure to breast feed for physical reasons is uncommon even in developed countries. One English hospital discharges 87 per cent of its new mothers successfully breast feeding, most of the remaining 13 per cent being unwilling rather than unable to breast feed.[66] Undoubtedly, emotion-al and psychological reasons most commonly underlie 'lactation failure', but many of these cases simply involve mothers losing confidence in their ability to perform what has been portrayed as a difficult and even distasteful duty. Com-pany promotion that frequently emphasizes 'when mother's milk is not enough, our product will help make up the difference' surely encourages and aggravates any possible lack of confidence. The promotional methods used are strikingly similar to those of the drug companies, although the milk companies approach not only health professionals but also mothers directly (*Fig. 5.10*).

Doctors and maternity unit nurses are often already 'primed' by their training to accept the use of breast-milk substitutes. Still today many medical students receive no instruction about breast feeding. On maternity wards the 'convenience'

Figure 5.10 The pressure of Western advertising. (Courtesy Richard Willson.)

for the nursing staff of routine bottle feeding is very likely to be viewed both by junior nurses and by mothers as an endorsement of this practice. Health professionals are then susceptible to the promotional activities of milk companies. They are visited by nurses and representatives who explain the 'benefits' of their products in much the same way as do the drug representatives. Indeed the drug companies are increasingly 'diversifying' into the baby-foods field. Those companies like Cow & Gate and Nestlé which do not market drugs create a relationship with the health profession through sponsoring and organizing conferences on, for example, nutrition, using such occasions to promote their products. The professionals now 'informed' about the 'advantages' of this or that milk, act, often unwittingly, as promotional agents.

In some underdeveloped countries it is, ironically, at the 'well-baby' or under-5s clinics that many mothers will first encounter information about bottle feeding, usually in the form of milk company posters which frequently decorate such buildings. Understandably, mothers are impressed by the well-clothed, clean, chubby baby in attractive surroundings. The feeding bottle which is part of this highly desirable overall image becomes for many mothers an attainable symbol or even a possible key to the whole package. And the presence of such posters in the clinic surely indicates that bottle feeding is good for babies. Promotion on press, television and radio is also used extensively by the milk companies. A Nigerian survey revealed that of the significant percentage of mothers who recalled media advertisements for baby milks, most remembered the positive statements about bottle feeding rather than the cautionary information.[67]

But it is perhaps the operations of the 'milk nurses' in underdeveloped countries that are most unethical. Nurses are employed by both Nestlé and Cow & Gate for sales promotion. Although they are instructed to emphasize the importance of breast feeding in the early months, it has been shown that the following serious abuses of this 'educational' approach occur:

'Medically unqualified sales-girls are hired and dressed in nurses' uniforms to give their sales pitch in the guise of nutrition advice.
'Mothers are encouraged to bottle feed their babies while they are breast feeding them satisfactorily and before there is any need for supplements.
'Qualified nurses are paid on a sales-related basis belying their educational role.'

Baby Killer[68]

That such promotional methods are effective was shown by Nigerian and Jamaican surveys. Mothers cited company nurses as an important reason for starting bottle feeding. And the great majority started bottle feeding long before it was necessary to give additional food. Nine per cent of the Nigerian and a much larger proportion of the Jamaican mothers had received samples either at a hospital or through nurses. It could not be determined whether these were real or company 'nurses'. The proportion of illiterate mothers receiving samples was almost the same as educated mothers, showing that no attempt had been made to ensure that mothers were affluent enough to be able to purchase adequate quantities, or sufficiently literate to make up the milk correctly. Some companies even offer a free feeding bottle with their product.

In May 1981, the campaign against the baby-foods industry scored a major success when the general assembly of the World Health Organization adopted a code of practice whereby the companies would stop advertising and stress the benefits of breast feeding. This was based on a code agreed in October 1979 between WHO and UNICEF and the International Council of Infant Food Industries, representing the companies.

But although the code of practice is a step forward there are still problems. For example, what constitutes advertising? Many baby-food companies reluctantly came round to supporting the code because they realized that there was nothing in it to stop them sending promotional 'information' to the medical profession. An even greater problem is whether the companies can be trusted to stick by the agreement. A few months after the October 1979 agreement campaigners against bottle feeding released details of 202 examples of advertising in violation of the code. One spokesperson said that 19 companies in 33 countries were involved.

'Mothercraft "nurses", wearing uniforms but without any medical training, are still being used by Nestlé to promote their products in South African clinics; tins of "Nan" infant formula which make no mention of the superiority of breast-feeding are still on sale in Mexico; plastic bags advertising Lactogen are being distribution to shoppers in Zimbabwe; babycare booklets advertising bottle-feeds are being distributed by Nestlé in Malaysia; and the Wyeth company is still advertising its SMA and S26 formulas in "African Buyers Guide" as being "Good for Babies, Good for Profits, Good for You".'

Since the code is voluntary it is difficult to police. The most effective way of enforcing it seems to be the approach adopted by a handful of countries like Mozambique and Papua New Guinea who have nationalized the import, distribution and marketing of baby foods. Often powdered milk formula is only available on prescription.[69] There is little effective alternative. A voluntary code is all very well but Nestlé has an annual turnover larger than the gross national product of any African country except Nigeria and South Africa. It spends more on advertising each year than the total budget of the World Health Organization — which is meant to police the code.

The companies have said that they will rewrite and redesign their product labels and educational materials to conform with the code. But altering labels will not improve the food supply or the availability of fuel for sterilizing bottles. The redesign of educational materials will not help the illiterate mother to follow instructions. And the companies have not yet suggested dropping the price of their baby milk so that mothers who over-dilute the mixture to economize may be able to give their babies the correct amount.[70]

Medical Equipment

The drugs industry is responsible for a significant slice of many countries' already inadequate health service budgets. The direct cost of the baby-foods industry falls on individual families rather than on countries' health budgets, although the treatment of childhood diarrhoea often associated with bottle feeding certainly imposes a financial burden on the health sector. In both cases though, the costs in terms of human suffering are high partly as a result of blatantly unethical marketing methods.

A third example of capitalist medical technology is that of *medical equipment*. The operations of the medical equipment industry are not frankly 'unethical' — and therefore do not attract investigation by the media — but they are important both in diverting health care resources and in influencing the shape of health services. Although the 'market potential' in the underdeveloped world is necessarily limited by its lack of purchasing power there are still some areas where such 'potential' exists and recently certain new markets have presented themselves.

Middle East Health, a new journal which describes its function as 'serving the needs of the rapidly expanding hospital and health-care market throughout the Arab world and Iran', notes that 'of all the areas of the world today, the Middle East countries are being looked at as having the fastest expansion rate and the greatest potential for trade and. . .enormous opportunities . . .exist in the region as an export market for manufacturers of medical and hospital supplies, equipment and pharmaceuticals from across the world'.[71] It goes on to add that:

'A recent press report valued the world medical market at more than £50 billion over the next 10 years and nowhere is this growth more apparent and conspicuous than in the Middle East region, enriched by substantial oil revenues. . . . Now more than ever, manufacturers should endeavour to capitalise on this vast health market. . . . There is no doubt that, providing correct procedures are undertaken for dealing with particular countries in the region, the Middle East provides an extremely valuable export market for manufacturers of medical and hospital supplies.'

And they substantiate these claims by providing information under the heading: 'Market Facts, Summary' (Tables 5.5 and 5.6). Thus while the drugs industry remains most significant in absolute terms, the rate of growth of the medical equipment, dressings and medical furniture components is especially rapid.

A similar venture whose role should be viewed in the light of the above 'Market Facts' is what is now called the British Health-Care Export Council (BHEC). As its glossy publication, *Health-Care, Equipment and Technology*, observes, *Health-Care* was substituted for the original *Hospitals* in 1976 to 'indicate more clearly the comprehensive nature of its coverage'. (Could it also have been a semantic manoeuvre to convey a more progressive image?) BHEC, a

Table 5.5 **The medical equipment market**

Country	Medical equipment	Dressings	Medical furniture	Drugs	Total (£000)	Total (US $000)
UK	11 168	3488	2753	43 097	60 506	108 910
France	2662	165	266	18 799	21 892	39 407
Germany	13 929	1128	1973	41 957	58 987	106 178
Japan	5304	424	121	2113	7962	14 330
USA	12 785	964	2656	24 925	41 330	74 393
1975	45 848	6169	7769	130 891	190 677	343 218
1972	16 391	1649	1920	51 635	71 595	128 871

Source: *Middle East Health*, Media Information File

Table 5.6 **Percentage growth from 1972 to 1975 of medical equipment sales**

Country	Medical equipment	Dressings	Medical furniture	Drugs	Total
UK	540	257	1140	236	284
France	289	259	505	122	137
Germany	37	205	48	121	91
Japan	314	266	10	342	301
USA	415	584	1177	130	203
Total	180	274	305	153	166

Source: *Middle East Health*, Media Information File

private organization supported financially by British industry, was started to 'promote the use of British goods and services for the design, construction, equipment, staffing and management of health-care facilities overseas'. It 'works closely with Government Departments, particularly the Department of Health and Social Security, the Department of Trade and the Central Office of Information'.[72] What kind of goods and services are promoted and what sorts of health-care facilities are thus encouraged by such initiatives?

MEH's stated editorial policy is 'to educate and inform its readers of the best and most recent developments in hospital supplies and services and in health-care at all levels from across the world, suitably highlighting their relevance to the Middle East'.[73] Thus it carries such news items as: 'Kuwait, which has one of the highest rates of kidney disease in the world, is to launch an all-out attack on the problem this year' (1977).[74] Led by an associate professor of medicine from Dublin, 'the campaign will be centred on an ultra-modern renal clinic to be built next to the 800-bed Al-Sabah Hospital.' It is questionable whether the 12 artificial kidney machines or indeed the ultra-modern renal clinic are the appropriate approaches to widespread kidney disease in such a country where the causes are likely to be rooted in the environmental conditions of underdevelopment. These are indeed examples of the 'most recent developments in hospital supplies and services in health-care. . .' (*Fig. 5.11*) but what is 'their relevance to the Middle East' or at least to the health problems of the vast majority of people?

Similarly, BHEC's 1978 'Medical and Surgical Equipment' asserts that 'ultrasound is now firmly established as an important clinical aid and no hospital can claim to be up-to-date unless it is equipped with ultra-sonic instrumentation.'[75] And conveniently juxtaposed to this article are advertisements for the various Sonic Aid Obstetric monitors! But it is perhaps in BHEC's 1978 'Intensive Care' publication that the 'relevance' of the advertised medical equipment to the health-care needs of underdeveloped countries is most strained. For the equipment demonstrated here ranges from the 'cardiovision mobile image intensifier'

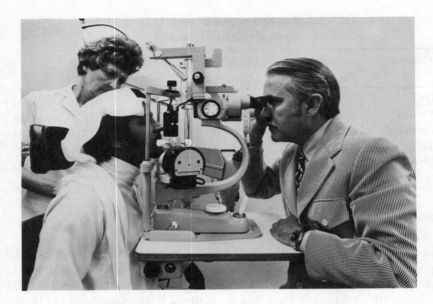

Figure 5.11   King Faisal Specialist Hospital, Saudi Arabia. (Courtesy Aspect Picture Library.)

through the 'Beaufort–Winchester flotation bed' to the truly indispensable 'hospital nurse call system equipment'.[76]

And though the Middle East is currently the most lucrative region for British medical capital, most of the medical technology used in underdeveloped countries comes from the developed world. For example, it has been estimated that 80 per cent of Latin American equipment is imported, mostly from the USA. So in Bogotá, Colombia, a city of over 2 million, where nutritional and communicable diseases predominate, the annual running costs of its three open-heart surgery units could provide a quarter of the city's children with ½ litre of milk daily for a year![77]

How is this grotesque situation brought about?

Doctors in particular and health workers in general are, through their practice and training, oriented towards individual, curative medicine. They are therefore susceptible to sophisticated, expensive technology which may be inappropriate to the needs of most people. So for example health workers trained in Britain or trained in countries where British curricula and methods have been followed are likely to have used British-made medical equipment and be easily influenced by those promoting its sale. These companies advertise in such publications as *Health-Care, Equipment and Technology* and *Middle East Health*, which, as the latter journal's circulation policy states, is 'circulated free of charge to medical and administrative personnel who purchase, or directly influence the purchase of, medical and hospital supplies and services (including equipment and pharmaceuticals)'. Like the drug and baby-food firms, they sponsor conferences which often attract an international contingent of health workers — mainly doctors — and which tend to focus on those aspects of medical care involving the use of up-to-date equipment — which invariably is displayed adjacent to the conference room.

But while it is largely the health workers of underdeveloped countries who act as a channel through which the medical equipment companies can direct their goods, it is not only they who are biased towards the urban-based, curative medical services. It is also the small ruling élites who push for such medical services. They tend to live in the urban areas, suffer developed country diseases, and may have had treatment (often private) in the super-technological hospitals of London, Paris, New York and so on. They argue that it is scandalous that their country, now independent of the former colonial power, should still be dependent on medical services overseas. As two sociologists researching in Zambia in the early 1970s explained:

'Their reference groups were their opposite numbers from neighbouring States and the whole world. In less than a generation they had genuinely forgotten the circumstances of life and death as experienced by the ordinary villagers as they, or at least their parents, had been.'

Sociology and Development[78]

Medical Aid

Another way in which the door is opened to the medical equipment (and drugs and baby foods) business — and this is most relevant to concerned health workers going to work in underdeveloped countries — is through foreign 'experts' and expatriate health workers. These people, often unconscious of the negative aspects of their approach, bring with them not just their ideas about health and health care, but their practical experience of using particular types of equipment. Hence they may become the unwitting agents of medical big business. Undoubtedly they are frequently seen as such by the companies concerned. As the *Middle East Health* editorial policy puts it, '. . . while the will and finance is there [the Middle East] the technology and expertise must be imported.' And an article in an early issue illustrates the point perfectly:

'According to its second 5-year development plan — currently in its third year of implementation — Saudi Arabia has a purse of $3.48 billion for new projects and an additional $1.4 billion for existing recurrent expenditures in the provision of medical and health services.
'There is, as in so many other sectors of this rapidly expanding economy, no shortage of money. But there is, more perhaps than in most other sectors, a shortage of expertise with which to tackle the problems of medicine and health care in the desert kingdom. . . .

'Clearly, the success of the plan still depends much on the import of
foreign doctors and nurses, most of whom are from the West. . .'.

Middle East Health[79]

The form in which medical aid is provided will help influence the approach
taken by the recipient to health and health care. For example, aid tied to technological inputs will reinforce the curative, technological approach to health
care. Britain's official aid programme is managed by the Overseas Development
Administration (ODA — now part of the Foreign Office). It involves more than
120 countries and in 1978-9 an estimated expenditure of £714 million.[80] In
1977 it represented approximately 1 per cent of total government spending. A
tiny proportion of this is health aid. Government disbursements for health projects in 1973-4 amounted to only about £8 million — which was only slightly
more than the amount of aid to the health sector provided by British voluntary
agencies.[81]

Health sector aid from British voluntary agencies is widely distributed to
more than 50 countries with most going to Africa and Asia.[82] In Asia, India and
Bangladesh receive most 'project' and personnel aid. In Africa, Malawi, Ethiopia
and Tanzania received most 'project' aid with Nigeria getting 32 per cent of
personnel aid, nearly three times more than any other African country.[83]

How then is *official* British aid apportioned? As a recent ODA leaflet stated:

'About 40% of the aid budget is directed to the developing countries via
international agencies such as the World Bank. ODA then decides how to
apportion the remaining 60% between the different countries and how
best to use it, for example, by providing finance or personnel, research or
training facilities. Whatever way it is used, it is in response to requests
from developing countries themselves. ODA doesn't initiate a country's
development plans. Any suggested project is, however, carefully and
expertly examined and appraised before acceptance.'

Britain's Aid Programme[84]

One phrase is often used both by governments and by voluntary agencies to
legitimize what might be inappropriate aid: '. . . it is in response to requests from
developing countries themselves.' But *who* in developing countries? The demands
of the mostly urban élites in underdeveloped countries are usually for health
care facilities which they perceive as appropriate to *their* needs. These are not
only inappropriate, but also frequently inaccessible to the vast majority of the
population. The leaflet later continues:

'. . . the use of experts from overseas remains an important part of the aid
Britain can offer. There are still not enough people in the Third World who
have had the opportunity to develop their skills and rural development
involves particularly intensive research, planning and appraisal. . . . So

technical co-operation — providing essential skills and helping to train local people — is vital and this is where people like you who are qualified to practise, teach or research, contribute to the aid programme as a whole.'

Britain's Aid Programme[85] (*see also Fig. 5.12*)

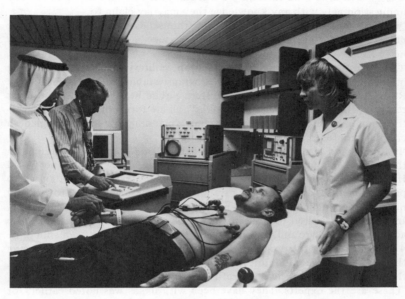

Figure 5.12   Technical co-operation. (Courtesy Aspect Picture Library.)

Certain skills are always necessary, but it is seriously questionable whether the ways in which many skills are applied are relevant to the majority in under-developed (and indeed many developed) countries. For example, underdeveloped country health workers are trained as physiotherapists who are able to work only in well-equipped units in hospitals. Such skills are inappropriate to the needs of the vast majority. On the other hand, many lower-level health workers could be trained to perform certain basic physiotherapeutic techniques which have been developed to treat common local deformities. This would be an appropriate skill.

During 1977 there were 8652 British professional men and women working in underdeveloped countries, partly or wholly financed by ODA, although only a small proportion of these were health workers.[86] In 1973–4, 1053 health personnel were supported in underdeveloped countries by voluntary agencies, 64 per cent of them nurses.[87]

The inappropriate contribution to health care by 'experts' is vividly illustrated in this account by a Bengali doctor:

'Recently in Dacca airport I met an acquaintance who said to me in the course of our brief discussion that he had counted 72 experts in Dacca on that one day alone. And yourself, I asked. "73", he admitted. It will be an up-hill road, overcoming this favourable bias towards the wisdom of the West. For a long time to come we will continue to credit foreign expertise unquestioningly with any knowledge they may lay claim to.

'Who are these experts that come from thousands of miles away with the perfect plan for a village they have never seen, and a culture they have never lived?

'Our "Western trained medical profession, sanitary inspectors originating in the British Empire, the malaria program established by the WHO, the Rural Health Centres devised by Western public health experts, and most recently, the family planning programs", all are forms of expatriate expertise that have left the health and family planning system of Bangladesh crippled, confused and utterly dependent. . . .

'It is accepted that Bangladesh needs barefoot doctors, people trained in the village and able to meet the needs of the villagers, but the World Health Organisation experts proposed an elaborate 3-year programme to produce medical assistants. This training will take place in the towns, and most of the students will have a background of 12 years formal education. In one centre visited, 65 out of 80 enrolled had had 12 years or more educational background, and nearly all felt that the course itself should be 4 or more years if the programme was going to equip them to "better serve the people". Serve, no doubt in Dacca, or Libya, as experience attests. But the expert advisers of the WHO refuse to see any other way.

'These are the experts. They have been with us, as was noted earlier, for some time. Will we sell ourselves out to them unconditionally now? There are real experts, however, and there is such a thing as appropriate aid. Neither is it impossible to discern the real from the "invested aid". Does it reach the real problems with realistic solutions? Does the plan provide for local responsibility in the foreseeable future? Is it honest in assessing its weaknesses as well as its strengths?'

Bangladesh Times[88]

He cited other examples of inappropriate aid and looked particularly at the field of medical research. He examined the operations of the world-famous Cholera Research Laboratory which made the breakthrough discovery of simplified oral therapy for cholera. This was still unavailable for most of Bangladesh. Further, the villages whose water was contaminated by material from the hospital had rates for cholera and diarrhoeal disease 20 times higher than the average.[89]

These are only some — perhaps particularly stark — examples of inappropriate health sector aid, although there are certainly many others in different countries. *Aid should in each case be critically evaluated for it is by no means always advantageous to the recipient.* Moreover, health-sector aid is nearly always dwarfed by health-sector trade, much of which is inappropriate to most peoples' needs. So, when on the one hand the British Overseas Development Administration argues for aid to be increasingly directed to the poorest, and on the other the British Department of Health and Social Security in co-operation with the BHEC launches an export drive for British medical equipment and expertise, this throws into question where the *real* interests of the British State lie.

Summary

As the capitalist economic and political system extended over the whole world, capitalist medicine was introduced into the underdeveloped countries. As in the developed countries, the starkly inappropriate health services have been primarily a result of the transformation of health care into a commodity. This has led to the neglect of health promotion, the stunting of preventive activities and the overblowing of the curative component. In most post-colonial countries both the health professions and the local élites have argued for Western-style health services. They have sealed this by adopting the educational curricula and institutions of the former colonial power in many cases. In this way the international saleability of the professionals' skills is ensured and with it their frequent international migration. The transmission of this approach to health and health care to lower-level health workers has created professional aspirations, upward migration and high drop-out rates.

This is further entrenched by medical business interests. The examples of the baby-foods business and the drugs and medical equipment industries show how the transfer of largely inappropriate technology aggravates the diversion of resources and the distortion of services in the interests of only a few. Much foreign 'aid' has similar effects, often benefiting the donor more than the recipient.

The transfer of capitalist medicine to underdeveloped countries has had other important effects. The medical profession, as in the developed world, comes predominantly from the higher social classes and frequently allies with both local and international business interests, particularly in the medical field. Behind the apparently reasonable argument of 'professional freedom', doctors insist on the right to private practice, sophisticated and expensive facilities and equipment, and unrestricted prescribing of expensive drugs. Their vested interests have led them to resist social change that would threaten the status quo nationally or internationally. For example, during the brief period of Salvador Allende's left-wing government in Chile in the early 1970s, many professionals resisted democratization of health care institutions.

The health professions internationally have given powerful encouragement to the idea that disease in the underdeveloped world is due to 'ignorance' and 'overbreeding', rather than underdevelopment. The medical contribution, while its major determining forces remain the medical profession, big business, and the State, rather than the people, is much more part of this problem of underdevelopment than part of its solution.

References

1. Robson, *Quality, Inequality and Health Care, Medicine in Society*, special edition, p. 11.
2. Barbara Ehrenreich and Deirdre English, *Witches, Midwives and Nurses: A History of Women Healers*, Glass Mountain Pamphlets, p. 15.
3. Robson, *Quality, Inequality and Health Care*, p. 11.
4. Ehrenreich and English, *Witches, Midwives and Nurses*, p. 12.
5. *Ibid.*, p. 17.
6. *Ibid.*, p. 17.
7. *Ibid.*, pp. 32–3.
8. *Ibid.*, p. 36.
9. Robson, *Quality, Inequality and Health Care*, p. 12.
10. Bernard Shaw, *The Doctor's Dilemma*.
11. Robson, *Quality, Inequality and Health Care*, p. 15.
12. *Ibid.*, p. 15.
13. *Ibid.*, pp. 14–18.
14. Ehrenreich and English, *Witches, Midwives and Nurses*, p. 28.
15. Much of the following discussion on health care as a commodity is based on M. Segall, Health care as a commodity, *Medicine and Society*, Vol. 2, No. 4, London.
16. J. P. Bunker and J. E. Wennberg (1973). Operation rates, mortality statistics and the quality of life, *New England Journal of Medicine,* **289**, 1249; quoted in Radical Statistics Health Group pamphlet No. 2, p. 24.
17. Unpublished report on Vermont Health Utilization Survey, 1973 Survey Research Program, University of Massachusetts and Joint Center for Urban Studies, Massachusetts Institute for Technology and Harvard University, 1973, quoted in Radical Statistics Health Group pamphlet No. 2, p. 25.
18. Radical Statistics Health Group pamphlet No. 2, p. 25.
19. H. G. Mather *et al.* (1976). Acute myocardial infarction: a comparison between home and hospital care for patients, *British Medical Journal*, **i**, 925; quoted in Radical Statistics Health Group pamphlet No. 2, p. 23.
20. Rob Crawford. *You Are Dangerous to Your Health – the Ideology and Politics of Victim Blaming*, HMO Packet No. 3, p. 13.
21. *Ibid.*, p. 7.
22. *Health of Towns Magazine and Journal of Medical Jurisprudence* (1847–8), p. 153.
23. Crawford, *You Are Dangerous to Your Health*, p. 7.
24. Radical Statistics Health Group, *Whose Priorities*, pp. 24, 26–7.
25. This and what follows is based largely on Segall, *Health Care as a Commodity*.
26. Robson, *Quality, Inequality and Health Care*, p. 21.

27. *See* Talcott Parsons (1972). Definitions of health and illness in the light of American values and social structure, in E. Gartley Jaco (ed.), *Patients, Physicians and Illness: A Source Book in Behavioural Science and Health*, New York Free Press.
28. A. Cartwright (1967). *Patients and their Doctors*, Routledge, London; quoted in *Science for People*, Health Issue Special, No. 58, Winter 1977-8.
29. Quoted in Ehrenreich and English, *Witches, Midwives and Nurses*, p. 19.
30. From J. R. Wilson *et al.* (1975). *Obstetrics and Gynaecology*, 5th edn., p. 43, quoted in *Science for People*.
31. *Women's Voice*, June 1978.
32. *Women's Voice*, March 1979.
33. Robson, *Quality, Inequality and Health Care*, p. 5.
34. *Ibid.*, p. 5.
35. *Social Trends* (1980). HMSO, London.
36. From *Who Needs the Drug Companies?* Haslemere Group, p. 6.
37. Robson, *Take a Pill*, Communist Party pamphlet.
38. *Ibid.*, pp. 18-22.
39. *Ibid.*, pp. 18-22.
40. *Ibid.*
41. The approach is similar to that in Robson, *Quality, Inequality and Health Care*, p. 3.
42. Vicente Navarro (1974). The underdevelopment of health or the health of underdevelopment: An analysis of the distribution of human health resources in Latin America. *International Journal of Health Services*, **4**, 10.
43. G. M. van Etten (1976). *Rural Health Development in Tanzania*, Assen, p. 161.
44. M. Segall, *Theoretical Problems of 'Middle-level' Rural Health Centres and of Rural Health in the Countries of East Africa (with special reference to Ethiopia and Tanzania)*, draft, unpublished.
45. *Who Needs the Drug Companies?* p. 9.
46. *Ibid.*, p. 9.
47. *Ibid.*, pp. 9-10.
48. *Ibid.*, p. 20.
49. Doyal, (1979). *The Political Economy of Health*, Pluto, p. 269.
50. *Who Needs the Drug Companies?* pp. 16-17.
51. J. Yudkin (1977). *To Plan is to Choose*, unpublished mimeo, University of Dar es Salaam, p. 9.
52. *Ibid.*, p. 13.
53. *New Statesman*, 15 August 1980.
54. Yudkin, *To Plan is To Choose*, p. 14.
55. *Ibid.*, p. 4.
56. *The Baby Killer* (1975). War on Want, London.

57. *Ibid.*, pp. 4–5.
58. Penelope Leach (1974). *Babyhood*, Penguin, p. 43.
59. S. J. Plank and M. L. Milanesi (1973). Infant feeding and infant mortality in Chile. *Bulletin of the World Health Organization*, **48**, 203; quoted in *Baby Killer*, p. 3.
60. *Baby Killer*, p. 17.
61. *Ibid.*, p. 3.
62. *Ibid.*, p. 7.
63. *Ibid.*, p. 6.
64. Gill Garb (1982). Babies mean business. *Africa Now*, June.
65. *Baby Killer*, p. 6.
66. *Ibid.*, p. 6.
67. *Ibid.*, p. 11.
68. *Ibid.*, p. 13.
69. *Guardian*, 13 May 1980; *New Internationalist*, April 1980; *Africa Now*, July 1981.
70. Garb (1982). Babies mean business.
71. *Middle East Health*, Media Information File, p. 22.
72. *Health-Care, Equipment and Technology*, BHEC, 1978, p. 1.
73. *Middle East Health*, Media Information File, p. 1.
74. *Middle East Health*, April 1977.
75. *Medical and Surgical Equipment*, BHEC, p. 13.
76. *Ibid.*, pp. 45, 98, 105.
77. Navarro, *The Underdevelopment of Health*, p. 11.
78. R. Frankenberg and J. Leeson (1974). The sociology of health: dilemmas in the post-colonial world. In de Kadt and Williams (eds), *Sociology and Development*, London, pp. 271–2.
79. *Middle East Health*, Media Information File, p. 1; *Middle East Health*, April 1977.
80. *Britain's Aid Programme Overseas*. ODM.
81. S. Cole-King (1976). *Health Sector Aid from Voluntary Agencies: the British Case-Study*. IDS discussion paper No. 97, University of Sussex, p. 18.
82. *Ibid.*, p. 61.
83. *Ibid.*, p. 64.
84. *Britain's Aid Programme Overseas*. ODM.
85. *Ibid.*
86. *Ibid.*
87. Cole-King (1976). *Health Sector Aid for Voluntary Agencies*, pp. 30–3.
88. Z. Chowdhury (1977). Research: a method of colonisation. *Bangladesh Times*, 13–14 January.
89. *Ibid.*

6 Changing Medicine, Changing Society

So far the focus has been on the negative aspects of the medical contribution. This has partly been a conscious attempt to correct the prevalent but unbalanced view that medical interventions no matter how small can *only* be good and that health workers always make a positive contribution to *health*.

What then should be the role of those concerned with health? What should be done by those who see the necessity for the promotion of health as well as the prevention and cure of disease? How, in short, can health workers both in developed and in underdeveloped countries become more part of the solution to underdevelopment and ill health than part of the problem?

Health problems both in the underdeveloped and in the developed world are rooted in social conditions. In the Third World these are determined by an international system that ensures underdevelopment.

The two most important measures to promote health in the countries that are now developed were improved nutrition and better environmental hygiene. Exactly the same measures are needed to promote health in the underdeveloped countries today. But the task of ending underdevelopment is not just a repetition of the development that took place in Britain and the other advanced capitalist countries. We have seen how the accumulation of capital for industrial development in those countries came from exploiting the colonial world. The underdeveloped countries today have no colonies to exploit – they have no easy source of capital and only small markets for their goods. Since the advent of imperialism, the economies of underdeveloped countries have become increasingly controlled by huge foreign-owned enterprises in alliance with a local ruling class.

The possibility of significant independent capitalist development as happened in nineteenth-century Europe no longer exists. There are, however, a few impressive examples of countries where underdevelopment is being successfully tackled and great improvements in their peoples' health achieved. The best known of these are Cuba and China where victorious popular struggles resulted in a change of economic and political systems. Long-stifled human potential was mobilized, foreign-controlled resources reappropriated and the ensuing wealth more fairly distributed, with particular emphasis on health and other social services. The last

factor — new approaches to *health care* — will be discussed later, but first here
are some of the ways in which health promotion grew out of the process that
reversed underdevelopment.

HEALTH PROMOTION. THE WAY FORWARD: THE CHINESE AND CUBAN EXPERIENCES

Two Americans, Victor Sidel, a physician specializing in community health
care, and Ruth Sidel, a psychiatric social worker, have visited China and studied
health and health care. They write:

> 'There is common agreement that prior to 1949 the state of health of large
> numbers of Chinese people was extremely poor and that the health services
> provided for them were grossly inadequate. The people of China in the
> 1930s and 1940s suffered from the consequences of widespread poverty,

Figure 6.1 Famine in China. (Courtesy Topham.)

poor sanitation, continuing war, and rampant disease. The crude death rate
was estimated at about 25 deaths per 1000 — one of the world's highest
death rates. The infant mortality rate was about 200 per 1000 live births;
in other words, one out of every five babies born died in its first year of
life. Most deaths in China were due to infectious diseases, usually complicated by some form of malnutrition. Prevalent infectious diseases included
bacterial illnesses such as cholera, diphtheria, gonorrhoea, leprosy, meningococcal meningitis, plague, relapsing fever, syphilis, tetanus, tuberculosis,
typhoid fever and typhus; viral illnesses such as Japanese B encephalitis,
smallpox and trachoma; and parasitic illnesses such as ancylostomiasis
(hookworm disease), clonorchiasis, filariasis, kala-azar, malaria, paragoni-
miasis and schistosomiasis.'

Health by the People[1]

Today the picture is rather different (*Fig. 6.2*):

Figure 6.2 Chinese workers today. (Courtesy Xinhua News Agency.)

'Although (official national) statistics are not yet available on the current
health status of China's population, recent visitors report a nation of
healthy-looking, vigorous people. While it is clear that the nation is still
poorly developed technologically and its people — particularly in the rural
areas — work very long and hard, there is no evidence of the malnutrition,
ubiquitous infectious disease, and other ill health that often accompanies
poverty.

'In one city, Shanghai, health statistics are becoming available. They show a crude death rate of 6 per 1000, an infant mortality rate of 9 per 1000 live births, and correspondingly low age-specific death rates at other ages. The life expectancy at birth now appears to be about 70 years. The leading causes of death are now reported to be cancer, stroke, and heart disease. Shanghai City is certainly not representative of the rest of China, or even of its other large cities, but the remarkable changes over the past two decades in Shanghai — the infant mortality rate in 1948 was estimated at 150 per 1000 — are probably indicative of rapid changes in health status throughout China'.

Health by the People[2]

All national statistics for China are estimates. Table 6.1 brings together estimates from some of the commentators who seem to have disagreed most, so probably it gives a broadly accurate picture.

Table 6.1 **Trends in vital statistics in China, 1949–80**

Statistic	1949	1955	1965	1972	1980
Population (millions)	540	608	705	775	875
Crude death rate (per 1000)	30	26	21	15	11
Crude birth rate (per 1000)	40	42	35	30	22
Growth rate (per cent)	10	16	14	15	11
Infant mortality rate (per 1000)	200	40–74	25	17–20	—

Source: adapted from Chabot, *The Chinese System of Health Care* (Chapter 3, reference 60)

In Cuba too the achievements have been impressive, though the nation's health at the time of the revolution in 1959 was considerably better than that of China before liberation. The health indicators in Table 6.2 give some idea of the advances.

With respect to China the Sidels conclude:

'These changes in health status are certainly not the result of changes in health care alone; improvements in nutrition, sanitation, and living standards are at least as important.'

Health Care Delivery System[4]

And this applies equally to Cuba.

Table 6.2 **Improving health in Cuba**

Mortality rates (per 1000)[3]

Crude death rate	6.5 (1958)	5.8 (1973)
Infant mortality rate	33.0 (1958)	27.0 (1973)
Mortality rate, age 1–4 years	2.6 (1958)	1.2 (1970)
Maternal mortality rate	1.2 (1962)	0.6 (1972)
Stillbirths	25.2 (1962)	13.0 (1972)

Disease-specific mortality rates (per 100 000)

Gastroenteritis	42.5 (1957)	18.4 (1970)
Tuberculosis	19.6 (1962)	7.3 (1970)
Typhoid	0.2 (1968)	0.0 (1971)
Poliomyelitis	32 cases (1960)	No cases since 1972
Malaria	Eradicated	

Morbidity rates (per 100 000)

Poliomyelitis	Eradicated (342 cases reported in 1961)	
Whooping cough	15.6 (1967/69)	7.2 (1970/72)
Tetanus	4.3 (1967/69)	2.3 (1970/72)
Tetanus neonatorum	49.0 (1959)	0.0 (1970) –
		1 case
Diphtheria	2.6 (1967/69)	0.0 (1971/73)
Tuberculosis	41.0 (1968)	17.8 (1971)

Nutrition

The improvement of nutrition was probably the most important factor in promoting the health of both the Cuban and Chinese people. This was the result of major political and economic changes. Privately owned agriculture, predominantly foreign, was reclaimed for the people and revenues from cash crop production were more equitably distributed or invested in social development. In the case of food crops, land was radically redistributed, more efficient farming techniques were subsidized and collective farming introduced. This ensured increased and more appropriate production. Storage and marketing facilities were extended to these collectivized units. Job opportunities grew and prices of foodstuffs were strictly controlled. Diets and thus nutritional status improved.

For example, in Cuba before the 1958 revolution, several surveys showed that undernutrition was widespread. One study indicated that one-third of the general population and 60 per cent of the rural population was undernourished. Therefore the percentage of children suffering from undernutrition was likely to be considerably higher. By contrast, a 1969 report by the United Nations Food and Agricultural Organisation (FAO) estimated the average daily calorific intake in Cuba to be 2650 kcal (11 MJ) per person, which is higher than both the Latin American average and the daily requirement of 2500 kcal (10.45 MJ). Also, surveys performed in 1967 in different rural areas, including the poorest, showed that severe undernutrition hardly existed and that only 6 per cent of children under the age of 6 had second-degree malnutrition (weight between 76 per cent and 90 per cent of international standards).[5]

Similarly, in pre-liberation China undernutrition and even starvation as a result of famine were common. Historical accounts describe 1828 famines between 108 BC and AD 1911, and recent evidence suggests that there was a major famine between 1959 and 1961, but none has occurred since then.[6] Children as always were worst affected and most illness and death from infectious and parasitic diseases were based on undernutrition. While detailed national data on nutritional status are as yet unavailable, it can be safely assumed that the massive fall in infant and child mortality since the time of liberation is due largely to the conquest of common and serious maternal and childhood undernutrition.

Evidence of good childhood nutrition is provided by the assessment of growth in pre-school children. Joe Wray, an American paediatrician who recently visited China, noted that growth 'seems to be closer to North American standards than that of Chinese children in Hong Kong and Singapore'.[7]

The improvement of nutritional status in the above cases strengthened people's response to infections, lessening the occurrence and duration of illness and thereby reducing the prevalence of infective organisms in the environment. Thus improved nutrition indirectly helped cut down exposure to infectious agents. But it was the addition of environmental improvements that led to a dramatic decrease in communicable diseases. While there are isolated examples from certain underdeveloped countries of impressive progress in improving living and working conditions, the situation in most of the underdeveloped world is seriously inadequate. Hence the achievements on a *national* scale of Cuba and China are well worth noting.

Airborne Disease

In reducing the incidence and seriousness of *airborne infections* the most important factors are nutrition and housing. With respect to housing too the progress made both in Cuba and in China stands in sharp contrast to most underdeveloped countries where large and increasing sections of the population live in urban slums or shanties or inadequate and overcrowded rural dwellings. In Cuba:

'11 089 homes were constructed each year during the 5 years following the Cuban Revolution. 40% of these were built in the countryside as part of a program which set the highest priority on rural construction, with the eradication of slums and tenements in both urban and rural areas as a second priority. From 1967 to 1969, construction increased to an average of 16 600 homes per year, bringing the overall construction figure for the period 1959 to 1969 to 140 000 new dwelling units. This figure, however, fell short of the estimated 400 000 dwelling units required for 1970'.

Health, Health Services and Health Planning[8]

There are no such readily available statistics for China but many visitors have confirmed the observations made by Wray during his recent visit:

'Nowhere in the PRC [Peoples Republic of China] did we see the contrasts, so striking in other developing countries, between a small affluent élite living in comfortable luxury, and poverty-striken masses living in crowded squatter slums. The standard of living, low by Western standards, seemed everywhere to be decent and minimally adequate. The homes and apartments we visited, both in urban and rural areas were small, somewhat crowded, and rather sparsely furnished. They were, however, invariably neat and reasonably clean. Kitchens and bathrooms, often shared in cities were clean; tap water and electricity were standard. Water is said to be potable everywhere; the countryside wherever we travelled was laced with electric power lines and electricity was available in all the communes we visited.'

Health and Nutrition Factors[9]

Improved nutrition and housing conditions are reflected in a dramatic reduction both in prevalence and in severity of those airborne infectious diseases previously common both in China and in Cuba. Diphtheria, whooping cough and measles have declined considerably as has tuberculosis, that classic indicator of living and working conditions.[10] In Cuba the mortality rate from TB fell from 19.6 per 100 000 in 1962 to 4.1 in 1973 and continues to decline.[11] In China before 1949 the prevalence in large cities lay between 3 per cent and 9 per cent, being highest in the densely populated Shanghai,[12] and in 1946, 60 per cent of all applicants for student visas for study abroad were found to be suffering from this disease.[13] The TB mortality rate in Peking fell from 230 per 100 000 in 1949 to 29.7 in 1963 and has almost certainly declined further. The fall in prevalence in TB in China and Cuba is reminiscent of that recorded for the developed countries, although in these two the rate of the decline has been considerably faster. How much this is due to the greatly improved social conditions and how much to the massive immunization campaign — 90 per cent of all newborn infants in China were inoculated by 1964 — is impossible to ascertain.[14]

Health education creates a popular awareness of how airborne diseases are transmitted. Two Australian doctors who visited China recently provide an illustration. In the lobby of a factory clinic they saw a blackboard on which was written information about meningococcal meningitis and how to prevent it. The first section was a simple description of the disease and how it was spread. The second was a list of preventive measures including making sure that living quarters were airy and well ventilated. It also recommended the preventive virtues of salt water mouth rinses and the use of garlic and herbal brews. The visitors concluded: 'Whilst one can remain sceptical about the salt water and the herbal methods (although we have no way of knowing whether such methods are effective), the statements concerning ventilation are sensible and correct.'[15]

Environmental Hygiene

Improved water supplies and sanitation are needed to reduce water-related and faecally-transmitted disease. It is perhaps in this area of environmental hygiene and the control of certain epidemic and vector-borne diseases that the most striking advances have been made in China and Cuba.

In Cuba in 1959 there were 303 urban communities of over 1000 people, 175 of which had sewage systems covering a total of 2 163 000 inhabitants. In 1967, there were 432 urban communities of over 1000 inhabitants, 223 of which had sewage systems, covering a total of 4 316 000 inhabitants. This represents a doubling of the population covered by sewage systems. In 1958 only 35 per cent of the total population was served by piped water systems. And in the rural areas, 75 per cent of all families obtained their water from rivers, wells and springs, with only 2 per cent receiving inside piped water. By 1969, however, 90 per cent of the urban population and 60 per cent of the rural population were covered by piped water systems.[16]

Similarly, at the time of liberation in 1949 in China sanitation and water supply was probably worse than in India today, where 91 per cent of the rural population lacks an adequate water supply.[17] In 1973 reports from China indicated that piped water is available to 90 per cent of the urban population and 70 per cent of the rural population have adequate water supplies and sanitation.[18]

The result in both these countries of improved nutrition and water and sanitation facilities has been a dramatic fall in incidence and severity of most water-borne and water-washed diseases. In Cuba, for example, the gastroenteritis mortality rate fell from 58.1 per 100 000 persons in 1962 to 9.7 in 1973, while poliomyelitis declined in incidence from 200–400 cases per year in the early 1960s to only three cases in the 9 years up to 1975.[19] Although specific national statistics are unavailable for China it is recorded that not a single case of cholera occurred in the 4 years following liberation.[20] A group of Australian health workers who recently visited reported that: 'many faecal-borne diseases still exist in China, although, as far as we could find out, at low levels of prevalence.'[21] This observation, in conjunction with the recent finding by Wray, that serious illness and death among children under 5 years are rare,[22] indicate impressive progress in the control of this group of diseases which is the cause of so much suffering and death in underdeveloped countries.

These impressive environmental improvements show clearly how health promotion and the political process necessary to reverse underdevelopment are interconnected. In the sanitation movements and successful mass campaigns against agricultural and disease-carrying pests in China the mobilization of long-stifled human potential is vividly demonstrated. It is this element that is crucial both to health promotion and to ending underdevelopment.

Mass Campaigns

In the early 1950s the Patriotic Health Campaign was launched. It was linked initially to the need to protect the population against the use of germ warfare by the Americans during the Korean War. In the first such campaign the 'four pests' were attacked — rats, flies, mosquitoes and sparrows, sparrows later being replaced by bed bugs. The people were mobilized to exterminate these pests under the guidance of health personnel. During this assault more than 74 million tons of garbage were cleared away and breeding grounds thus eliminated.[23] In fact, in 1960 it was reported that 1590 million rats, 100 million kilograms of flies and 11 million kilograms of mosquitoes had been collected![24]

In later years the Patriotic Health Campaigns were replaced by 'shock attacks', short-lived but highly intensive campaigns, often carried out on a regional scale, and each dealing with a specific problem. Campaigns then became regular seasonal affairs directed towards eradicating all the major communicable diseases as well as the 'four pests' and at the improvement of sanitary conditions (*Fig. 6.3*). For example, in the 1958 campaign it was reported that 63.27 million public latrines were constructed or repaired — one for every ten people.[25]

Perhaps the most remarkable achievement is the massive reduction in schistosomiasis or bilharzia. This contrast sharply with several underdeveloped countries, especially in Africa, where the prevalence has risen explosively. In her report on the 10 years of public health work from 1949 to 1959, China's Minister of Public Health stated that schistosomiasis had practically been eradicated in 65.4 per cent of the affected areas,[26] and a more recent study reports a drop in prevalence from 97 per cent before 1949 to 3 per cent in 1968 in some areas.[27] The snails that harbour the infective larvae of this chronic and debilitating disease grow at the edges of ponds, dams and irrigation ditches. Although the Chinese do use some chemical molluscicides, the main method of control is by burying snails with earth. Millions of people have been mobilized to dig irrigation canals adjacent to those infested with snails and fill in the old ones, so burying and exterminating the snails. This campaign affords a classic example of the use of mass organization in health promotion, an approach quite different from that employed in those countries where schistosomiasis remains a scourge. In these countries 'longitudinal campaigns' are headed by 'experts' — often foreign — and utilize chemical or biological techniques. The involvement of the mass of the affected population is quite exceptional. Most people are not aware

Figure 6.3 Weekly road cleaning as part of a 'patriotic mass movement'. (Courtesy
World Health Organization.)

of the need or the means to interrupt the transmission of a disease. Nor are they
encouraged to participate in the appropriate collective activity. China's anti-
schistosomiasis effort is particularly instructive, for it mobilized the population
in several directions: to eradicate snails, to co-operate in case finding and treatment and to improve environmental sanitation.

For example, Yukiang County in Kiangsi Province had been plagued by
schistosomiasis for more than 100 years. About one in five peasants was infected.
In 1953 an anti-schistosomiasis station was set up. The first stage was to publicize
the aim of the campaign, using broadcasting, wall newspapers, blackboards,
exhibitions, lantern-slide shows and dramatic performances. The next stage was
a 'people's war' against the snails. From 1955 to 1957, 20 000 peasants in
Yukiang County filled up old ditches and ponds, dug new ditches and expanded
the area for cultivation by about 90 acres. But even after this, it was still necessary to check for the recurrence of snails as well as controlling water supply and
waste disposal. The people were educated in the treatment of human excreta,
the provision of safe drinking water and improved personal hygiene.[28]

Other parasitic diseases that have been assailed with considerable success are
malaria, filariasis, kala-azar and hookworm. These, together with schistosomiasis,
were singled out for attack during the 1956 National Program for Agricultural
Development when certain health interventions were incorporated with farming
improvements. For example, to combat breeding of mosquitoes, rivers and

canals were widened and straightened to promote fast-flowing water. Stagnant pools in paddy fields were eliminated and larva-eating fish such as carp were introduced.

Another illustration of the integration of agricultural and health interventions is the handling of human excreta. In China this 'night soil' is collected and placed in storage tanks where fermentation of the urine/faeces mixture produces heat which destroys most organisms. The mixture is then placed in a compost pit with vegetable matter and allowed to decompose further before being used as fertilizer.[29] In this way, valuable fertilizer is provided for agriculture, hence ultimately contributing to improved nutrition, and the spread of most faecally-transmitted and water-related diseases is interrupted.

This sort of measure can only be realized on a mass scale by the active participation of people who are conscious of the reasons for it and convinced that it is in their collective interest. It is the mystification of technical knowledge that keeps most people ignorant of the reasons for such health-promoting interventions. This situation is maintained by medical professionalism. It is the structure of privileges and highly unequal social and economic relationships that acts as a barrier to the development of a collective commitment to the community. These obstacles need to be eradicated if the whole population is to act in a collective and self-reliant way to promote health and other activities that combat underdevelopment. This necessarily involves fundamental social change. This is borne out on the one hand by the experiences of China, Cuba and North Vietnam and on the other by the well-documented failures in many different underdeveloped countries to harness the collective potential of the people.

Malaria Control

A good illustration of this point is provided by malaria control programmes. Substantial progress has been made since 1957 when a global malaria eradication programme was started. But the situation remains serious in many areas, with 30 per cent of the world's population living in originally malarious areas being still affected and with a toll of 1½ million deaths each year.[30] In Africa the prevalence of malaria has not been changed very much in the past 20 years and in sub-Saharan Africa about 270 million people still remain exposed and unprotected. Since the early 1970s there has been a resurgence of malaria in Central and South America and in Asia, particularly India where there are now estimated to be over 5 million cases whereas at the peak of the success of the eradication programme there were only 100 000 sufferers.[31]

Why these difficulties and failures? And how does the persisting problem of malaria control illustrate the crucial importance of conscious and active popular participation in the promotion of health?

There are several points in its cycle of transmission at which malaria can be attacked but the most significant impact can be made by an effective attack on the adult mosquito. This is not to discount other methods such as those comprising removal of breeding sites, destruction of mosquito larvae, or protection of the human host by mosquito netting, repellents or regular drug prophylaxis. But by far the most effective method in the control of malaria is reducing the average life-span of the mosquito vector by spraying with insecticide the surfaces on which it is likely to rest after biting. In fact the impetus to the 1957 world-wide eradication programme was the early success achieved with insecticides (*Fig. 6.4*).

It soon became clear, however, that total eradication of the disease was possible only in those countries where malaria was unstable or epidemic as opposed to stable or holoendemic — with the exception of a very few small islands where the elimination of mosquitoes has been relatively easy. In stable areas — which include most African countries and some areas of Asia — the malaria parasite is present in the blood of a high proportion of the population for most of the time and consequently a high level of natural immunity exists so that malaria does not *appear* to be the problem that it actually is. The serious complications, cerebral malaria (affecting the brain) and death, especially affect those whose immunity has not yet developed — infants and small children — or is impaired — the very undernourished and pregnant women.

Because of the much greater difficulties of eradication in stable malarial areas, and, more recently, the development in some areas of insecticide resistance by the mosquitoes, malaria *control* has replaced the earlier objective of eradication.

Figure 6.4 Malaria control team: insecticide spraying seemed to work, but not where the disease was endemic. (Courtesy USIS.)

In control, the aim is the reduction of the amount of malaria so that it no longer constitutes a public health hazard. However, for the success not only of eradication but also of control the initial attack phase must be followed by fastidious surveillance. This involves active participation by the whole of the exposed population in reporting new cases, eliminating breeding sites, ensuring conscientious prophylaxis and, most importantly, assisting in maintaining the effective spraying of a high percentage of dwellings. It is precisely this *continuing control* that failed in projects such as that in India, which for several years consumed massive material and human resources and whose achievements have now been almost reversed. By contrast, all reports from China, where the equivalent geographical and biological conditions prevail in some areas, indicate that malaria control is well established.[32] The success of surveillance and continuing control of malaria depends on those same factors that are essential to the success of other campaigns and health-promoting activities.

Venereal Disease

The eradication of venereal disease (VD) in China provides another example of the indivisibility of progressive social change and health promotion. At the time of liberation, as in many underdeveloped countries today, the prevalence of syphilis was said to be 5 per cent in the cities and 1–3 per cent in the countryside, reaching 10 per cent in the national minority areas.[33] Within a few months of taking power the new government passed a law that closed all brothels and set up special medical boards to treat all prostitutes suffering from VD. These women were given special education and later suitable alternative work, if necessary by moving equipment such as sewing machines into the brothels and converting them into factories. Thus prostitution, which was responsible for much of the spread, was eliminated. In the early 1950s programmes for detection and treatment were co-ordinated on a national scale by the newly formed Central Institute of Dermatology and Venereology.[34] As with other mass campaigns active popular participation was encouraged. Large numbers of paramedical personnel were chosen from the local population and taught, often for no longer than 7 days, to diagnose, treat and report infected individuals. Communist Party cadres, medical people and voluntary workers gained the active participation of the people using film, radio, wall posters and newspapers. The achievements of this campaign and its relationship to social change and political organization are summed up in a Christian Medical Commission publication entitled *Health Care in China:*

'Venereal diseases have now been eliminated as a major threat to the health of the nation. The campaign relied upon a thorough health education program, which took place in a society that was traditionally as reluctant as any to speak openly of health problems related to sexual relations. The educational work was combined with highly organised and effective mobilization of the masses, and a detection and treatment program that seems to have relied as heavily on local community pressure as upon enforced action. It succeeded, in other words, because the people wanted it to succeed, rather than simply through political pressure from above, and it succeeded because of the progressive atmosphere of the times and the new sense of community.'

Health Care in China[35]

Occupational Health

In both Cuba and China the achievements in overcoming the disease pattern of underdevelopment have been phenomenal. But particularly in China the legacy of underdevelopment still remains in some areas and is reflected in health. This is particularly visible in industry.

The Australian doctors who visited recently reported that it was common in heavy industry to see sophisticated machines interspersed with groups of workers hammering or trimming the product. Often processes were semi-automated and required manual assistance from several workers. 'In short', they comment, 'the picture was exactly what one would expect in a developing economy geared to maximum output of manufactured products and with enormous social pressures to meet quotas. Under such circumstances it could be predicted that arrangements for the health and safety of workers may not be so prominent as in Western industry. And this is what our impressions tended to confirm.'

One sight that worried the Australians was women with long pigtails close to machinery. Operators of lathes and grinders often did not have goggles or gloves. Noise levels were high, especially in silk-weaving shops. They were told that deafness was a problem among weavers, but there was no attempt to monitor noise or provide ear muffs.

It was admitted that accidents were frequent. The Shanghai Machine Tool Factory estimated that every 100 working hours there were one or two accidents serious enough to warrant treatment at a clinic. 'A doctor remarked that the relatively high rate of serious accidents was one reason why the Chinese had developed an excellent reputation in the management of limb reimplantation and burns.'

This picture would be familiar enough in the underdeveloped world. But the Australian visitors did come across efforts to improve occupational health which compare favourably with other countries at a similar stage of industrial development. Large factories had a technical safety department to design safer machines and improve the work environment. Each workshop had a safety officer, trained primarily in first aid. The Australians came across several doctors doing rounds on the shop floor 'to detect and deal with health problems and contribute to preventive teaching of workers'.[36]

Immunization

Popular awareness of health issues in China has made possible a programme of immunization far ahead of most underdeveloped countries. When most countries still only had smallpox vaccination on a wide scale, China had immunization nationally against the six immunizable childhood diseases.

In recent years the WHO and UNICEF have launched an international campaign for countries to adopt the Expanded Programme of Immunization (EPI), which also covers the six immunizable diseases. Things have undoubtedly improved in many countries as a result. But still the contrast with China is striking. In most countries coverage in towns may be good but it rapidly deteriorates the further one goes into the rural areas. In Zimbabwe and Mozambique, both countries with a substantial commitment to primary health care, it is estimated that the number of children immunized is 50 per cent and 10 per cent respectively.[37]

In China, on the other hand, Wray recently found that in many districts 100 per cent of children had been immunized and that rates were consistently above 90 per cent.[38] Several visitors have confirmed these high rates of immunization and a group of Australian health workers who recently visited China reported that 'compliance rates of various groups are freely displayed in local clinics, and are very good by Australian figures'.[39]

Similarly in Cuba, immunization programmes covering the whole population were established within a few years of liberation. Moreover, the efficiency of these campaigns contrasts sharply with that which characterizes immunization campaigns in most other underdeveloped countries. Thus 80 per cent of all Cuban children under 15 years of age (over 2 million children) were immunized against poliomyelitis in 11 days in 1962. In 1969 a similar task was accomplished in just 72 hours, and in 1970 it was completed in only 1 day.[400] And in Nicaragua where the popular mobilization for the successful liberation struggle has been maintained and channelled into social programmes, a number of reports indicate immunization rates of almost 100%. In 1984, only 5 years after independence, a total of only 17 measles cases and none of polio were recorded!

Summary

This discussion has attempted to show how the promotion of health is intimately related to the process of ending underdevelopment. This relationship is not confined to the economic level – that is, the freeing of resources which are then available for the improvement of social conditions and thus health. It is most importantly a political relationship, for it is the political dimension – specifically popular pressure – which is both responsible for the reclaiming of resources in the first place and can ensure their direction to areas of pressing social need.

It could be argued that in focusing on specific disease control campaigns and finally on immunization, discussion has strayed into the area of 'the medical contribution'. This would be a justifiable observation, But it should be apparent by now that the division between 'health promotion' and 'the medical contribution' is to some extent an artificial one. The success of the medical contribution — that is the application of medical technology to the benefit of society — is crucially dependent on the political context in which it is applied.

Thus while research and technology for malaria control may be highly advanced, their successful application is hindered by political considerations. Similarly, the unrivalled achievements of China, Cuba and Nicaragua in the field of immunization have depended on the active and conscious participation of their people and on transport, communications and refrigeration facilities, ensuring the effective coverage of most of the population.

Smallpox — a Typical Disease?

Some would question this argument by pointing to the much-heralded success of the smallpox campaign. This dangerous and disfiguring disease has recently been eradicated from the area where it was especially prevalent — India and Bangladesh — countries that have by no means overcome underdevelopment. The World Health Organization has now declared smallpox totally eradicated. But it is misleading to hail the smallpox experience as a path-breaking success, implying that the same could be done for other infectious diseases. Smallpox exhibits certain specific features that are not present in most other infectious diseases and that make it easier to eradicate:

(1) The disease spreads slowly with a long, 2-week incubation period. Almost all cases display symptoms that are easily recognizable to the untrained eye and are infectious only during this period.
(2) There is no carrier state. Smallpox is not highly infectious and only those in contact with active cases are at risk. The chain of infection can be simply broken by surrounding each case with people who are freshly immunized.
(3) There is a safe and effective vaccine that is easily transported, needs no refrigeration and can be inoculated with a simple, cheap and unsterile device — the bifurcated needle (*Fig. 6.5*). Under field conditions more than 95 per cent of those vaccinated are protected for at least a year by a single dose.

These factors add up to a rare instance of a medical intervention which is largely independent of the political and social context in which it is applied.[41] In contrast, there are economic and political constraints to the success of malaria control. These would still operate even if an effective malaria vaccine were available. Malaria can only be recognized by laboratory tests, so it would need universal immunization. This would depend on both an efficient infrastructure and popular co-operation.

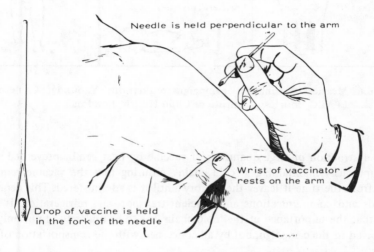

Needle is held perpendicular to the arm

Wrist of vaccinator rests on the arm

Drop of vaccine is held in the fork of the needle

Figure 6.5 Simple technology — the bifurcated needle. (Top, courtesy Oxfam; bottom, TALC, courtesy Institute of Child Health, London.)

The fact that preventive activities depend on political and economic factors is best illustrated by considering measles. The logistic problems of giving measles vaccine are greater than for any other used on a wide scale. A study in Cameroon showed how a measles vaccination campaign can be largely ineffectual (*Fig. 6.6*). Vaccine was given to all children between the ages of 6 months and 6 years — including those who had already suffered from measles.[42] This waste can be effectively reduced by ensuring that careful histories are taken from mothers as to whether their children have already had measles. But this requires locally based health workers who have the confidence of mothers and can convince them of the importance of such information and can recognize local descriptions of this disease.

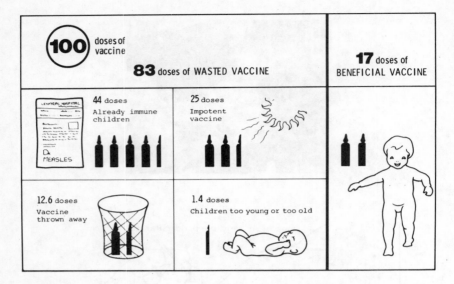

Figure 6.6 Measles vaccination campaign evaluation, Yaoundé, Cameroon. (TALC, courtesy Institute of Child Health, London.)

The destruction of large quantities of vaccine by heat can be prevented only by scrupulously maintaining a 'cold chain', ensuring that the vaccine remains frozen from the time it leaves the factory until it is administered. This depends on roads and communications and efficient transport and refrigeration. It also means that the importance of the 'cold chain' has to be understood not only by all involved in the campaign, but by all concerned with the transportation of the vaccine.

Summary

In Chapter 5 it was argued that Western health care systems are dominated by the medical profession, business interests and the State – in opposition to the people. Far from contributing to *health*, they assist in many ways in maintaining the system that perpetuates underdevelopment and ill health.

To change the nature of the medical contribution means creating a situation in which health care is no longer a commodity owned and purveyed by doctors and other health workers. This can only be by establishing an economic system that differs from the capitalist one, which is based on the generalized production and exchange of commodities for private profit. Indeed, it is only in those countries where the *capitalist system has been overthrown and the economic system is oriented to social need rather than private profit, that the medical contribution has changed fundamentally. Changes in the health sector follow rather than precede fundamental social change.*

Medicine in China

China has a health care system that has developed in a society where fundamental political, economic and social change has occurred. We shall look at China for two reasons. First, because the changes in its health care system have been so innovative and striking; secondly, because the Chinese experience has had a profound impact on thinking about appropriate approaches to health care in the underdeveloped world, especially for those countries which like China have predominantly rural populations.

The impressive improvements in the health of the Chinese population since liberation in 1949 have been discussed. These changes included, in addition to a marked decline in the burden of ill health and death, a change in the population structure. As a result of this and new social conditions the disease pattern itself is becoming more similar to that of a developed country.

The process has many similarities to that which occurred in England and Wales, although the historical, political and economic circumstances are quite different. One reflection of this is that there is much less disparity in health between different social groups in China in comparison with English society at the same stage. Furthermore, the time scale over which these changes occurred has in China's case been telescoped into 25 years.

But what is perhaps most striking is the comparison of China with other underdeveloped countries and especially its neighbour India. Despite India's greater agricultural, mineral and industrial wealth both at independence in 1947 and today, the vast majority of its population is trapped in the morass of under-development. The health of most Indians remains much as it was in colonial days – and as it was in China in 1949.

In the late 1960s and early 1970s when Western visitors were admitted to China, revelations about the achievements in health became irrefutable. Among the most influential visitors were professional health workers, many of whom were greatly impressed by the effective and widespread use of primary health workers, the most numerous of whom were the 'barefoot doctors'. Perhaps because barefoot doctors were such a novelty for the visitors, and perhaps because people in the developed world tend to think that the improvement in their own population's health was because of the medical contribution, the impression has been given that the use of barefoot doctors in large numbers was responsible for the rapidly improved health of the Chinese people. The next section will critically examine this notion and its underlying assumption, that somehow the barefoot doctor experience (and indeed the health sector as a whole) can be isolated from the political and social context in which it emerged.

The Barefoot Doctor

Joshua Horn, an English surgeon who worked in China from 1954 to 1969, observed that in 1949 there were 'probably fewer than 30 000 modern-type doctors to care for the health needs of more than 500 million people, and most of them were concentrated in a few coastal towns. In the vast rural areas, where five out of every six Chinese lived, there were virtually no modern-type doctors and only a sprinkling of traditional doctors'.[43] It has been estimated that at the end of 1966 there were about 150 000 doctors of Western medicine in China — an increase of over 100 000 doctors in less than 20 years,[44] although they still tended to be concentrated in the cities. Another major source of health care personnel, following the Soviet model, were the 'secondary medical schools' which had increased in number to 230 by 1965.[45] In these schools were trained large numbers of assistant doctors, nurses, midwives, pharmacists, and radiology and laboratory technicians. And the forerunners of the 'barefoot doctors' were trained in the late 1950s and the early 1960s in the rural areas around Shanghai.[46]

However, despite these strides and the major successes in controlling such diseases as cholera, plague, smallpox, nutritional diseases, opium addiction and venereal diseases, the health sector remained flawed in a number of ways:

(1) Although 80 per cent of the population lived in the countryside, urban health services still received a disproportionate share of the health resources.
(2) Curative medicine received much more attention in research, teaching and practice than did preventive medicine.
(3) There was increasing concern with 'raising of standards' rather than on the provision of adequate health care to everyone in the society.
(4) Traditional Chinese medicine still had less status and was undervalued compared with 'scientific' medicine.

Other problems included a bureaucratic managerial structure that was unresponsive to criticism from below and valued intellectual work more than manual.

In the late 1960s, under the pressure of popular struggles against growing bureaucratization, the Chinese Communist Party under the leadership of Mao Zedong initiated the Cultural Revolution of 1966-9. In one of the forerunners to the Cultural Revolution Mao singled out the Ministry of Health for criticism:

'Tell the Ministry of Public Health that it only works for 15 per cent of the entire population. Furthermore, this 15 per cent is made up mostly of the privileged. The broad ranks of the peasants cannot obtain medical treatment and also do not receive medicine. The Public Health Ministry is not a people's ministry. It should be called the Urban Public Health Ministry or, the Public Health Ministry of the privileged or even, the Urban Public Health Ministry of the privileged.
'Medical education must be reformed. It is basically useless to study so much. How many years did Hua T'o (a third-century physician) study? How many years did Li Shih-chen of the Ming dynasty study? Medical

education does not require senior middle school students, junior middle school students or graduates of senior elementary school. Three years are enough. The important thing is that they study while practising. This way doctors sent to the countryside will not overrate their own abilities, and they will be better than those doctors who have been cheating the people and better than the witch doctors. In addition, the villages can afford to support them. The more a person studies, the more foolish he becomes. At the present time the system of examination and treatment used in the medical schools is not at all suitable for the countryside. Our method of training doctors is for the cities, even though China has more than 500 million peasants.

'A vast amount of manpower and materials have been diverted from mass work and are being expended in carrying out research on the high-level, complex, and difficult diseases, the so-called pinnacles of medicine. As for the frequently occurring illnesses, the widespread sicknesses, the commonly existing diseases, we pay no heed or very slight heed to their prevention or to finding improved methods of treatment. It is not that we should ignore the pinnacles. It is only that we should devote less men and materials in that direction and devote a greater amount of men and materials to solving the urgent problems of the masses.

'We should keep in the cities those doctors who have been out of school for a year or two and those who are lacking in ability. The remainder should be sent to the countryside.'

See How They Grow[47]

In the Cultural Revolution the health sector was radically reorganized. The Sidels report how higher medical schools began to admit students with work experience and less formal schooling. Usually they were selected by the people they worked with. The curriculum was cut from 6 years to about 3½ years and restructured to emphasize practical aspects and Chinese medicine. Medical research also followed this new emphasis and concentrated far more on common illnesses.

Mobile health teams, which had previously operated on a small scale, now travelled all over the countryside. Urban health workers had to take part in these — not just to bring health care to the rural areas but also to change their own attitudes. At any given time about a third of urban health workers were serving outside the cities. These teams trained peasants who could provide environmental sanitation, health education, preventive medicine, first aid and primary medical care while continuing their farm work. These were the 'barefoot doctors' (*Fig. 6.7*) — so-called because in the rural areas around Shanghai much of the farm work is done barefoot in the rice paddies.

The Sidels report that the barefoot doctor, helped by more junior health aides, has responsibility for disposal and later use of human faeces as fertilizer, purity of drinking water and pest control. Immunization is another important responsibility. He or she is skilled in first aid and can deal with medical emergen-

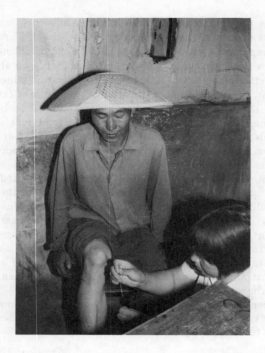

Figure 6.7 The barefoot doctor at work. (Courtesy World Health Organization.)

cies. As the Sidels comment: 'Perhaps most important, his fellow workers know him well and trust him.'

One measure of what the barefoot doctor does is the drugs he or she uses — ranging from herbal remedies to antibiotics, adrenaline, reserpine and other powerful modern drugs. Other powerfully toxic drugs such as digitalis and adrenal corticosteroids are not generally used. The Sidels report: 'Visitors discussing these items with barefoot doctors have been impressed by their remarkably detailed knowledge of the nature of the medications, the indications and contraindications and the possible adverse reactions.' Training takes place for an initial 3 months, often in the commune hospital or county hospital, with subsequent supervision and training to improve their skills. According to the Sidels:

'Barefoot doctors are encouraged to use a wide range of both traditional Chinese and Western medicines and some have become skilled enough to perform limited forms of major surgery. The complex system of supervision and referral appears to ensure that there is adequate control of technical quality as well as rational deployment of manpower and access to services.'

Health Care Delivery System[48]

In a commune visited by Joshua Horn, first-year barefoot doctors had learned to prescribe 40 drugs and to use 50 acupuncture points for common local diseases. By the end of 2 or 3 years' training a barefoot doctor usually can treat about 100 diseases, perform 30 clinical techniques such as blood transfusion and acupuncture and prescribe 80–90 kinds of Chinese and Western medicines. After only 10 months, students can recognize 75 common diseases and 160 acupuncture points.[49]

The Sidels report how in countryside, factories and towns Chinese health care is decentralized as far as possible. 'China's countryside is divided into communes; these are divided into production brigades, which in turn are divided into production teams. The barefoot doctors — now numbering more than a million — usually work in health stations at the production brigade level, but do much of their work, both medical and agricultural, with their fellow members of the production team.' They are selected by their fellow peasants. As with all the peasants in the commune the barefoot doctor's income depends on the total income of the brigade and the number of 'work points' he or she earns. Work points are collected for medical as well as agricultural work.

'Worker doctors' in the factories play a similar role to the barefoot doctor. They are also selected by their fellow workers and receive a short initial training. Continuing supervision comes from the factory doctors. Like the barefoot doctor, the worker doctor does health work part time and is paid a similar wage to other factory workers. The Sidels tell how a similar system operates in the cities:

'The cities of China are divided into districts of several hundred thousand people, the districts are divided into neighbourhoods or "streets" of about 50 000 people, the neighbourhoods are divided into "residents' committees" or "lanes" of about 5000 people, and the residents' committees into "groups" of about 100 people. Services are decentralized to the lowest level at which they can be given. Many social services are provided at the group level by elected group leaders and deputy group leaders. Residents' committees usually have health stations in which the personnel are local housewives or retired people trained for short periods and called "Red Medical Workers". These workers are trained and supervised by the doctors and assistant doctors who work in the clinic or hospital at the neighbourhood level; they can refer patients to those facilities or directly to the district general hospital when necessary.'

Serve The People[50]

This section has focused on the innovations in the Chinese primary health care service. It is not only in this area of the health sector that great advances have been made. Technical achievements such as the successful treatment of widespread severe burns and the implantation of severed limbs are well known, as well as new uses of techniques derived from traditional Chinese medicine. These include acupuncture anaesthesia and the study of a number of traditional herbal medicines in an attempt to isolate and identify their active ingredients and evaluate their effectiveness.[51]

The Lessons of China and Cuba

To return briefly to the questions we posed earlier. Has the use of large numbers of primary health-care workers — and particularly barefoot doctors — been responsible for the unparalleled advances in the health of the Chinese population? And can the barefoot doctor experience be somehow isolated from the social process in which it evolved and, by implication, be successfully transplanted to societies whose political and economic situations are quite different?

The answer to the first has already been implied by the review of the wide range of health-promoting interventions — many from outside the health sector — which were so vigorously and successfully applied in China in the 1950s and 1960s. This was *before* the substantial strengthening of the primary health care services through the barefoot doctor and his or her urban counterparts. Indeed, the early revelations about the vastly improved health of the Chinese population largely pre-dated the widespread increase in primary health care facilities.

As to the second question: the underlying answer rests in the fundamental change in the organization of the Chinese economy from one based on individual production for private profit — much of which was appropriated by foreign exploiters — to an economy predominantly based on collective production for social need. Thus the health service is financed largely by central government whose goal has been to provide a free service for everyone. As well as financing the construction, upkeep and staffing of central hospitals and supporting county hospitals, the national budget finances a medical insurance scheme for all State employees as well as maternity costs and leave for State-employed women. About 25 per cent of the urban population is catered for by State insurance. Finally, government funding for preventive activities includes support for sanitation projects and immunization programmes.

To pay for rural health services, co-operative medical schemes which operate most often at the brigade level have been developed. Each brigade member pays an annual fee, roughly equivalent to one day's wages, and the brigade fund contributes the additional financing. The total sum goes to build and maintain the facilities, cover treatment costs, buy services not available and cover referral payments. There are still instances, however, when fees are collected from the individual for medicines and treatment. In some areas brigade members also support health care actively by building their own facilities, collecting medicinal herbs and making their own medicines.[52] Although this co-operative scheme does bring health care within the reach of most rural people it has not been without its financial difficulties. The financing of communal health is supposed to come from the agricultural base. In bad years the funds available for rural health programmes contract, for agricultural production especially in times of bad weather is often too near subsistence level to provide the necessary surplus.

The political accompaniments of collective production at local level have been a growth in collective participation in decision-making and the widespread development of previously absent local control. This increase in popular participation was a result of the protracted struggle against a common enemy. However it has been seriously distorted by the large degree of bureaucratic control.

In both Cuba and China the revolution was the result of long years of struggle involving large numbers of workers and peasants. But in neither case was the seizure of power achieved by a fully democratic political party accountable to those workers and peasants. And just as importantly, in neither case was the old dictatorial order replaced with new popular democratic structures comparable with, say, the Soviets or workers' councils which ruled for a few brief years after the 1917 revolution in Russia. Cuba and China have this in common but they also have important differences. In China it was a centralized and bureaucratic Communist Party that took power, stifling political opposition from the beginning. In Cuba, the revolutionaries formed a far more amorphous and imaginative movement which may since have assumed many of the features of the ruling caste in Moscow and Peking, but which is still by no means an ossified and unchangeable bureaucracy.

This should not be too surprising. Capitalist countries are ruled by a wide selection of fascist, military and democratic goverments. Post-capitalist societies have shown a similar variety, and socialist democracy is not easy in a hostile, capitalist world. Nevertheless, this cannot excuse the shortcomings that are caused by a lack of political participation. In a paper on health care in Cuba, David Werner summarizes the realities of 'popular power' in a way that could equally be applied to China:

> 'The "power of the poeple" ("*poder popular*") to influence official decision making — while it may function moderately well with regard to *details* in the implementation of established policy — functions poorly if at all with regard to policy making *per se*. It appears that major policies are rarely debated upon by, or even in, the public. They are decided upon by top officials, and then announced.'

> *Health Care in Cuba Today*[53]

The example already quoted of work hazards in China illustrates the point. Given a free hand, what worker would ever vote for unsafe machinery and procedures? Democracy here, as in all cases, should proceed from the assumption that workers themselves are in the best position to decide.

Werner reports how in Cuba this lack of popular control affects the sort of health care the people get. For example, diarrhoea in children, always described as 'gastroenteritis', is invariably a cause for medical intervention. Although mothers of children with diarrhoea are given thorough and impressive education

into the causes of diarrhoea and how to avoid it, they are not told of the importance of giving plenty of fluids to prevent dehydration. One doctor told Werner
why: 'We don't want to tell mothers anything that might lead them to put off
getting adequate medical attention at once'.[54]

This lack of confidence in people's capacity to use knowledge even extends to
the health service. Werner asked one 'health brigadist' what she would do if someone who was stung by a bee went into allergic shock and lost consciousness. She
said that she would take the person to the clinic — which would be too late to
save his or her life. The *brigadista* had not been taught how to combat allergic
shock by injecting adrenaline since that would entail her being allowed to use a
prescriptive medicine.[55]

China's health service relies far more heavily on community-based health
workers who are far more responsive to local needs. But there too there has been
a general reorientation in recent years which seems to be turning the health
service back towards the professionalized Western model. Since the mid-1970s,
and especially since the death of Mao in 1976, there have been factional changes
in the ruling bureaucracy and a drive to 'modernize' in all spheres of life. The
guiding slogan has become the 'four modernizations'. In foreign policy and
technology this has meant increased contact with the West. Mao's old dictum
of 'politics in command' has been abandoned. Instead the experts are in command.[56]

This change has been felt in health care as in all other walks of life. Entrance
to medical school is no longer governed by having a peasant or working-class
background and the right political commitment. Instead candidates have to pass
a written examination — which favours those from the towns with parents who
are literate. The medical curriculum has been standardized and lays increasing
stress on clinical subjects at the expense of the social content of medicine. Staff
at Chengdu Medical College boast that they have cut political education from
324 hours a year to 200.[57] Barefoot doctor training has been standardized too
and examinations instituted. If they pass, barefoot doctors are given preference
at medical college. It is likely that this will encourage many to try to climb the
medical hierarchy and not be satisfied with their part-time role in the countryside. The barefoot doctor seems to be turning into an auxiliary. Or, as the Sidels
ask, is the barefoot doctor being given shoes?[58]

Perhaps most dangerous in the long term is the alienation and cynicism that
infects people when there is a political monopoly that excludes and oppresses
them. In the Soviet Union one way in which it is expressed is by alcoholism, in
China by cigarette smoking, in Cuba by vagrancy and emigration. One young
Cuban, who had been persecuted for saying his school course was rigid and
dogmatic, summed this up for Werner:

'I've been called a counter-Revolutionary, but I'm not. I'd do anything to
make the Revolution really succeed, not just in terms of giving everybody
the same opportunity for housing and clothes and food and medicine, but

in giving everybody the same chance to be himself, to think his own thoughts, and to take part in deciding the things that affect his own life and the lives of everybody. I greatly admire the leaders of the Revolution — Che, Fidel, Camilo. I think they had the same human ideals as I do. I think Fidel still has them. But I think the power has gone to the heads of many in control today. No, I'm not saying they're corrupt. Our leaders are enormously committed to creating the "New Cuba" and the "New Man". But they want to do it their way, to mold the population into their own image, as if people were clay. . . Cuba has accomplished some marvelous things. It has met the basic physical needs of an entire population — something few other countries have done, and certainly no other country as poor as ours. But it has tried to force us all into a common mold — to make us think common thoughts rather than our own.

Health Care in Cuba[59]

A Chinese electrician called Wei Jingsheng said something similar. In response to the leadership's campaign for the 'four moderizations' he produced a wall poster saying that what China needed was a fifth modernization: democracy. He was thrown in jail for his pains.[60]

But China and Cuba do display *some* elements of democratic participation, at least at the grassroots level. This participation is important because it was the tool that was used to break the power of the health professionals. It enabled the previously powerless majority to select responsive primary health care workers and make them accountable to the community. It also ensured that popular health concerns rather than professional competitiveness influenced the type of training and research carried out in the health sector.

This is why attempts to transplant the barefoot doctor experience into countries like Iran in the early 1970s have been unsuccessful.[61] The economic resources are not there to sustain such services. There is no grassroots democracy so the 'barefoot doctor' cannot be selected by the community or be answerable to it. A qualitatively changed health sector depends on fundamental social change and that has not occurred.

Should the concerned health worker therefore abandon health work and become immersed solely in the politics of progressive social change? Clearly this is one possible approach. Indeed, there are several examples of concerned health workers who, after recognizing the roots of ill health, saw their primary roles as agents of social change. Such people include the late presidents of Angola and Chile, Neto and Allende, the Argentinian revolutionary Che Guevara, the Martinican psychiatrist Fanon and President Machel of Mozambique. All these were qualified health workers.

In his *Reminiscences of the Cuban Revolutionary War* Guevara recalls the choice facing the socialist health worker. In the first days of the war the embryonic revolutionary army was ambushed by government troops:

'This was perhaps the first time I was faced with the dilemma of choosing between my dedication to medicine and my duty as a revolutionary soldier. At my feet were a pack full of medicines and a cartridge box; together, they were too heavy to carry. I chose the cartridge box, leaving behind the medicine pack. . . .'

Reminiscences of the Cuban Revolutionary War[62]

But for most of us, partly because of our own class backgrounds and social experience, the understanding and the commitment necessary for such a role is absent. Also some health workers would reasonably argue that their skills gained from lengthy and expensive training should not be wasted but should be applied in the most useful way to prevent and cure disease and to ease suffering.

Is there then a way of ensuring the more effective performance of useful and necessary medical interventions and also assisting in creating the conditions for the promotion of health? In other words, is there a way of both providing effective health care and stimulating within the health sector the growth of popular pressure which could contribute to a movement for progressive social change?

CHANGING THE MEDICAL CONTRIBUTION AS A MEANS TO CHANGING SOCIETY

The present form of the medical contribution in underdeveloped countries and in the developed ones that dominate them has been determined by the influences of the medical profession, business interests and the State, influences that have been overwhelmingly more dominant than that of the people.

Clearly it is necessary to devise some way of changing this relationship of forces. And, if promotion of health is the object, then it is important that such an initiative be part of a wider process aimed at stimulating progressive social change. The essential character of the medical contribution will only be changed when the present economic and political system is transformed. But changes in the balance of power within the health sector — reforms — can help spread popular pressure for thorough-going social transformation. Increasing the power of *people* (i.e. non-professionals) within the health sector is a necessary part of a struggle for popular control of all areas of society.

Possible general approaches in the health sectors in both developed and under-developed countries include weakening the monopoly control of the medical profession over medical knowledge, which allows it to maintain control over health care; fighting for democratic control over health care by representatives of the majority of people rather than appointees of the State; and limiting the excesses of medical business interests by exposing their operations to the scrutiny of the public.

How can health workers do this, while at the same time contributing the caring and medically useful functions for which they have been trained?

The Village Health Worker — a Possible Link?

The high cost of training doctors and the need for improved coverage by official health services lay behind the creation of the auxiliary grade. Although health care for many people in underdeveloped countries has been improved through the use of auxiliaries, their expected contribution has, to a great extent, not materialized. This has been partly because they are often not responsive to the communities they service, move upwards in the medical hierarchy or just drop out altogether. Their social background and 'professional' approach often make them more part of the problem than the solution. Partly as a result of this disappointment and as a response to the success of the barefoot doctor in China, the village health worker (vhw) has been devised.

The vhw performs many of the same tasks as the auxiliary, and indeed in many countries and projects is nothing more than the auxiliary renamed. However, the vhw we are suggesting as a possible link between health care and social change differs fundamentally from the auxiliary. David Werner, who was involved for many years in helping establish a primary health care network in a remote mountainous sector of Mexico, summed up the differences between medical professionals and the vhws he observed in visits to many rural health programmes in Latin America (Table 6.3 overleaf).

The vhw we describe and suggest as a means of increasing the impact of the people within the health sector is distinguished from the auxiliary in the following crucial respects. The vhw:

(1) *Should be selected by the people from among themselves and should be responsible primarily to them, not to the health professionals.*
(2) *Should be part time and able therefore to subsist by performing agricultural or other work, possibly receiving a subsidy from either the local community or the national health service.*
(3) *May be someone who has already been a traditional healer or birth attendant and should preferably be trained in the community in not only curative but also preventive and promotive functions.*

These criteria show what distinguishes the vhw from the professional health worker. There is, nevertheless, considerable variation in the length and content of their training and in the duties performed by vhws, in the many different projects where they have emerged in the past few years.[63]

Table 6.3 **The doctor and the village health worker**

	Conventional doctor (with a few exceptions)	Part-time health worker (at his or her best)
Class background	Usually upper middle class; if not, moves into that group during training	From the peasantry, known for years by those he serves. May have grown up with them
How chosen	By medical school, depending on exam results, and attendance at the 'right' schools. Helped by influential relatives	By the community, for interest, compassion, knowledge of community, ability for hard work. Already a respected person
Preparation	Through institutions, 12–16 years' schooling, 4–6 years' medical training. Training concentrates on physical and technological aspects of medicine, and gives low priority to human, social and political aspects. While lip service is paid to prevention, the successful role models are in curative care	Mainly from experience. Limited key training appropriate to serve all the people in a given community; management and treatment of important diseases; prevention; community health; teaching skills; health care in terms of economic and social realities, and of needs (felt and long-term) both of individuals and of the community; humanization (conscientization) and group dynamics
Qualifications	Highly qualified to diagnose and treat individual cases. Especially qualified to manage uncommon and difficult diseases. Less qualified to deal effectively with the more important diseases of the majority of a given community. Poorly qualified to supervise and teach the part-time health worker. (Well qualified in clinical medicine, but not in other more important aspects of health care: he tends to favour imbalance; wrong priorities)	More qualified than the doctor to deal effectively with the important sicknesses of most of the people. Non-academic qualifications are intimate knowledge of the community, language, customs, attitudes towards sickness and healing, willingness to work and earn at the level of the community where the needs are greatest. Not qualified to diagnose and treat certain difficult and unusual problems: knows those conditions he or she must refer

Orientation	Disease/treatment/individual patient-oriented	Health/community-oriented. Seeks a balance between curative and preventive. (Curative to meet felt needs, preventive to meet real needs)
Primary job interest	The challenging and interesting cases. (Often bored by day-to-day problems)	Helping people resolve their biggest problems, because he is their friend and neighbour, and has grown up with them
Attitude towards the sick	Superior. Treats people as patients. Turns people into 'cases'. Underestimates people's capacity for self-care	On their level. Treats patients as people. Mutual concern and interest because the part-time health worker is village selected
Attitude of the sick towards the doctor or part-time health worker	Hold him in awe. Blind trust (or sometimes distrust)	See him as a friend. Trust him as a person, but feel free to question him
How does he or she use medical knowledge?	Hoards it. Delivers 'services', discourages self-care, keeps patients dependent	Shares it. Encourages informed self-care, helps the sick and family to understand and manage their problems
Accessibility	Often inaccessible, especially to poor. Preferential treatment of 'haves' over 'have-nots'. Does some charity work	Very accessible. Lives right in the village. Low charges for services. Treats everyone equally and as *his or her* equal
Consideration for economic factors	Overcharges. Expects disproportionately high earnings. Feels it is his or her God-given right to live in luxury while others are hungry. Often prescribes unnecessarily costly drugs. Overprescribes	Reasonable charges. Takes the person's economic position into account. Content (or resigned) to live at economic level of his people. Prescribes only useful drugs. Considers cost. Encourages effective home remedies

Table 6.3 *(continued)*

	Conventional doctor *(with a few exceptions)*	Part-time health worker *(at his or her best)*
Relative permanence	At most spends 1–2 years in a rural area and then moves to the city. Even if he or she wishes to stay, family pressures and schooling of children force a return to the city	A permanent member of the community in which he or she has grown up. Unlikely to leave as he or she is a respected and successful farmer
Continuity of care	Can't follow up cases because doesn't live in the isolated areas. Is not motivated and is too busy	Visits neighbours in their homes to make sure they get better and assists them to learn how not to get sick again
Cost-effectiveness	Too expensive ever to meet medical needs of the poor, unless used as an auxiliary resource for problems not readily managed by the part-time health-worker	Low cost both of training and of practice. Higher effectiveness than doctor in coping with primary problems. In childhood great frequency of common conditions
Resource requirements	Hospital or health centre. Depends on expensive, hard-to-get equipment, and a large subservient staff, to work at full potential	Works out of home or simple structure. Requires little equipment or drugs which have to be imported. People are the main resource

Present role	On top. Directs the health team. Manages all kinds of medical problems easy or complex. Often over-burdened with easily treated or preventable illness, his or her excuse for poor coverage	On the bottom. Often given minimal responsibility, especially in medicine. Regarded as an auxiliary (lackey) to the physician
Impact on the community	Relatively low (in part negative). Sustains class differences, and mystification of medicine. Depends on expensive outside resources. Drains resources of poor (money)	Potentially high. Awakening of people to cope more effectively with health needs, human needs, and ultimately human rights. Helps community to use resources more effectively, and to develop new resources
Appropriate (future?) role	On tap (not on top). Functions as an auxiliary to the part-time health worker, helping to teach him more medical skills and attending referrals at this worker's request (the 2–3 per cent of cases that are beyond the part-time health worker's limits). He is an equal member of the health team	Recognized as the key member of the health team, but remains responsible to the health committee. Assumes leadership of health care activities in his village, but relies on advice, support and referral assistance from the doctor when he needs it. He is the doctor's equal, although his earnings remain in line with those of his fellow villagers

Source: From David Werner (1977) *Village Health Worker, Lackey or Liberator?* Hesperian Foundation; adapted by David C. Morley and Margaret Woodland (1979), *See How They Grow*, Macmillan, London, pp. 210–14 (Chapter 2, reference 7)

Qualifications

The qualifications held by vhws vary in different situations. In Jamkhed, South India, for example, many of the vhws are illiterate while in Chimaltenango, Guatemala, the average level of education of the health promoters is the third grade of elementary school. In the former case vhws are selected by the village council and in the latter by the community health committee. In China, bare-foot doctors – and even medical students – are chosen by the people whom they will serve. Political orientation and a desire to 'serve the people' are import-ant in their selection.

The vhw may be a traditional healer. This is probably the most useful way of integrating traditional medicine with Western techniques. But the criterion for selection must be the same as for anyone else: the trust of the people. As one commentator remarks, talking of Mozambique: 'The currently fashionable debate in international health and academic circles tends to make the romantic assumption that if practitioners are "traditional" then they are "of the people". In an idealised classless rural community, the *curandeiro* is envisaged as a kind of people's doctor, standing ready for instant transformation into a village health worker acceptable to all.'[64]

In reality peasant communities – as well as townships and shanty towns – have considerable divisions of wealth and status and traditional healers may be drawn from among the richest or the poorest. In colonial Mozambique *curan-deiros* were sometimes even visited by the Portuguese and could charge high fees which placed them in the same social position as the Western doctor. Traditional doctors, like their Western counterparts, will tend to guard their medical know-ledge jealously. They have been drawn into the money economy and have a commodity to sell like anyone else. To that extent they are a conservative influence.

However, when traditional practitioners are willing to depart from their own brand of 'medical professionalism' they will often have the confidence of the people they serve and will be suitable candidates for vhw.

Training and tasks

There is a great variation in the length and depth of training given to vhws. Vhws at Maradi in Niger are given 10 days of mainly practical training at the nearest dispensary or health centre. The courses cover: general health concepts, emergen-cies and referrals, epidemic diseases, health education (including nutrition), elementary health care, environmental sanitation and some record keeping.

The aim, according to a group of visitors from the World Health Organization, 'is to prevent diseases and wounds from becoming complicated while awaiting referral of the patient and to refer patients who cannot be treated with the elementary means available to better equipped health facilities in time. Village health workers are also intended to improve environmental health conditions in the village.' Each year the vhws go on a 10-day refresher course, where they will be introduced to new items such as the treatment of malnutrition and the preparation of weaning foods.

The vhws have proved able to treat most common diseases such as malaria and diarrhoea, superficial wounds and some skin and eye diseases. They receive small quantities of drugs: an antiseptic, eye drops and chloroquine, aspirin and guanidine tablets. Some are distributed free of charge, some sold to patients at low prices and the money used to re-stock the pharmacy.[65]

Gonashasthaya Kendra (Peoples' Health Centre), a rural health and community development project at Savar, Bangladesh, gives an illustration of the use of vhws which differs somewhat from the Niger example. Dr Chowdhury, who initiated the project, and his co-workers recognize that 'ideally, the candidates for the training as primary health workers should be proposed and selected by their own community'. This, however, has not proved advisable in Bangladesh where 'a few wealthy families control resources and public opinion' and thus community selection would 'lead to one of two extremes: either if the job carried prestige and adequate remuneration, the sons, daughters or other relatives of the few better-off families would be chosen, or, if the job was considered beneath their dignity it would be left to the poor and uneducated who would carry little authority for the duties they would be intended to perform'. Therefore selection has been left with the staff of the health centre who 'apply criteria which refer to the necessity for impartiality of service, intimate communication with the common people of the village and dedication rather than insisting on scholastic achievements although basic literacy seems to be a definite necessity'.[66]

The basic training period lasts for 6 months to 1 year, depending on the time of arrival. All paramedics (the term used in this project for primary health workers) perform agricultural labour daily as part of their duties and undergo an apprenticeship and attend evening classes given by senior paramedics and doctors. Before a paramedic is finally selected the villagers where s/he has been working are consulted. If strong objections are voiced then these will outweigh even strong recommendations from other sections of the project. The paramedics' duties towards their villagers are:

'(1) Registration of births and deaths.
(2) Identification of pregnant women and establishing at-risk cases.
(3) Identification of at-risk children (defined as children with either malnutrition and diarrhoea, or children with chronic diarrhoea and night blindness).
(4) Immunization: BCG for children under 1; DPT (diphtheria, pertussis, tetanus) for children under 5; tetanus toxoid for women of childbearing age to combat neonatal tetanus; primary smallpox for all.
(5) Nutrition and health education.
(6) Treatment of diarrhoea and dysentery, teaching preparation and use of oral rehydration fluid, treatment of scabies.
(7) Motivation, supply and follow-up of FP (family planning) clients.

These services are carried out entirely by house to house visits by the para-medics. Usually, paramedics are assisted by a particular contact person in each village, be it just a talkative woman with time on her hands who likes to be the first to impart all the local gossip, or one of the 20 dais (village midwife) who have taken some training in hygiene and FP at the Centre and receive a small monthly remuneration for their ongoing services. The trained paramedic is often accompanied by a trainee colleague on his/her village round. Trainees assist in all their tasks and in clinic work for 6 months before being given the responsibility of their own.'

Organization, Supervision and Evaluation of Primary Health Workers[66]

After completing 6 months of basic training some of the female primary health workers are trained for 2 months in performing female sterilization by tying the Fallopian tubes (*Fig. 6.8*). By December 1977 a total of 2826 such tubectomies had been performed, 2351 of these by 21 different paramedics, 475 by 12 doctors and three medical students. 'Among the cases operated by doctors and medical students, 42 (8.8%) experienced wound infections; among the cases operated by paramedics 133 (5.6%) became infected.'[66] There have been only three tubectomy failures; two of them had been performed by paramedics and the other by a doctor.

The achievements of some primary health care services based on vhws are impressive so far. In Gonashasthaya Kendra the successes have been ascertained by surveys of sample villages and by more random observation of disease inci-dence. There has been a dramatic decrease in the incidence of severe diarrhoea with dehydration. This has probably been a result of extensive teaching of oral

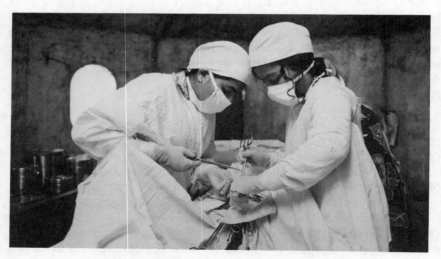

Figure 6.8   Village health workers at Gonashasthaya Kendra perform a steriliza-tion operation. (Courtesy Oxfam.)

fluid therapy to mothers of small children, who institute this treatment at the first sign of diarrhoea (*see* below). Since childhood diarrhoea remains the commonest cause of death in Bangladesh, this success in preventing serious cases may well account for the lower overall death rate in the project area – 12 per 1000 as opposed to the national average of 17 per 1000. There has also been a great decrease in scabies and other skin diseases. And care of at-risk pregnant women (e.g. with pre-eclampsia) ensured nil maternal deaths in the area during 1977.[67]

Appropriate Technology

The success of the smallpox vaccination campaign depended not only on the specific characteristics of the disease which rendered it relatively easy to control, but also on two important operational factors. The first was the use of local *vaccination agents* who, although not medically qualified, were familiar with the local geography, conditions and customs. Secondly, the bifurcated needle developed for smallpox vaccination is a good example of *appropriate technology*: cheap, simple, effective and easily understood and applied by 'front-line' health workers such as the vhw, or even by individuals in the community.

The development of appropriate technologies for health and health care is an important element in the successful operation of a primary health care scheme. Below are a few selected examples of important appropriate technologies that have been developed to facilitate the sort of *integrated* – curative, preventive and promotive – primary health care that vhws can help spread.

Curative

Rehydration

Diarrhoea is a common cause of ill health and death in underdeveloped countries. Dehydration with its accompanying blood and tissue electrolyte imbalance is dangerous and progresses rapidly in the young child. Therefore in underdeveloped countries where poor transport means considerable delays in reaching a health care facility, conditions such as diarrhoea often result in death or require expensive, complex treatment in sophisticated hospitals.

Early treatment is therefore essential both to prevent deaths and to abort potentially serious attacks. This means treatment at or very close to home. To correct dehydration a simple but practical method of rehydrating children (and adults) has been developed, using the knowledge that glucose absorption by the small bowel remains intact in diarrhoea. The glucose is linked to sodium absorption in such a way that a molecule of salt, and with it water, are absorbed by a mechanism that is independent of the process of excretion of electrolyte stimulated by the infecting organism (*Fig. 6.9*).[68]

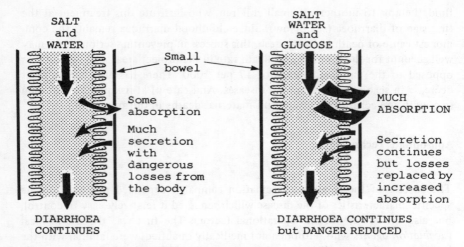

Figure 6.9 Replacement of fluids by mouth in acute diarrhoea. (TALC, courtesy
Institute of Child Health, London.)

Thus a simple hydration kit (*Fig. 6.10*) for the use of the vhw *and easily
taught to mothers* consists of a calabash (or other local container) and lid to
hold water, a mug, spoon and tins of salt and sugar. A thumb and two-finger
pinch of salt and a four-finger scoop of sugar (*Fig. 6.11*) plus a squeeze of orange
juice (to provide potassium) dissolved in 1 pint (0.61) of clean water make an
adequate rehydration solution.

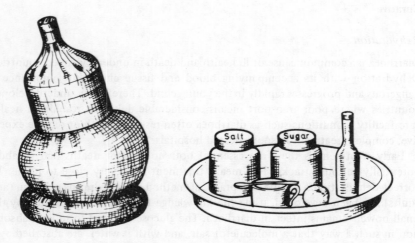

Figure 6.10 A simple rehydration kit. (TALC, courtesy Institute of Child
Health, London.)

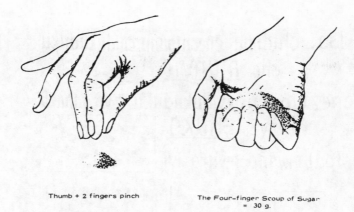

Thumb + 2 fingers pinch   The Four-finger Scoup of Sugar
                                            = 30 g.

Figure 6.11   An adequate solution for rehydration. (TALC, courtesy Institute of Child Health, London.)

A more reliable local method has been devised in Zimbabwe using 750 ml water in an empty oil bottle or 'Mazoe Crush' bottle – this is a fruit drink that is sold everywhere. A half a level teaspoon of salt and six level teaspoons of sugar are mixed in. (Fig. 6.12). The advantage of this technique over the use of packaged rehydration salts is that all the items are readily available and identifiable by parents. This rehydration method is reinforced in Zimbabwe by its use even in hospitals so that its promotion in the community is not regarded as 'second-best' treatment. It could be repeated elsewhere using a similar local container. [69]

The use of such prompt oral rehydration to prevent severe dehydration in diarrhoea has been shown to be successful. It was reported from the Jamkhed (South India) project in 1977 that 'as a result of this teaching' (to village mothers) 'and the presence of these village health workers in the 18 villages they serve, over the last 4 years there have been no dehydrated children brought to the hospital. All the dehydrated children now come from villages not yet served by such workers'.[70]

Drugs and Medical Equipment

The common conditions causing ill health and death in underdeveloped countries are limited in number and have a fairly uniform pattern, as is also the case in the developed world. For this reason, and for reasons of expense, the World Health Organization has recently developed a recommended drug list for underdeveloped countries.

This comprises a reduction in the number of items stocked and restriction of the use of proprietary names. Further, it is increasingly accepted that a relatively short list of basic drugs and equipment will adequately equip most primary health care units.[71]

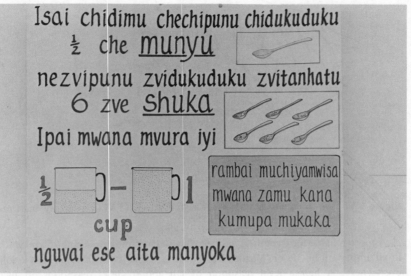

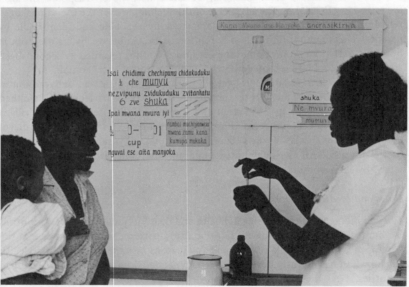

Figure 6.12   Zimbabwe – a nurse instructs a mother in the preparation of sugar-salt solution in Harare Central Hospital's rehydration unit (courtesy Ministry of Health, Zimbabwe).

In most primary health care schemes involving vhws these workers are equipped with a kit (often portable) containing carefully chosen, basic, yet effective, drugs (and, if refrigeration is available in the village, vaccines) as well as basic equipment. This enables them to treat early the majority of episodes of ill health in the community.

In the Jamkhed project the vhws are taught to use seven drugs and seven vaccines. The vhw in *Fig. 6.13* was asked detailed questions by a paediatrician who spoke Maharati, the local language, on how she would use these medicines and in what way they could be dangerous.[72] She gave very satisfactory answers, although she is illiterate, as are most of her colleagues. In the project at Chimaltenango in Guatemala, health promoters whose formal education ended on average after the third grade of elementary school are trained in group sessions once a week for a year. Then they are permitted to dispense medicines and give injections. A study made by an American university's department of community medicine 'showed a low percentage of error in treatment, about 9%'.[73]

Figure 6.13 Village health workers weigh a child in Jamkhed. (Courtesy Oxfam.)

Preventive

Malaria

In many underdeveloped countries malaria is a major cause of low birth weight. This can stunt mental potential and increase susceptibility to infection in infancy. It is particularly dangerous to population groups whose immunity is impaired – children under the age of 5 and pregnant women. Protection from the effects of malaria without impairing the development of natural immunity can be easily achieved by suppression with a low dose of an antimalarial drug such as pyrimethamine.[74] In malarious areas, vhws, in addition to administering drugs to treat common illnesses, can prevent severe malaria by prescribing a suppressant to at-risk groups.

Measuring Undernutrition

Protein–energy malnutrition is, as we have seen, probably the most widespread health problem in underdeveloped countries and the basis for the severity of most infectious diseases. The road-to-health chart is a very useful simple technology to assess undernutrition and monitor growth in all children.[75] Unfortunately, such charts and reliable weighing scales are often not available nor will the precise age of many children be known. It is known, however, that the circumference of the upper arm changes very little between the ages of 1 and 5 years, the most critical period in terms of nutrition and growth (*Fig. 6.14*). Using this observation, a simple technology has been devised to measure the arm circumference. It is usually called a Shakir strip after the man who suggested it:

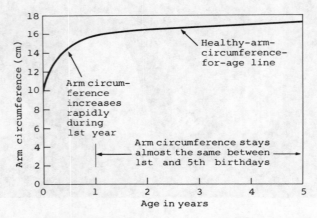

Figure 6.14 An arm-circumference-for-age graph. (TALC, courtesy Institute of Child Health, London.)

'The Shakir strip is usually a piece of plastic or string, but any material can be used which is flexible and does not stretch. The strip is marked with numbers (as on a tape measure) or sometimes with colours. There is scope for ingenuity, depending on local conditions. For example, old used X-ray film has been found to be particularly satisfactory. It is soaked in caustic soda solution for 24 hours after which the emulsion can be simply rubbed off. The clear film is scratched with a sharp point and the spaces between the scratches are coloured, using felt-tipped pens which are not water soluble. The zones are coloured red (for danger when the arm circumference is below 12.5 cm), orange or yellow (between 12.5 cm and 13.5 cm) and green (for good nutritional status above 13.5 cm). Such a strip is shown in the figure below [*Fig. 6.15*]. Research has shown that no advantage is gained by measuring the mid-point in the upper arm as long as the health worker takes care to use the strip in what he considers to be the mid-point between the acromion and olecranon.'

See How They Grow[76]

If a child's upper arm circumference is in the danger zone, a note must be put on the child's road-to-health chart or one must be started if the child does not have one. The Shakir strip can be used by a part-time health worker and easily taught to senior schoolchildren and other members of the community. This is a good example of the application of scientific data to the development of a simple technology which can be used by a community to assess a major health problem in its midst.

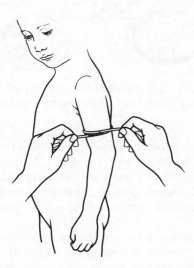

Figure 6.15 Using the Shakir strip. (TALC, courtesy Institute of Child Health, London.)

Nutrition Supplementation and Rehabilitation

Until fairly recently major emphasis was placed on deficiency of dietary protein
in causing protein–energy malnutrition. Indeed, still today it is widely taught
that kwashiorkor is caused by a diet seriously deficient in protein but adequate
in carbohydrate, whereas marasmus is attributed to deficiency in all constituents,
but particularly carbohydrates. Recent research, however, has shown that the
primary problem in both these as well as in the much more common 'moderate
undernutrition' is *energy deficiency*. For, when the total food intake is inadequate in energy terms, protein is not utilized for replacement and formation
of body cells, i.e. growth, but to satisfy energy needs.

The main reason for this energy deficit is that in underdeveloped countries
the unrefined cereal or root staple has a low energy density, particularly when
cooked in water as is usually the case (*Fig. 6.16*).[77] Typically, such diets have a
crude energy density of $1 \, \text{kcal} \, \text{g}^{-1}$ ($4.2 \, \text{kJ} \, \text{g}^{-1}$). This means that a 1-year-old
child would have to eat a kilogram of food each day simply to meet his or her

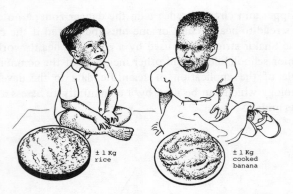

Figure 6.16 The volume a child has to eat to consume 1000 calories. (TALC,
courtesy Institute of Child Health, London.)

energy needs. This is between two and three times the amount that an English
child of the same age has to eat (*Fig. 6.17*).[78] Insufficient energy intake by
many children is therefore a result of this bulky nature of foods and the low
frequency of meals — which is related amongst other things to the sheer volume
of time-consuming work performed by most mothers in underdeveloped
countries.

This new thinking has profound implications for nutrition supplementation
and rehabilitation. It is now increasingly accepted that energy-rich foods — fats
and oils — are more important in correcting undernutrition than the previously
stressed protein. For, in addition to being useless as 'tissue building food' until
energy requirements have been satisfied, protein provides less energy per unit

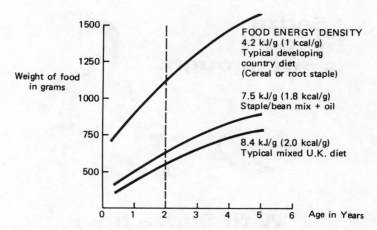

Figure 6.17 Britain and the underdeveloped world -- food intakes in relation to
energy density. (TALC, courtesy Institute of Child Health, London.)

weight than fat or oil. In fact, both protein and carbohydrate provide
$4 \, \text{kcal g}^{-1}$ $(16.7 \, \text{kJ g}^{-1})$ as opposed to fat or oil which provides $9 \, \text{kcal g}^{-1}$
$(37.6 \, \text{kJ g}^{-1})$. Therefore by adding high-energy food such as oil to a cooked
staple, the volume of food that the young child needs to eat can be greatly
reduced to an amount similar to that eaten by the European child. Furthermore,
the oil also has an important softening effect on the food. This means that less
water needs to be added in order to provide a food of soft consistency that can
easily be eaten by a young child. Oil also has the important function of keeping
food soft as it cools. 'A porridge or pap which is liquid at 45 °C rapidly becomes
thicker as it cools towards 35 °C. The addition of oil dramatically reduces this
rate of change throughout the temperature range at which food is normally
eaten, so that even at 35 °C the food remains in a liquid state easily eaten by the
young child.'[79]

Hence the strategy in nutrition supplementation and rehabilitation should be
to increase the energy content of the local staple/legume (bean, groundnut) mix
by the addition of oil or fat. Vegetable oil is generally cheaper and easier to use
than animal fat. A simple formula for the composition of the optimal nutritional
mix would be:

staple : legume
  3   1   plus small volume of oil

This general approach to the prevention of undernutrition among young children
is easily transmitted to the vhw who in turn can teach mothers to 'measure, mix
and mash' the child's portion of food and serve it in 'more meals'.

One place where this approach has been successfully adopted is Zimbabwe.
At the end of the country's long liberation war it faced severe food shortages.

Figure 6.18 Zimbabwe – encouraging local high-energy foods. (Courtesy Children's Supplementary Feeding Programme.)

Particularly badly affected were 1–5 year olds in the outlying areas. A Ministry of Health survey found that in some areas four out of every five children in this age group were undernourished. Altogether more than 150 000 were at risk.

A feeding programme was planned in response to this need. In the worst-affected areas, children at risk were identified using the mid-upper arm circumference measure. Any child whose arm measured less than 13 cm was included in the programme. The choice of supplementary meal was based on the understanding that it is lack of energy in the diet, not lack of protein, that underlies protein–energy malnutrition. It was also more appropriate to use food that could be grown locally rather than artificial foods. Hence maize meal, beans, groundnuts and oil were chosen. The quantities used were calculated to provide each child with approximately 530 kcal (2.2 MJ) daily and about 16 g protein. Feeding points were chosen close to people's homes and there the mothers of the affected children prepared a meal each day to be eaten on the spot. A poster was produced to reinforce the message that high-energy foods that could be grown locally would provide a nutritious meal for young children if they were added to the staple of maize meal porridge. Thus the relief and rehabilitation exercise contained an educational message (Fig. 6.18).

But education is only a small part of the solution to undernutrition. It will have an effect only when the necessary resources are available — above all land. In Zimbabwe one of the problems is that although groundnuts are grown almost everywhere, most of those produced in the peasant areas are sold. Economic pressures have turned a potentially nutritious food into a cash crop. Some communities approached the organizers of the Children's Supplementary Feeding Programme and asked for groundnut seed to enable them to grow the crop for their children. The Ministry of Health gave seed and fertilizer to those communities that were organized to cultivate collectively on a plot next to a pre-school centre. If production was collective it was far less likely that the crop would be sold. Unfortunately the harvest from these plots was badly hit by drought, but where it succeeded it became an important part of the daily meal given to children attending the pre-school centre.

This, then, was a community-based programme which incorporated rehabilitation (through supplementary feeding), prevention (nutritional education) and promotion (collective food production).[80] It provides a good example of a comprehensive (or integrated) approach to malnutrition within a primary health care framework.

Promotive

Water Development

Water-related illnesses are important in underdeveloped countries, particularly where undernutrition is also common. Most faecal–oral disease is not classically water-borne but is, together with diseases of the eyes and skin, water-washed, and it is this group of diseases that causes most serious illness and death in underdeveloped countries, especially among young children. These water-washed infections and infestations are reduced by increasing the quantity, availability and reliability of the water supply, almost irrespective of its quality. It is clearly of little use to increase the quantity of water available if it is not going to be used. Here the distance to the water source is crucial. Research has confirmed the importance of providing plenty of water close to peoples' dwellings. Therefore, water supply programmes should, most importantly, aim at bringing abundant quantities of water near to or into dwellings throughout the year.[81]

While the most desirable means of supplying water would be to pipe it into or near to peoples' homes, this is not economically feasible in many underdeveloped countries, at least for the poor who constitute the majority of their populations. It is for the most part only in those underdeveloped countries where thorough-going economic and social changes have occurred that the problem of water provision has been effectively addressed. However, for other underdeveloped countries certain technologies have been devised to maximize, within these financial limits, the potential for water provision. It is not possible here to detail the many different designs for water systems since these depend on such considerations as local sources, physical, geological and climatic factors and population distribution. It is, however, the proper construction, operation and maintenance of water facilities that are usually the determining factors in the success or otherwise of a water system. And it has been shown that partici-pation by the community at all stages of the development and maintenance of a water system is crucial to its acceptability and successful functioning.[82]

Sanitation

A few simple modifications to the basic idea of a pit latrine make an effective and cheap way of disposing of human faeces. A ventilation pipe extracts smells from inside the latrine so that flies are attracted to the top of the pipe rather than the latrine itself. The upward flow of air in the ventilation pipe is encourag-ed by the warmth from the fermentation process and the suction of wind passing the top. The pipe is painted black so that it absorbs heat, thus warming the air which then rises. A fly trap at the top prevents flies from entering and leaving it. Flies that do get into the pit through the entrance are attracted to the light at the top of the pipe and so try to get out that way rather than through the squat-ting plate, which is in darkness. There are a number of different designs for this sort of ventilated pit latrine. Probably the best one has a spiral superstructure, no door and is made of mud wattle and thatch at a cost of under US$10. This design gives the user total privacy.[83]

In one Central American country women would not use the public latrines, even though they had had health education. It was found that the women were shy to use them because the walls did not cover their feet.[84] Like all appropriate technology, latrines cannot be imposed from outside. They must be designed and built in consultation with the people who will use them.

Effects of Primary Health Care Systems Involving the vhw

Health workers based in the community can extend useful and necessary health care to very many people who would otherwise derive little benefit from the health services. And their potential to prevent and cure disease and ease suffering can be greatly enhanced through the use of simple technologies.

However, it is the less immediately obvious effects of the use of vhws that are perhaps more important. It is through the vhw that a shift can be made in the balance of forces determining the nature of the medical contribution. What follows is a discussion of how the vhw can weaken the monopoly control of the professionals over medical knowledge, represent the interests of the people rather than act as a representative of the medical profession and the State, and help limit the usually unbridled operations of medical business interests. Finally, and most importantly, how can the vhw contribute towards a movement for progressive social change and thus the promotion of health?

Chapter 5 examined some of the reasons behind the relative lack of success of the auxiliary. They are biased to curative care, often unresponsive to the health needs of their communities, and tend to drop out or migrate upwards. These features result from a number of factors, many of which are connected with them being regarded as professionals, responsible in the end to the doctor 'above' them. The vhw, by contrast, is *selected* by the people through a representative body such as a village council or committee and is answerable to them, not the medical profession. Furthermore, the qualities sought in selection – if it is left to the community – are often not academic, but rather are compassion or trustworthiness. This relationship is further strengthened by the fact that the vhw while working part time as a health worker is partly *subsidized* by his or her community either in cash or in kind. These mechanisms of selection and payment help to ensure control over the vhw by the community rather than by the medical profession and such a health worker is more likely than the auxiliary to remain responsive to his or her community's health needs. If, moreover, the selection of a vhw results in the nomination of a woman, or member of a social or racial minority (for example, a *harijan* or 'untouchable' in India) then not only is the domination of the medical profession challenged, but so also are some of society's frequently unquestioned hierarchies which help maintain existing power arrangements and inequities.

In Pimpalgaon, a small village near Jamkhed in India, Lalanbai Kadam was chosen as a community health worker (CHW) in 1973. She is a *harijan* and a widow – about the lowest of the low in Indian society. With the other *harijans* she lived outside the main village and was not allowed to go into the temple or into other people's homes. At the training sessions she heard new, unfamiliar ideas about equality. When she had finished her training Lalanbai had acquired a new confidence. She attended public meetings – previously all-male occasions – and went to people's homes to make suggestions about health promotion. Then a young man in the village died of a cerebral haemorrhage. People felt that it was a curse on them for allowing a *harijan* widow into their homes. Many wanted to chase Lalanbai out. She stayed in the village but stopped her health work.

'That same day, one of the village women went into labour, and Lalanbai was called. She refused to attend the delivery, however, on the grounds that the villagers had asked her to stop working. Mothers brought children for medicine, but were obliged to go to the CHW in the next village because Lalanbai could no longer dispense medicine. Within 2 days the whole village realized the importance of the role played in their lives by Lalanbai. She was presented with a petition pleading her to resume her health work. Finally, after a public apology for the shabby way she had been treated,

Lalanbai was formally reinstated. A total transformation in the attitude of the whole community to this poor "outcaste" widow had taken place.'

Practising Health for All[85]

The *training* and range of skills acquired by vhws are important in increasing both their effectiveness and their potential to act as catalysts for social change. Young and illiterate health workers in Bangladesh quite competently perform abdominal operations, and illiterate vhws in South India dispense drugs with great precision. David Werner in his survey quoted earlier found that:

'. . . the skills which village health workers actually performed varied enormously from program to program. In some, local health workers with minimal formal education were able to perform with remarkable competence a wide variety of skills embracing both curative and preventive medicine as well as agricultural extension, village co-operatives and other aspects of community education and mobilization. In other programs — often those sponsored by Health Departments — village workers were permitted to do discouragingly little. Safeguarding the medical profession's monopoly on curative medicine by using the standard argument that prevention is more important than cure (which it may be to us but clearly is not to a mother when her child is sick) instructors often taught these health workers fewer medical skills than many villagers had already mastered for themselves. This sometimes so reduced the people's respect for their health worker that he (or usually she) became less effective, even in preventive measures.'

The Village Health Worker[86]

Equipping vhws with curative skills does not simply provide health care to more people, more quickly and more cheaply, but it also gives the vhw greater credibility in the eyes of the community. Moreover, if through education and the use of appropriate technologies the vhw is able to equip members of the community with both an understanding of and skills in health care then the medical profession's monopoly of knowledge and expertise is challenged. The power of the doctor, often based on mystification, can in this way be weakened. And if certain appropriate health technologies become widely incorporated into health practice their use can stimulate a critical approach to the expanding range of inappropriately sophisticated, expensive and mystifying technologies. Perhaps the best example is that of drugs. Encouragement of the use of a standardized, short list of inexpensive drugs (known by their own name, not a trade name) can reduce bad prescribing practices and begin to undermine the operations of the drugs industry.

Perhaps the most important potential of the vhw is his or her ability to stimulate the growth of a movement for progressive social change. David Werner puts it thus:

'If the village health worker is taught a respectable range of skills, if he is encouraged to think, to take initiative and to keep learning on his own, if his judgement is respected, if his limits are determined by what he knows and can do, if his supervision is supportive and educational, chances are he will work with energy and dedication, will make a major contribution to his community and will win his people's confidence and love. His example will serve as a role model to his neighbors, that they too can learn new skills and assume new responsibilities, that self-improvement is possible. Thus the village health worker becomes an internal agent-of-change, not only for health care, but for the awakening of his people to their human potential. . . and ultimately to their human rights.'

The Village Health Worker[87]

The vhw's special qualification to play this role as an agent of social change derives from two sources, both equally important. First, he or she, through the mechanisms of selection and payment, is more likely to represent truly the people rather than the medical profession or the State. Secondly, the vhw can endorse people's ideas that the sources of their ill health are rooted in their living and working conditions. For, contrary to many misguided assumptions, sociologists have established that 'villagers do know that disease is caused by food (or its lack), bad sanitation and hygiene, poor water supplies, excessive work, and bodily weakness'. If the vhw is regarded by the community as *their* representative and respected for his or her responsiveness and health care capabilities, his or her effect in confirming the community's understanding of the sources of its ill health has a powerful potential.

A good example of this potential of the vhw is given by David Werner, considering the possible approaches to diarrhoea:

'Each year millions of peasant children die of diarrhoea. We tend to agree that most of these deaths could be prevented. Yet diarrhoea remains the number one killer of infants in Latin America and much of the developing world. Does this mean our so-called "preventive" measures are merely palliative? At what point in the chain of causes which makes death from diarrhoea a global problem . . . are we coming to grips with the real underlying cause. Do we do it. . .
'. . . by preventing some deaths through treatment of diarrhoea?
'. . . by trying to interrupt the infectious cycle through construction of latrines and water systems?
'. . . by reducing high risk from diarrhoea through better nutrition?
'. . . by curbing land tenure inequities through land reform?
'Land reform comes closest to the real problem. But the peasantry is oppressed by far more inequities than those of land tenure. Both causing and perpetuating these crushing inequities looms the existing power structure: local, national, foreign and multinational. It includes political, commercial, and religious power groups as well as the legal profession and the medical establishment. In short, it includes . . . ourselves . . . .

'Where, then, should prevention begin? Beyond doubt, anything we can do to minimize the inequities perpetuated by the existing power structure will do far more to reduce high infant mortality than all our conventional preventive measures put together. We should, perhaps, carry on with our latrine-building rituals, nutrition centers and agricultural extension projects. But let's stop calling it prevention. We are still only treating symptoms. And unless we are very careful, we may even be making the underlying problem worse . . . through increasing dependency on outside aid, technology and control.

'But this need not be the case. *If* the building of latrines brings people together and helps them look ahead, *if* a nutrition center is built and run by the community and fosters self-reliance, and *if* agricultural extension, rather than imposing outside technology encourages internal growth of the people toward more effective understanding and use of their land, their potentials and their rights . . . then, and only then, do latrines, nutrition centers and so-called extension work begin to deal with the real causes of preventable sickness and death.

'This is where the village health worker comes in. It doesn't matter much if he spends more time treating diarrhoea than building latrines. Both are merely palliative in view of the larger problem. What matters is that he gets his people working together.

'Yes, the most important role of the village health worker *is* preventive. But preventive in the fullest sense, in the sense that he help put an end to oppressive inequities, in the sense that he help his people, as individuals and as a community, liberate themselves not only from outside exploitation and oppression, but from their own short-sightedness, futility and greed.

'The chief role of the village health worker, at his best, is that of liberator.'

The Village Health Worker[88]

And this ideal, the liberating potential of the vhw, the people's representative, is quite the opposite of the negative potential of many health professionals who transmit the idea that social conditions causing ill health are natural and unchangeable and that any solutions rest with the individual.

Problems of Schemes Involving vhws

While some schemes involving vhws have so far proved very successful, the majority of attempts have failed. There are many reasons for these failures, some specific to certain schemes, but others common to many. Here are some more general problems that vhw schemes often encounter.

Economic

We noted that in China in bad agricultural years the funds available for rural health programmes contract. In those countries with poor rural (and urban) communities and where production is mostly on an individual basis, frequently no surplus exists from which a vhw can be subsidized. Further, it is often the case that on occasions when a surplus has been created, poor people understandably choose to invest in items that they regard as more vital than health care. In fact they often choose to invest in land or farming implements which undoubtedly contribute more to their health than does health care. In Mozambique, for example, where a new category of primary health worker, the *agente polivalente*, has been developed, who work in communal villages, 'in some villages there has been too little communal production to support the Agente, who then has to spend most of his/her time producing essential food for the family.'[89] Most of the successful vhw schemes either receive substantial funding from a nongovernmental — usually foreign — agency, or, after an initial period of reliance on such outside funding, workable health insurance schemes have been devised. But whether such schemes can be sustained depends in the long term on how much surplus is produced within the community and who controls it.

Political

Popular, democratic control is a crucial ingredient for the success of a primary health care scheme based on the vhw. In communities where most people are poor and often illiterate the tendency is for the better-off and better-educated to dominate. This has implications for both the selection and control of the community-based health worker. Indeed, it calls into question the very notion 'community', a term that is very freely used and suggests a homogeneous, conflict-free group of people. This is almost never the case. It is not simply that villagers as a homogeneous whole are divided from professionals. Villagers are also divided among themselves. Hence Professor Banerji of the Jawaharlal Nehru University in India is quite doubtful of that country's new community health worker programme. He says that the social structure of Indian villages is such that rich landlords will usurp the benefits of the new health workers and allow very little to trickle down to those who most need their health. He notes that as village councils are dominated by the rich landlords, the selection of health workers by the community merely means selection dominated by local vested interests.[90]

The example of Botswana shows how economic constraints can combine with political problems, and how government control can reinforce local divisions of status. Since 1970 Botswana has been training a type of village health worker called the Family Welfare Educator (FWE). The idea was that they should come from the poorer families and be paid to compensate them for their loss of earnings. But by placing them on a local government salary scale the Ministry of Health has turned them into low-level bureaucrats, auxiliaries by another name, and they have become financially and socially removed from their 'communities'.

Now the government is using the FWEs to popularize a new tribal land grazing policy which will worsen the inequality in rural incomes. FWEs increasingly describe the poor as 'difficult to understand' and 'lazy' and 'uncooperative'. It has been remarked:

> 'The FWE has been lifted out of her background of poverty and coopted into the bureaucratic structure. She has lost her ability to identify with the people she is meant to serve and, therefore, her effectiveness as a vehicle for change. The FWEs who have retained their original identity are finding life difficult. The result of the FWE status promotion has been to take the political element out of rural health care, the cost of it being a decrease in its effectiveness.'

Ideas and Action[91]

It is in situations where the old order and power structures are being contested or have recently been overthrown that primary health care schemes involving vhws are likely to take root. In such conditions popular participation in decisions and collective rather than individual self-reliance grow and flourish. Zimbabwe, which won its independence after a long war of liberation, provides a good example. Sister Margaret Nhariwa runs one vhw scheme at Bondolfi mission in Victoria Province. She explains the origins of the scheme:

> 'It's the people who organise themselves and do the choosing; but the way it sprung up in this area was through the party (Zimbabwe African National Union). Not that the party officials came in and said let's do this. But you see during the war there weren't any clinics from here to Mozambique and the people were sick. So the comrades took it on themselves to do public health. In this area they were doing public health thoroughly, going visiting homes. When the ceasefire came, these people had just taken people on to help them. And some of the women were working in the bush hospital treating the guerrillas. Then the people realised that when the guerrillas went they would lose what they had gained in public health. So they approached myself and Father Graf (Father Superior of Bondolfi Mission) and they asked if we could train these people.'

The area was well organized into one political district with 28 branches. Each branch had a committee of sixteen who were popularly elected. Of these sixteen, two were responsible for community health matters. Training commenced for these 56 branch health leaders in May 1980. Their six months' training included both theory and practical work, the latter being done after planning with their committees. Due to this project's popularity and increasing community demands, the people decided to have an unpaid vhw for every one to three villages, resulting in the selection and training of 293 vhws, thirty-five being from other districts.

In the words of Sister Nhariwa, vhws at Bondolfi (*Fig. 6.19*) are:

Figure 6.19 Bondolfi — 'people choose whom they trust'. (Courtesy Lesley McIntyre.)

'. . . selected by the people, voted in. People choose whom they trust, whom they say is kind and whom they say is able and is committed to the community. I think it is the commitment that is looked for much these days, at least in this area.'

It is important to note that selection and control of these workers was at village and branch level with ongoing popular participation.

The vhws are not paid:

'When they were trained it was a fighting sort of affair. There were party committees and one doesn't get paid for belonging to a party. So they came in this knowledge that they were doing this for their own people, for the development of their country and that they had been chosen by the people.'

From this project sprang up a Development Committee, organized by the people themselves.

'Its aim is to co-ordinate the work done by vhws in different areas, and organize other development projects that are not directly involved with health. . . . The formation of the Development Committee has strengthened the health projects and intensified these projects making the people more determined than ever.'

But this Zimbabwean scheme is in danger of collapse. Between 1980 and 1982 District Councils were established. These local government structures are composed of councillors elected by each ward and are served by a full-time, salaried, District Administrator. Such full-time, local government officials are responsible to the Ministry of Local Government and Town Planning, and councillors, although elected every few years, are neither answerable to their electorate on a day-to-day basis nor subject to recall (voting out of office) for unsatisfactory performance. With this extension of the central State to local level, and through the resources available to District Councils, the popular committees have become in many instances marginalized.

In late 1981, the government began training vhws. The aim is to have about 12 000 vhws countrywide. By early 1984 about 3000 had been trained. These vhws are supposed to be selected by their own communities in consultation with the District Council. In some areas there *is* real popular involvement in the selection of these workers, this being done at ward level (although many wards would be far too large to allow effective popular participation). However, in many areas it is done by the District Council and in some it is acknowledged that 'there is some nepotism; councillors choose their wives and friends. . . .' Further, the payment of these vhws ($33 per month) is made by District Councils from a grant received from central government. This means, inevitably, that vhws are subjectively responsible to their District Councils rather than the villagers they serve, although with widespread rural poverty it would be impossible for many communities to fund their own vhws. (This possibility depends on the success of the government's rural development strategy for the majority — the poor peasants and workers.)

When the government scheme was set up, ten of the Bondolfi vhws who were working at the time were taken on and trained.

The government vhws receive a more formal training, spending more time in the clinic or hospital, than the Bondolfi vhws. Because of their much lower concentration in the population they have to cover a larger area than the Bondolfi women. This means that, in effect, most of them are full-time workers. The Bondolfi scheme, although still functioning, by mid-1984 involved only about 100 vhws. There are a number of reasons for this drop-out, but as one local vhw organizer said:

'When the government scheme started, and some were paid $33 a month, others stopped working because they were not paid.'[92]

Here again a general political problem, similar to the Botswana example above, is illustrated. In contrast to the original village health workers, who were directly selected by meetings in the villages and answerable to the local people, the government vhws are chosen and paid by the District Councils. These bodies are democratic — but only in a distant and representative way. If responsibility for the vhw is delegated to a remote State structure, then the crucial element of popular mobilization is missing. The vhw is no longer directly answerable to the poor people of the community and cannot be recalled by them. He or she becomes just another health service employee — more appropriate perhaps, but still answerable to an outside body. Once again, 'communities' are not homogeneous units but are divided into conflicting classes and interest groups. It will always tend to be the richer and more powerful sections of the community who dominate local government bodies which are only infrequently re-elected. Direct control over vhws at the grassroots level is the best way of ensuring that they are answerable to the poor.

Disagreements can develop between local communities and health ministries even when the government is a new one thrown up by popular struggle. This has happened in Nicaragua. David Werner reports how in 1982, when a team of vhws from Mexico was in Nicaragua conducting a training course on teaching methods, the local health *brigadistas* and *multiplicadores* suddenly got orders from the Ministry of Health to change their plans and interrupt the course.

'The health workers replied that they would always seriously consider suggestions from the Ministry of Health, but that they took their orders from the community. The community committee for the defense of the revolution voted not to interrupt the course, and the health workers followed the community's request.'

'The fact that the local community and its *brigadistas* had the courage to stand up to the health ministry is impressive. The fact that the Ministry of Health accepted their decision is even more encouraging and gives hope that in time the Ministry of Health will move towards decentralized control and a stronger community base.'

David Werner[93]

So there is no need to be totally negative about the possibilities contained within vhw schemes, although their lasting success is dependent on the presence of certain economic and political prerequisites.

One sobering index of a primary health scheme's potential to threaten the status quo was given recently in the Gonoshasthaya Kendra Project in Bangladesh. Here one of the best health workers was killed by an assassin hired by some of the local quack doctors and politicians.[94] Clearly they perceived this paramedic to be more than just another health worker. He seemed to them to be a threat, an agent of social change.

References

1. Victor W. Sidel and Ruth Sidel (1975). The health care delivery system of the People's Republic of China. In Kenneth W. Newell (ed.), *Health by the People*, World Health Organization, Geneva, p. 1.

2. *Ibid.*, pp. 10–11.
3. S. Gomez *et al.* (1975). Cuba's health care system. In V. Djukanovic and E. P. Mach (eds), *Alternative Approaches to Meeting Basic Health Needs in Developing Countries*, World Health Organization, Geneva, pp. 56–7.
4. V. Sidel and R. Sidel (1975). The health care delivery system of the People's Republic of China, p. 11.
5. Vicente Navarro (1972). Health, health services and health planning in Cuba. *International Journal of Health Services*, **2**, 403–4.
6. Edgar Snow (1961), *Red China Today: The Other Side of the River*, New York, Random House; quoted in Joe D. Wray (1974), *Health and Nutritional Factors in Early Childhood Development in the People's Republic of China*, mimeo.
7. Wray (1974). *Health and Nutritional Factors*, p. 65.
8. Navarro (1972). *International Journal of Health Services,* **2**, 401.
9. Wray (1974). *Health and Nutritional Factors*, p. 9.
10. V. Sidel and R. Sidel (1975). The health care delivery system of the People's Republic of China, p. 26; Chabot (1976), The Chinese system of health care, *Tropical and Geographical Medicine*, **28**, S115.
11. A. F. Tejeiro Fernandez (1975). The National Health System in Cuba. In Newell (ed.), *Health by the People*, p. 26.
12. Chabot (1976). The Chinese system of health care. *Tropical and Geographical Medicine,* **28**, S115.
13. J. S. Horn (1969). *Away with All Pests*, Monthly Review Press, New York, p. 125.
14. Chabot (1976). The Chinese system of health care. *Tropical and Geographical Medicine,* **28**, S115.
15. *New Doctor*, September 1977, p. 16.
16. Navarro (1972). *International Journal of Health Services,* **2**, 4010.
17. *World Health Statistics Report* (1973). Vol. **26**, World Health Organization, Geneva.
18. G. F. White (1974). Domestic water supply: right or good. In *Human Rights in Health*, Ciba Foundation Symposium 23 (New Series), Elsevier, Amsterdam.
19. Tejeiro Fernandez (1975). The National Health System in Cuba.
20. Ray Wylie (ed.) (1972). *China, the Peasant Revolution*, WSCF Books, London, p. 68.
21. *New Doctor*, September 1977, p. 15.
22. Wray (1974). *Health and Nutritional Factors*, p. 50.
23. Wylie (ed.) (1972). *China, the Peasant Revolution*, p. 68.
24. *Health Care in China* (1974). Christian Medical Commission (CMC), Geneva, p. 58.
25. Wylie (ed.) (1972). *China, the Peasant Revolution*, p. 68.
26. Chabot (1976). The Chinese system of health care. *Tropical and Geographical Medicine,* **28**, S115.

27. V. Sidel and R. Sidel (1974). *Serve the People, Observations on Medicine in the People's Republic of China*, Beacon Press, Boston, pp. 104–5.
28. *New Doctor*, September 1977, p. 14.
29. *Ibid.*, p. 15.
30. L. Bruce-Chwatt and Professor Gillette in a symposium on malaria at the London School of Hygiene and Tropical Medicine, 13 May 1976.
31. *Ibid.*
32. Chabot (1976). The Chinese system of health care, *Tropical and Geographical Medicine*, **28**, S115; CMC, *Health Care in China*, p. 65; World Bank, *Health Sector Policy Paper*, 1975, p. 40.
33. CMC, *Health Care in China*, pp. 60–1; V. Sidel and R. Sidel, *Serve the People*, p. 160.
34. CMC, *Health Care in China*, p. 62.
35. *Ibid.*, p. 63.
36. *New Doctor*, September 1977, pp. 18–19.
37. Informal estimate by Zimbabwean health officials.
38. Wray (1974). *Health and Nutritional Factors*, p. 47.
39. *New Doctor*, September 1977, p. 17.
40. Navarro (1972). *International Journal of Health Services*, **2**, 401; personal communication with Nicaraguan health officials, January 1985.
41. S. I. Music (1976). *Smallpox Eradication in Bangladesh — Reflections of an Epidemiologist*, dissertation presented for the Academic Diploma in Tropical Public Health, London School of Hygiene and Tropical Medicine, June, pp. 3–4.
42. A. M. McBean, O. S. Foster, K. L. Herrman and C. Gateff. Evaluation of a mass measles immunisation campaign in Yaoundé, Cameroon. *Transactions of the Royal Society of Tropical Medicine and Hygiene*, **70**, 206.
43. J. S. Horn (1971). Experiments in expanding the rural health service in People's China. In *Teamwork for World Health*, Ciba Foundation Blueprint, J. & A. Churchill, London, p. 77.
44. V. Sidel and R. Sidel, *Serve the People*, p. 23.
45. *Ibid.*, p. 24.
46. *Ibid.*, p. 79.
47. Mao Zedong, 1965 directive, quoted in Morley and Woodland (1979). *See How They Grow*, Macmillan, London, p. 12.
48. V. Sidel and R. Sidel (1975). *The Health Care Delivery System of the People's Republic of China*, pp. 7–8.
49. For an expansion of this *see* Horn, *Away with All Pests*.
50. V. Sidel and R. Sidel (1974). *Serve the People*.
51. CMC, *Health Care in China*.
52. *See* for example S. Rifkin (1978). Politics of barefoot medicine. *Lancet*, i, 34.
53. David Werner (1979). *Health Care in Cuba Today: A Model Service or a Means of Social Control — or Both?* The Hesperian Foundation, p. 28.

54. *Ibid.*, p. 20.
55. *Ibid.*, p. 22.
56. S. B. Rifkin (1980). Health care in China: the experts take command. *Tropical Doctor*, **10**, 86–90.
57. *Ibid.*
58. V. W. Sidel and R. Sidel (1983). *The Health of China – Current Conflicts in Medical and Human Services for One Billion People*, Zed, London; *see* also J. E. Rohde, Health for all in China: principles and relevance for other countries, In D. Morley, J. Rohde and G. Williams (eds), *Practising Health for All*, Oxford University Press.
59. Werner, *Health Care in Cuba Today*, pp. 33–4.
60. *Socialist Challenge*, 12 April 1979; *Amnesty International Report 1979*, p. 89.
61. H. A. Ronaghy and S. Solter (1974). Is the Chinese 'barefoot doctor' exportable to Iran? *Lancet*, **i**, 1331.
62. Che Guevara (1969). *Reminiscences of the Cuban Revolutionary War*, Pelican, London, pp. 43–4.
63. Some of these projects are described in Newell (ed.) (1975). *Health by the People* (World Health Organization, Geneva), and more recently in Morley *et al.* (eds) (1983), *Practising Health for All*, Oxford University Press.
64. Carol Barker (1983). A long-term check. *Africa Now*, January.
65. Djukanovic and Mach (eds) (1975). *Alternative Approaches*, pp. 80–1.
66. Z. Chowdhury (1976). *Organisation, Supervision and Evaluation of Primary Health Workers*, mimeo, presented at the IXth International Conference on Health Education in Ottawa, Canada, 29 August–3 September.
67. *Ibid.*, p. 10.
68. Morley and Woodland (1979). *See How They Grow*, Macmillan, London, pp. 97–110.
69. Isabel de Zoysa, *Diarrhoea and Oral Rehydration in Zimbabwe*, mimeo.
70. *See* TALC slide set on Jamkhed.
71. M. Segall (1975). *Pharmaceuticals and Health Planning in Developing Countries*, IDS Communication 119, University of Sussex; also *The Selection of Essential Drugs*, (1975) Technical Report Series 615, World Health Organization, Geneva.
72. *See* TALC slide set on Jamkhed.
73. Quoted in Carroll Behrhorst (1975). The Chimaltenango Development Project in Guatemala. In Newell (ed.) *Health by the People*, p. 39.
74. Morley (1973). *Paediatric Priorities in the Developing World*, Butterworths, London, pp. 252–4.
75. For a description of the background and use of the growth chart *see* Morley and Woodland (1979). *See How They Grow*, Macmillan, London.
76. *Ibid.*, pp. 176–81.
77. J. C. Waterlow and P. R. Payne. The protein gap. *Nature (Lond.)*, **258**, 113–17.

78. D. Morley and P. Harman (1979). The Third World: What the child eats and how this has changed our approach to malnutrition. *Nursing Times*, 1 November.
79. *Ibid.*
80. David Sanders (1983). Community participation in integrated health care. In *Major Maternal and Child Health Problems in Zimbabwe*, Maternal and Child Health Workshop, 20-30 June, Zimbabwe Ministry of Health; *see* also Richard Carver (1982), Letter from Zimbabwe, *Times Health Supplement*, 19 March.
81. For a discussion of this *see* R. Feachem, M. McGarry and D. Mara (1978). *Water, Wastes and Health in Hot Climates*, John Wiley and Sons, London, pp. 12-13.
82. *See* Safe Water — Essential to Health, *Contact* 52, CMC, Geneva, August 1979.
83. Piers Cross and Neil Andersson. Sanitation and rural development, *Ideas and Action*, No 145.
84. Piers Cross (1983). Latrines and Liberation. *Journal of Social Change and Development*, May 1983, Harare.
85. Maitrayee Muhhopadhyay (1983). Human development through primary health care: case studies, from India. In Morley *et al.* (eds) *Practising Health for All*, Oxford University Press, p. 138.
86. David Werner (1977). *The Village Health Worker — Lackey or Liberator?* Hesperian Foundation, pp. 3-4.
87. *Ibid.*, p. 5.
88. *Ibid.*, p. 8.
89. *People's Power in Mozambique, Angola and Guinea-Bissau* (1979), **13**, Spring, 41.
90. Quoted in Anil Agarwal (1978). New strategy for world health. *New Scientist*, 22 June.
91. Skimming the skills off the poor, *Ideas and Action*, No. 145.
92. Drawn from an interview of Sr Nhawira by Richard Carver (1980) and David Sanders (1984). The state and popular organization, *Journal on Social Change and Development*, No. 8, Harare, p. 8.
93. David Werner (1983). Health workers and their relationship to the social and political dimensions of a country. Paper presented at the seminar *Working Towards Health Care in an Independent Namibia*, London, 10 October.
94. Agarwal (1978). New strategy for world health. *New Scientist*, 22 June.

7   Postscript: The Role of the Concerned Health Worker

The role of the foreign expert in conventional development ideology is simple — and quite ineffective in bringing about social change. He or she has multiple constraints of culture, language, training and perhaps social class which make it difficult to work directly with the poor. It will always be easier to work with a narrow, westernized medical stratum who speak the same language as the visiting health worker — literally and metaphorically. They will have read the right WHO publications and be able to use the right rhetoric. Their intentions will frequently be the best. But, as we have discussed, they do not challenge the social order that produces ill health and usually do little to improve the health of the people.

The concerned health worker from abroad who wants to adopt a different approach faces severe difficulties. He or she will always be an outsider and always have the aura of the visiting expert — however much he or she may want to identify with the people and their struggles. These problems are best borne in mind.

The concerned health worker may arrive in a village, overflowing with brilliant, progressive ideas for preventive or promotive schemes, only to discover that the inhabitants are obstinately uninterested in them. Maybe they want a health worker who hands out drugs, not one who builds latrines. And the visiting health worker must accept that more often than not the villagers are right; they have lived there all their lives and are most likely to know what their health needs are. But, most difficult of all, the concerned health worker must be a servant to the people even when they are mistaken. Society will only be transformed and ill health combatted when people are free to make their own mistakes.

Health in the underdeveloped world can only come by the actions of the people themselves — it will not come from outside. But that does not mean that the concerned health worker has nothing to offer. She or he may have skills to put at the people's disposal.

The village health worker can act as a link not just between medicine and progressive social change, but also between the outside health worker and the people. But often a genuine vhw scheme will not exist. If this is the case, and if the concerned health worker is in a position to help bring such a scheme into

218

existence, then it is worth trying to identify areas and communities that show a degree of popular self-organization. This is an important ingredient in the success of vhw schemes.

If the possibility of working with a vhw exists, concerned health workers should show themselves to be in solidarity with the people by putting their skills at the disposal of those acting with the poorest and most powerless. Encouraging democratic control over the provision of health care and showing oneself to be willing to submit to the will of the majority, rather than asserting one's professional autonomy, is crucially important. And its accompaniment, constantly attempting to demystify medical knowledge and practice, is the second principle. These principles, demystification and democratization, form the basis of any attempt to change the medical contribution. This is no light responsibility. If there is resistance by groups who see their interests threatened, then it will usually be the vhw or members of the community who will be most vulnerable to reprisal.

The concerned health worker may, however, find him/herself working in an institutional framework — hospital, clinic or university — where there are no possibilities of working with the poorest and most powerless through a vhw. In this situation, while the language and cultural constraints are often less, the possibilities for 'becoming more part of the solution than part of the problem' are undoubtedly more limited. However, the same principles of democratization and demystification still apply, although the institutional framework may make it more difficult to break through the professional barrier. It is none the less possible and important to begin by breaking down hierarchical divisions *within* such institutions, and through this to build up a group of health workers who could help develop this process. Democratization, usually fiercely resisted by higher level health workers, is fundamental.

There are very few data in underdeveloped countries, especially for the poorest sections of society. It is always useful to collect statistics relating to disease. This material, particularly if coupled with information about relevant social conditions, can be of great value to those struggling for improved health.

A good example of this sort of work is provided by the Health Information Centre, a group of concerned health workers from Johannesburg, South Africa. Their experience is worth looking at because it shows some of the things that concerned health workers can do in towns, whereas the last chapter concentrated almost exclusively on the rural parts of underdeveloped countries. The Health Information Centre began in 1982 with a pilot project around sewerage in an East Rand township. The Centre trained a group of local people to do a survey and gave some informal seminars on the relationship between health and housing, including sewerage. The group managed to get the authorities to fill in a ditch which had sewerage water in it where children used to play. The Centre concluded: 'The interaction was very constructive for the group and ultimately the issue of funeral services (there is a lot of corruption around funerals which are a very costly affair) was taken up: a local committee of street representatives was formed and an embryonic residents' association is consolidating, thus meeting the initial objectives of the activists in that area.[1]

The Health Information Centre has held a series of weekend seminars on health and safety with shop stewards and branch organizers from the Metal and Allied Workers' Union. It is dealing with requests for advice from a number of unions on new government health and safety legislation. The Centre's most tangible achievement came when the Commercial, Catering and Allied Workers' Union (CCAWUSA) came to it for information on maternity rights. Between them the union and the Centre drew up a draft maternity agreement. The health workers provided information to back up each demand and photocopies of articles from medical journals to give 'expert' weight to the arguments. CCAWUSA has won the maternity rights it was seeking from one major company, OK Bazaars, and is negotiating with others. A number of other unions have approached the Health Information Centre to provide similar advice.

Finally, the concerned health worker can document the activities of medical business interests such as the drug and medical equipment companies and baby-foods industry. Also, since non-medical business interests, such as the agricultural multinationals, are often far more significant in undermining people's health, then it is important to work *outside* the health sector too in gathering and publicizing such information. For example, in the case of the hazardous Asbesco plant in Dar es Salaam, cited in Chapter 3, it was a foreign researcher who took samples of the factory's waste for analysis and undermined the management's claim that the operation was safe.[2]

In Developed Countries

The multinational corporation is the embodiment of the increasing economic interdependence of the world's nation states. Chapter 3 showed how this has been accompanied by an increasing political interdependence, so that events in one area of the world almost inevitably have an effect in other countries, especially if there is a historical, often colonial, link. The internationalization of the medical contribution has had similar economic, political and ideological effects in many different parts of the world. Struggles in the developed world may affect the ability of people to be healthy not only in that country but also in other developed countries and in the underdeveloped world. Hence the concerned health worker, unconstrained by cultural and language barriers in his/her own country, can almost certainly contribute more significantly there both to the development of more appropriate health care and to the movement for progessive social change. The effects of any actions are unlikely to be limited within the particular country in which they first started.

The most effective demonstration of international concern over the multinationals and their effect on health has been the campaign against 'The Baby Killer'. Campaigning bodies and *ad hoc* committees in many countries, with an unprecedented degree of international co-ordination, have forced the baby-food companies to accept a code of practice directly against their own interest and to the benefit of the health of children in the underdeveloped world. An important part in this campaign was played by returning health workers monitoring the use of baby foods and documenting their experiences. The companies may have already violated the agreement on countless occasions, but that only indicates that the process of monitoring and campaigning must continue. Such methods could be repeated in many other cases: drug dumping and the sale of inappropriate medical equipment, for example.

In many developed countries, and particularly in Britain today, the most important instances of popular pressure within the health sector are the struggles against the cuts in health care — and other areas of public expenditure. The reduction in public expenditure is taking place in the context of the latest of capitalism's recurrent crises. Because the provision of universal health care free at the time of need is seen as a real gain by most people in Britain, and because the NHS does indeed satisfy certain health care needs, these struggles are being supported by most progressive health workers. Often they have involved not only health workers from the institutions threatened with closure but also other health workers, and perhaps more importantly non-health workers. This has sometimes meant the difference between defeat and victory, such as when the miners supported anti-closure struggles in South Wales. However, many of these struggles have been finally defeated when senior members of the medical profession withdrew their support under pressure from the State, which often included offers of hospital beds elsewhere. This confirms in a different way the crucial necessity for democratic control by the majority of people — 'patients' and other health workers — over those who continue to monopolize responsibility for the care of their health.

However, movements against cuts in public expenditure, self-care groups and international solidarity campaigns, as well as other struggles in areas related to the health sector, have another possible political dimension. For it is in popular movements such as these that people are most self-confident and susceptible to new ideas. It is here that the concerned health worker and all those concerned with health could introduce the issue of how ill health is produced in our societies — and how any struggle for progressive social change and against the old order and power structures is also a struggle for health.

References

1. This, and the other material on the Health Information Centre's activities, is drawn from a mimeographed report produced by the Centre, dated 1 August 1983.
2. Deadly dust threatens workers. *Africa Now*, February 1983.

Selected Bibliography, Films and Addresses

Below is a list of books which might be useful to anyone who wants to pursue the issues discussed in this book. Many of them are referred to in the text but this is not an exhaustive list of sources. The lists of films and organizations later is intended as an aid to further discussion and action.

These lists first appeared in a shorter form in *Links*, the magazine of Third World First.

BIBLIOGRAPHY

Bull, D. *A Growing Problem*, Oxfam, 1982.

Campaign Against Depo-Provera. *Depo-Provera: a Report*, 1981

Chetley, A. *The Baby Killer Scandal*, War on Want, 1979.

Counter Information Service. *The NHS − Condition Critical*, Report No. 26, CIS/Pluto.

Craig, M. *Office Workers' Survival Handbook − a Guide to Fighting Health Hazards in the Office*, BSSRS, 1981.

Doyal, L. *The Political Economy of Health*, Pluto, 1979.

Ebrahim, G. J. *Child Health in a Changing Environment*, Macmillan, 1982.

Ehrenreich, J. (ed.). *The Cultural Crisis in Modern Medicine*, Monthly Review Press, 1978.

Food and Agriculture Organisation (FAO). *Rural Health*. Special issue of *Ideas and Action*, FAO, Rome.

Garner, L. *The NHS − Your Money or Your Life*, Pelican, 1979.

George, S. *How The Other Half Dies*, Pelican, 1976.

Gilmurray, J., Riddell, R. and Sanders, D. The struggle for health. *From Rhodesia to Zimbabwe*, No. 7, CIIR, 1979.

Heller, T. *Poor Health, Rich Profits*, Spokesman, 1977.

Horn, J. *Away with All Pests − an English Surgeon in People's China 1954−1969*, Monthly Review Press, New York, 1969.

Human Health Committee. *A Barefoot Doctor's Manual*, Routledge-Kegan-Paul, 1978.

Iliffe, S. *The NHS: A Picture of Health?* Lawrence and Wishart, 1983.

Illich, I. *Limits to Medicine — Medical Nemesis: the Expropriation of Health*, Pelican, 1976.

Kinnersley, P. *Hazards of Work: How to Fight Them*, Pluto, 1974.

Le Serve, A. and Doyle, M. (eds). *Health and Safety in the Workplace*, WEA, 1980.

Lobstein, T. and the Namibia Support Committee Health Collective (eds). *Namibia: Reclaiming the People's Health*, AON Publications, London, 1984.

MacKeith, N. (ed.). *New Women's Self-Health Handbook*, Virago, 1978. Virago, 1978.

Mass, B. *Population Target*, Zed, 1976.

Medewar, C. *Insult or Injury?* Social Audit, 1979.

Melrose, D. *The Great Health Robbery*, Oxfam, 1981.

Melrose, D. *Bitter Pills*, Oxfam, 1982.

Morley, D. C. and Woodland, M. *See How They Grow*, Macmillan, 1979.

Morley, D. C., Rohde, J. and Williams, G. (eds). *Practising Health for All*, Oxford University Press, 1983.

Muller, M. *The Baby Killer*, War on Want, 1974.

Muller, M. *Tomorrow's Epidemic*, War on Want, 1978.

Muller, M. *The Health of Nations*, Faber, 1982.

National Union of Agricultural and Allied Workers (now TGWU). *Not One Minute Longer! The 245-T dossier*, 1980.

Navarro, V. *Medicine Under Capitalism*, Croom Helm, 1976.

Parish, P. *Medicines: A Guide for Everybody*, Penguin, 1976.

Phillips, A. and Rakusan, J. (eds). *Our Bodies, Our Selves*, Penguin, 1978.

Politics of Health Group. *Food and Profit — It Makes You Sick*, 1980.

Politics of Health Group/Fightback. *Going Private: The Case Against Private Medicine*, 1981.

Politics of Health Group. *Cuts and the NHS — What Are We Fighting For?*

Revolutionary Practice in Health. *People's Power in Mozambique, Angola and Guinea-Bissau*, No. 13, 1979.

Rogers, B. *The Domestication of Women*, Tavistock/Methuen, 1980.

Shirley, O. (ed.), *A Cry for Health — Poverty and Disability in the Third World*, Third World Group and AHRTAG, London 1983.

Sidel, V. W. and Sidel, R. *Serve the People — Observations on Medicine in the People's Republic of China*, Beacon Press, USA, 1973.

Sidel, V. W. and Sidel, R. *The Health of China*, Zed, 1982.

Silverman, M. *The Drugging of the Americas*, Berkeley, 1976.

Stimson, G. and Stimson, C. *Health Rights Handbook*, Penguin, 1980.

Thunhurst, C. *It Makes You Sick: The Politics of the NHS*, Pluto, 1982.

Townsend, P. and Davidson, N. (eds). *Inequalities in Health — The Black Report*, Penguin, 1982.

Weir, D. and Schapiro, M. *Circle of Poison: Pesticides and People in a Hungry World*, IFDP, 1980.

Werner, D. *Where There Is No Doctor*, Macmillan, 1980.

Werner, D. and Bower, B. *Helping Health Workers Learn*, Hesperian Foundation, Palo Alto, California, 1982.

White, A. *British Official Aid in the Health Sector*, IDS Discussion Paper No. 197, University of Sussex, 1977.

Whittemore, C. *The Doctor-Go-Round*, Oxfam, 1976.

Women and the Informal Sector, Institute of Development Studies Bulletin, Vol. 12, No. 3, Sussex, 1981.

FILMS

A Fair Share of What Little We Have
GB/1976/colour/45 min/Concord
Optimistic look at health system in Tanzania.

The Chicago Maternity Care Story
USA/1977/b&w/60 min/Other Cinema
How private ownership distorts health care in America.

Seeds of Health
GB/1977/colour/45 min/Film Forum
The Chimaltenango Development Project in the highlands of Guatemala is revolutionizing community medicine there (or at least it was until 1977!).

Minamata
Japan/1971/b&w/122 min/Contemporary
A case study of one of the most unpleasant examples of industrial pollution: mercury poisoning.

Tomorrow's Epidemic?
GB/1980/colour/15 min/Concord
Smoking, tobacco growing and the multinationals in the underdeveloped world.

Blood of the Condor
Bolivia/1969/b&w/English subtitles/74 min/Other Cinema
Narrative reconstruction of the US Peace Corps' attempt to sterilize Indian women.

The Great Health Robbery
GB/1981/colour/22 min/Concord
A look at baby-milk and drug promotion in the Yemen, complementing the book of the same title.

Guess Who's Coming to Breakfast?
Obtainable through Oxfam America. USA/1977/tape-slide show/25 min
A look at the operations of a multinational corporation and its effects on health
in the Dominican Republic.

Into the Mouths of Babes
USA/1978/colour/30 min/Concord
Report on promotion of powdered baby-milks in the underdeveloped world.

In Sickness and in Wealth
GB/1980/colour/37 min/Other Cinema
A history of public and private health care in Britain.

Barefoot Doctors of Rural China
USA/1975/colour/45 min/Contemporary
Shows traditional Chinese methods being used to cure both humans and animals.

The Pharmacy
France/1976/colour/81 min/Other Cinema
Looks at Pharmacy No. 3, Shanghai, known for its outstanding attempts to serve
the people.

Mukissi
Congo/1975/colour/25 min/Concord
How a traditional African society treats mental illness in a young woman.

The Struggle for Health
GB/1983/colour/54 min/Central TV
Problems and progress in health care in post-independence Zimbabwe. Includes
the politics of undernutrition and medical education.

Distributors

Concord Films, 201 Felixstowe Road, Ipswich, Suffolk IP3 9BJ.
Booking/accounts: 0473 76012. Film despatch: 0473 77747.
Contemporary Films, 55 Greek Street, London W1. 01 734 4901.
Film Forum, 56 Brewer Street, London W1. 01 437 6487.
Other Cinema, 79 Wardour Street, London W1. 01 734 8508.

ADDRESSES

The following organizations and groups are working on issues raised in this book.
Their resources and scope vary widely, but most will try to deal with specific

requests as far as possible. Some of the large agencies involved in overseas programmes have individual areas of expertise.

Appropriate Health Resources and Technology Action Group,
85 Marylebone High Street, London W1. 01 486 4175.
Baby Milk Action Coalition,
34 Blinco Grove, Cambridge. 0223 40483.
Campaign Against Depo-Provera,
374 Gray's Inn Road, London WC1. 01 278 0153.
Catholic Institute for International Relations,
22 Coleman Fields, London N1. 01 354 0883.
Christian Aid,
PO Box 1, London SW9. 01 733 5500.
Fightback,
30 Camden Road, London NW1. 01 485 8610.
Health Action International,
IOCU, PO Box 1045, Penang, Malaysia.
International Contraception, Abortion and Sterilisation Campaign.
Co-ordination Group, 374 Gray's Inn Road, London WC1. 01 278 0153.
Mozambique/Angola Committee (MAC),
35, Wellington Street, London WC2 7BM.
National Union of Public Employees,
Civic House, Aberdeen Terrace, London SE3.
Oxfam,
274 Banbury Road, Oxford. 0865 56777.
Politics of Health Group,
9 Poland Street, London W1. 01 437 2728.
Radical Nurses Group,
c/o Gill Black, 9 Ryland Road, London NW5.
Radical Statistics Health Group,
c/o BSSRS, 9 Poland Street, London N1. 01 437 2728.
Returned Volunteer Action,
1 Amwell Street, London EC1R 1UL. 01 278 0804.
Social Audit,
9 Poland Street, London W1. 01 734 0561.
Socialist Health Association,
9 Poland Street, London W1. 01 439 3395.
Society for Anglo-Chinese Understanding,
152 Camden High Street, London NW1. 01 485 8236.
Third World First,
232 Cowley Road, Oxford OX4 1UH. 0865 245678.
War on Want,
467 Caledonian Road, London N7. 01 609 0211.

Index